Geranium Justice

The Other Side of the Table

Published by Piscataqua Press
An imprint of RiverRun Bookstore, Inc.
142 Fleet St., Portsmouth, NH, 03801

www.piscataquapress.com
www.riverrunbookstore.com

ISBN: 978-1-939739-35-3

Printed in the United States of America

Visit the author: geraniumjustice.blogspot.com

Geranium Justice

The Other Side of the Table

Barbara Hanson Treen

For Teddy Boy, Annette and Ted, and to the memory of my mother whom I promised I'd tell the story.

Praise for *Geranium Justice:*
The Other Side of the Table

"The book will prove particularly satisfying to anybody who, like myself, enjoys discovering what happens, deep backstage, in the world of the media, such as at a big newspaper office, and also in the worlds of New York State and City government. Barbara Hanson Treen, the author, worked for years at Newsday, a leading metropolitan New York newspaper, later at New York City's Rikers Island Penitentiary, followed by 12 years as a Parole Commissioner, a member of New York's Parole Board. With disarming candor, Treen has penned a very up-close-and-personal narrative of her journey to now, one generously sharing events in her own backstage life through two marriages and single parenting, and her experiences as participant-observer in New York's jails and prisons.

"For Treen, who originally trained as a sociologist, news of the carnage at Attica Prison at the hands of the New York State Police while ending the famous 1971 riot, crossed her desk at Newsday, revolted her, and ultimately propelled her to work in criminal justice, particularly in the prison system. After her long service on the Parole Board, Treen minces no words, describing the Board as the 'Star Chamber'.

"The reader will recognize any number of significant crimes, prosecutions, and convictions discussed in the book, and their aftermath, covering New York's last half century. There is the Queens murder of Kitty Genovese by Winston Moseley in 1964, the poster case for urban anonymity where it was reported that 36 neighbors of the victim heard her screams, but nobody called the police. Another case grew out of the assassination of Malcolm X in 1965 and resulted in the later appearance before the Board of one of the convicted assassins, Muhammad Al-Aziz a/k/a Norman Butler. The book also addresses the killing of

John Lennon by Mark David Chapman in 1980 and his later appearance before the Board, as well as the case of Jean Harris, and the appearance before the Board of Jason Ladone, a convict in the notorious Howard Beach race assault and homicide case of 1986.

"Geranium Justice is a fascinating book, one which, in my opinion, is deeply rewarding in its insights, its truthfulness, and its humanity. Most of all, it successfully promotes the cause of governmental transparency."

—William M. Erlbaum

Justice, New York State Supreme Court (Retired), Adjunct Professor of Law, Brooklyn Law School, Adjunct Professor of Behavioral Sciences, York College of the City University of New York

Table of Contents

Introduction

Sitting on top of my bookshelf over the computer in my den, there's a framed photograph of the sky showing a cloud mass that looks like an angel smiling down. This is a gift from two of my former clients who are now married to each other and are my friends. This picture makes me smile at the wonder of its image and the gift givers and how they became part of my life. Scotch-taped next to it is a picture of Bobby Kennedy and a quote from his speech in South Africa in 1966. He said, "Each time a man stands up for an ideal, or acts to improve the lot of others, or strikes out against injustice, he sends a tiny ripple of hope. And crossing each other from a million different centers of energy and daring, those ripples build a current which can sweep down the mightiest walls of oppression and resistance." It's the inspiration of these that kept me going in the most brutal of jobs with the unkindest of people.

This is the story of the trajectory that led me, an ordinary woman, to an extraordinary job as a commissioner on the New York State Parole Board, on the other side of the table from what most people read about. My chair behind the table was as hot a seat as the one in front, sat in by the 77,000 inmates whose liberty I decided during my tenure. My career path didn't seem to have as predictable an outcome as that the criminals were leading up to, but once on my side of the table, it made sense and was something I'd been practicing for all my life. Although, interviewing killers, rapists, addicts, muggers, molesters and burglars in prison basements 10 hours a day for 12 years wasn't anything I could have envisioned,

I wanted always to make things better but never thought about it in such wholesale ways. The violence of hearing the inmates' stories over the years penetrated my soul but seldom did they tell their stories with the intensity I absorbed them. I think their years of retelling their histories separated them from the events and created calluses as protection. The victims, the communities, and the politicians never distance from the immediacy of the crime.

The following chapters tell my story: the fumbles, the unwitting capers, the hopes, the ironies, and the search for justice. And in this search, is always the story of being a woman in this unconventional job playing in the big leagues with the good ole boys who would have liked me to stay on the bench. The language of punishment is taken from a man's dictionary while my style of common sense decision-making invited criticism of emotionality from others. The questions about how I got to the table are numerous. My life happened at the intersection of coincidence and opportunity, of making choices every day like everyone else. Although I became an authority figure, I am no less human or perfect; a single mom, a daughter, a lover, a student of life, doing the best I know how every day with my personal life weaving through my work. It tells what I saw and heard with parole decisions made in the face of truth-telling versus politics; of justice versus revenge, of sound judgment versus pressuring news headlines, of correction versus punishment, and in some cases, of men versus women.

In my thirty-five years in criminal justice, I've seldom talked about the stories I heard or the misery warehoused behind prison walls. I've always felt that to talk about a case 'out of the office' exploited the crime, the offender and the victim, for violence is so daunting and the pyramid of its damage so enormous, that in the end it is extremely personal. After so many years in the trenches and some more since I've been above ground, I still feel compelled to work for justice. Although I've never talked about 'my day at work,' I tell these tales now to let the reader decide if justice does indeed exist and who interprets it. This is my story. This is a woman's story.

1 | In The Beginning

As I hop on the Second Avenue bus going uptown to visit John Lennon's shooter, I'm awed at how I got here. With a newspaper in my hand, I try to look blasé as if this trip to Bellevue Hospital where Mark David Chapman, the acknowledged killer, is being detained is something I do on an everyday basis. Although this is my work, Chapman is a special kind of customer. I investigate to make sure that the least among us in New York City's jails are treated by The Department of Correction in accordance with the law. I do this for New York City's watchdog agency, the Board of Correction. While I'm thinking on this ride of the part I'm playing in this caper and prepping myself for my conversation with him to make certain he's being treated fairly, I'm mentally hop-scotching notches of my past. Answering my own question about how I got here, I reason it's a job I seemed to have quite naturally trained for all my life. And if there were a crystal ball on the bus with me, I'd know that there was so much more to come my way.

My earliest memories remind me that I've always believed in fairness. And I've always rooted for the underdog. Some people say that they were born 'ready'. Unlike them, back then I never felt prepared, smart enough, informed enough, good enough. My adoring father wrote in my autograph book in elementary school "To my darling little pish posh who always spills the milk or ink." It was upgraded at the turn of the sixth grade in 1950 to, "Bobby Dear, Both you and I are glad school is over. However, always be glad to go to school or else you will not only be beautiful, but you will be dumb also. And who wants to be beautiful and dumb? Dad." And growing up in the shadow of a perfect older, smarter and obedient sister didn't help. But it probably served me well. There was so much room for my improvement. I was terror struck by authority as a tiny kid and believed that if I deviated from what I was told, there'd be dire consequences; that if I bit my nails my appendix would burst, that if I crossed the city streets without permission, I would be hit by a car, and that if I laughed too much during dinner it would turn to tears. So I lugged these negative messages around.

Early on I figured out that if I didn't feel good speaking out for myself, I could find a voice for others. So it followed that I became a natural at being an advocate for others in ways that I couldn't help myself. By extension I began to feel pretty good plus I had a lot of reinforcement for being supportive. My mother told me when I was in the fourth grade, how proud she was of me for befriending Joyce Levetin, who was friendless. This compliment was the exception to the years to come of her criticizing every other detail of my life (her way of pushing for excellence). And so it was stunning to me to find in her wallet upon her death in 2001, a clipping from a Hadassah newsletter dated 1984. It said, "Congratulations to my daughter upon her appointment as Commissioner to the New York State Parole Board."

I was influenced as a young kid and tested early by very obvious social inequities. I had to choose which clique to be part of in a tiny Maine summer community where my family had a second home. The locals of the village were Christian and a great many of the tourists were Jews who

I went to school with. Come summer, the beach was flooded with the kids from away. There were huge differences between these seasonal groups of friends: the local kids worked and their families didn't have money, and the summer kids came from money and spent their time playing. And these different groups of kids had nothing to do with one another. Even a nine year old could figure out that something was out of balance here. Though my two neighborhoods were far apart, many of the same people inhabited both. I think I had a sense of guilt about privilege and wanted to even it out. At the beach, the separate groups sat far apart each with disdain for the other. It was a regular Gaza Strip. Although this town was perfect in most other ways, it had vestiges of anti-Semitism and the hotels displayed signs that said "Gentiles Welcome." My father told the story of arriving in town for the first time with our little family in tow for a weekend but found it hard to book a room. He finally went to a door of a home with a 'For Rent' sign posted and introduced himself, saying right up front that he was Jewish. The woman said, "Come right in, Mr. Firestone. Our Lord was a Jew." The next year my parents built their dream home. This was the place where I came of age.

I found myself occasionally the subject of this anti-Semitism during those earlier summers. It was a confusing issue to me as I identified much more with the values of the town kids but was loyal to my school friends and had no tolerance for the discrimination. But I did agree with the reasons the City Kids were disliked: they were spoiled, they were rude, and they were snobs and acted as if the local people were there to serve them. These attitudes had not a thing to do with religion but everyone was labeled according to their ethnicity, not their behavior, so the dislikes and separateness continued. What was a kid to do? I did the obvious: I became the ambassador between them. I brokered friendships, I included outsiders, and I like to think that I moved the beach blankets closer together.

My winter experience was a harsher one spent in an affluent community of Boston where I possessed none of the attributes that makes one a star. While I had friends and continued to champion Joyce Levetin in high school, I was not a good student, I was not a beauty, my dad was not a captain of industry and to top it all, when we played sports in gym and 'chose up,' the loser got me. Not incidentally, this high school spawned many luminaries: judges, athletes, governors, movie stars and cultural icons. A decade later, I worked with a guy at a newspaper who wrote the book, *Is There Life After High School?* His name was Ralph Keyes and the conclusion was that high school could be the beginning of a disappointing life pattern. Fortunately for me I can say, "Yes! There was, much more!" I would have hated for life to stop at my exit from Brookline High School for I felt I was invisible there.

This split identification and understanding of others has helped me in my work throughout life but it was invented through necessity to get along. My reputation as a conciliator followed me years later when on the parole board during one of my first hearings, a 'good ole boy' commissioner, snarling and fuming smoke through a pipe between his teeth, quizzed me about my intentions. "I understand that you have a social work background. What are ya' gonna do with the inmates? Jump over the desk and take them home with you?" Quite a welcome. But I'm getting ahead of my story.

I worked summers starting at the age of 13, first as a mother's helper, then for a couple of years as a stable "boy" until graduating to waitressing (a plum of a job in a resort town.) The work ethic was a status symbol for me back then and I loved it. I returned as a full-time resident to this town ten years ago after an absence of 36 years and learned some interesting things; among them, that my salary at the stable was paid for by my dad. He had arranged it with the manager, Bob Perkins, who was one of those irresistible bad boys, and a drinker. My dad was in the liquor business so how convenient for Bob to have me as a stable hand and a trail guide in exchange for booze. I'm so grateful my father did this as I loved the horses, and the work, and being really good at something (I should have recognized the shoveling of manure as the omen of what was to come on the parole board.) I had fantasies of becoming a jockey but I grew. Years later, whenever I met a jockey coming up for parole, I gave a naïve lecture disbelieving that drugs could possibly be part of that perfect life on the back stretch. The track life I learned, is very far from perfect; starts at 4:30 in the morning, is filled with blood, sweat, tears, and sometimes drugs, and is the most rigorous job imaginable. Meanwhile today, Bob Perkins is a kindly most respectable grandfather, and we sit side by side as board members of an historical society silently chuckling about all that's gone 50 years before.

The waitressing was tough work and at 14 it felt very important. I did it until I was the victim of an attempted rape walking home from the restaurant one night. My screams during the attack scared off the perp and alerted the neighborhood. Once home, after running the block as fast as I could with him giving chase, my mother berated me for being provocative in my dress. This was a generation of the victim-blame school of justice and in some quarters it still exists in crimes of family violence (what did you do to provoke him?). After this attack, I had such fear that I left town and returned to our city apartment for the rest of the summer. My leanings toward restorative justice and reconciliation as ways of ending violence have always been translated by others as those of a liberal who'd never been mugged. Ah, let me count the *many* ways. I've been a victim more than most, as you'll find out, but it never affected my beliefs about crime and subsequent justice.

These summers of growing consciousness included many firsts: up close and personal views of unfairness but also first kisses (in a cemetery) and first boyfriends. When I came of age I quickly discovered the 'bad boys.' There was a real attraction to these brave characters that didn't live by mother's teachings. While I never actually breached the guidelines, I lusted after the guts to be able to do so (maybe the beginning of going where angels feared to tread.) To my surprise my number-one heartthrob, Mike P., was unfaithful. I went to see him one stormy afternoon when he had the day off from his job of crewing on a boat. As I walked in to his tiny cottage with his bedroom door ajar, I found him in bed with Montgomery Clift. This was an arts and theatre community after all, and the shenanigans and hijinks never ended. Much of the color and drama of daily life in town was enriched by the gay population before the national spotlight and civil rights were ever focused on it. So this added to my education and acceptance of differences in people. I was more hurt that Mike would be interested in someone else than surprised that it was with a man. I think the celebrity somehow made it more understandable to me (after all, I told myself, I was only a degree of separation from Monty!).

Much water has passed under the bridge as I think about those years, but as I thoughtfully trace my steps, the segues seem clear and predictable. I'm on this bus three days after the shooting. For all of us, for Mark David Chapman, for John Lennon, and for me, the fix was in long ago, all culminating on the night of December 8, 1980.

A Monday in December at 10:40 in the night and I'm walking hand in hand with a date on Central Park West. We can't help but notice blockades, people, and police activity on the corner of W. 72nd Street where the Dakota apartment building sits. This is commonly home-base for celebrity watchers and autograph seekers, as many well-knowns live here. But this scene feels very different, somehow haunted and ominous. We're told by onlookers that John Lennon has been shot. After taking in the scene, we believe that if the crowd's report is true, the victim needs some privacy and the police need room to do their job. And so we move on. To bolster this decision, I confess that I'm not a huge Beatles fan, am no stranger to crime scenes, and am not a voyeur. And so we head for one of the many cafes in the neighborhood.

I don't think that on the walk to the restaurant we utter anything other than an occasional 'wow.' This seems the only thing to say in the absence of having any further information. My date, Joe Russo, is a criminal attorney and I work for the watchdog agency over at the NYC Department of Correction, monitoring 'conditions of confinement' at Rikers Island. We're hardwired to be in tune with what's going on in the street but we don't want this date night to be full of shop talk. Our usual professional position is mopping up after the bloodletting, legally in jail or court. We know that speculating about a crime is a waste of breath as the initial rumor and innuendo are never accurate. Once we're settled in at the restaurant, it's like watching a forest fire sweeping through the tables as we hear the patrons in the Museum Cafe catch the buzz about the murder up the street. We can't help being human on our night off and we join in the hearsay.

The next few days the media is spilling over with all angles of the murder. People have set up camp and cameras in Central Park, soon to be named 'Strawberry Fields.' Memorials abound. The shooter surrendered at the scene so there's no manhunt. The public is lusting after Chapman's blood as he's taken their hero from them. In another age, we might have seen a lynching. But I remind you that my agency is responsible for making certain that safety and security is in place for all prisoners and that the jail minimum standards dictated by the court are met. In the coming days I find out much more about Mark David Chapman and about how he's living. I don't have any inkling now that he'll be a focus for me through two jobs. And now writing this, three.

On Thursday morning, the 11th, a few days after the shooting, I report to my office across the street from City Hall. I'm told to check out Chapman's lockup at Bellevue Hospital, where they're holding him. What? No Rikers Island? Corrections is housing him at the hospital in the jail ward for his protection, thinking the public won't know. This is a huge case and no one is risking any liability for the City by putting a prisoner in danger. All of us are used to responding to emergencies but this assignment is unusual for me. I'm a veteran of suicides, riots, knife fights and all sorts of unusual incidents but not a celebrity murder. During the three days since the shooting, he's been booked, printed, questioned, held and housed. The media has continued broadcasting the event 24/7.

I'm a bit astonished over the coincidence, having been in the crowd Friday night, and realize that I'm 'up close and personal' meeting history. After getting my orders I put the tools of my trade together: my badge, a business card, and my wits. And, I think about the personal slant this has for me. Not incidentally, I'm stinging over my recent divorce from a newspaper reporter, a 'golden boy.' He had entrée to everything and everybody which eclipsed me during our marriage of slights, violence and competition. And here I am— about to meet his hero's shooter. I feel validated after years of his elevated status that froze me out professionally. This will certainly show him. But, as I head out the office door toward the elevator, I know how unseemly and selfish I sound, even to myself, in the face of these circumstances. I try to edit myself and my feelings but I'm human and lapse into thoughts of how this will play out for me.

I'd normally drive a city car up the two miles of Second Avenue to 23rd Street and Bellevue Hospital. Not today. No traffic other than buses and police are allowed. I hop the first bus that comes along. I'm cool as I scan the riders in the bus. I sit down and glance at the newspaper I'm holding hoping to find out any new updates in print that I may have missed about the case. I feign reading but really as I've told you, I'm putting the pieces of my life together. The bus is packed. The silence along the route is deafening. Horses, wooden and real, holding people back, line Second Avenue. Hundreds of Lennon fans in mourning are waiting to witness what they hope will pass before them: a cavalcade chauffeuring a different kind of celebrity. How do they even know that Chapman is in this neighborhood? The jail is out on Rikers Island, an appendix of the Bronx. At 23rd Street I stand up to exit the bus only to be told by the driver that no one is getting off here and he's not stopping per orders of the NYPD. There's a little verbal scuffle between us and with his foot on the brake and the bus slowing, a cop at the closed door is waving him on. Until I flash my shield all around. It works like Dracula with a cross. He stops, opens the door, and I get off with the cop assisting me.

The day is murky in every way possible. The sky is distinctly gray. There's a muddle of sounds echoing angry screams, sad moans, and excitement on the street. The vision of Bellevue Hospital alone emits fear wrapped in doom like fog. There's a gauntlet of reporters and photogs that I have to cross through…from the bus to the hospital door. The police framing the entrance are keeping the screaming mob away from me. Am I the wife? "Just who are you?" News has carried about Chapman; that he's from

10

Hawaii, that he's married, that he grew up with a childhood like Lennon's. The reporters are clearly confused as to who I am and why I'm being admitted. "Are you Gloria?" they ask and I suddenly become the story. I scan the crowd filling the lawn between the street and this little-known side entrance to see if perhaps my former husband, the reporter who I can finally out-do, is in the crowd. No. His not being there gives me a lot more confidence.

The monotone gray continues as I enter the door that opens only into an elevator which takes me up a few floors to the prison hospital ward. It's manned by a corrections officer who matches the steely gray surroundings. It creeks to the jail hospital floor as my moment in the sun swiftly passes. Without a word exchanged, the corrections officer brings the boxy elevator even with the floor where I will meet John Lennon's killer. As the door slides open, there's nothing to be heard at all. There's no clanking din of gates, no undercurrent of men's voices as is heard in 'real' jails. There is only a sense of tension in the void shared by officers flanking the hall to the left and to the right, bookending the CO sitting behind a sign-in desk. In back of the desk are a few rooms. I'm expected, and in as little time as it takes for me to print my name in the log book, I hear a familiar voice greeting me. Breaking the mood and the silence is a pipe-smoking, smiling Ed Hershey, who is the Department of Correction's public relations director. In the narrow, dark corridor, he says, "Hi Barbara. Come here often?" This is the perennial pick-up line and an obvious stab at humor in this most unlikely of settings. Could this be any more inappropriate? I had known and dated Ed when we both worked at *Newsday*

11

and now we are both obviously displaced and trying to make a joke of this strange situation. He ushers me into his office to await my interview with Mr. Chapman and my required tour of the security of the ward. Ed tells me that Chapman isn't in the building...yet. He leaves the office to answer a phone call and now I'm alone with little understanding of where the inmate is. On his desk is a radio transmitter that's carrying a running narrative from Chapman's escorts as they leave the arraignment in Criminal Court. They're headed up the FDR Drive in an unmarked car. Chapman's wearing a bullet-proof vest and is on the rear floor of the car for his safety. This is a highly secretive operation and the Department is pulling out all the stops to guard his security. No way is any onlooker on Second Ave. seeing him.

I wait in the office by the 2-way until I hear that he's in the building. The PR guy returns to tell me that Chapman is being asked if he wants to see me. This reminds me of an old Gene Shepherd story where he projects about his unmet blind date, joking about how awful she'll be, until he meets her and realizes that *he's* the blind date! They are not guarding *me* from this alleged killer. They are protecting *him* from me. He has agreed to meet me. And so the time has come for me to talk to him, check out his surroundings and make sure he's safe. They're doing all the right things.

I'm instructed to begin my slow walk down the hall. My pace is timed with the opening and closing of the barred gates I pass through. We come from opposite ends of the cement glazed hall, going through four separate iron gates to meet in the middle. From each of our vantage points, we are both striped by light reflected through the barred windows from the individual cells lining both sides of the corridor. Two men walking together approach a card table set up for this meeting. The silhouettes show one tall and straight, and one short and rounder. Our gate keepers time our passage to arrive at the table simultaneously.

The taller man is from Corrections, already a trusted confident of the prisoner and has told Mark that I am there to explain his rights to him. We introduce ourselves, shake hands, and sit down. We sit facing one another while he tells me in the friendliest of ways how well he is being cared for, and acknowledges that it's probably more than deserved considering his crime. I liken the staff to being his canaries in this Bellevue mine. Even without formal psychiatric training, it's no reach for me to conclude that he's mentally ill and has been for a while. His manner is meek, respectful, and vulnerable. He tells me that his voices had been plotting this for a long time. He's been fixated on Lennon's celebrity and his own inadequacies, he's had suicidal ideations and other classic symptoms of mental illness. As he talks, he seems to fold into himself. He says with frustration that he and Lennon are so alike that he had to get one of them out of the way to exist and begins again to mention the 'voices.' I interrupt, and am careful not to discuss the reason he's here and remind him why I'm here. My intention is not to become witness for the prosecution and I fear he's telling me far more than I need to know. As a human being, I can't help but feel pity for this so obviously disturbed man. Certainly he'll be separated from the public for a long, long time, and due to the victim, perhaps forever. In this testosterone-filled prison psych ward of Bellevue Hospital, I don't want to display publicly any compassionate attitude but Chapman could use a few kind words and remarkably he's the one giving it out...to his jailers. I focus on discussing how he's being treated and give him my card should he need to be in touch with my office. I've told him about his rights here and I've looked and listened for over an hour. I've done my job as required but wish I could also do what I did in my last job when I was a prison social worker. Then I would have done a full psycho-social intake so I could understand this guy better. It's time to go.

Being a woman in this profession is challenged all the time. It's never lost on me that the officers guarding Chapman are all men, that their faces reflect a studied machismo for the occasion, that they're wondering who sent this girl to do the job. I know they'd like to mop up the floor with their prisoner as avengers, but no, they're actually doing a good job protecting him by the rules. But still, there is no eye contact connecting them to me, even when they talk to me. When I mention some problem with the lock-in system and the log, they resist my corrections. Do their mothers, their wives, their sisters have such trouble with them? I remind them that we're really working together and I finally get what I want. They'll talk about me after I leave, I'm sure.

When Chapman's safely returned to his cell, I'm given a tour by the acting warden, inside and out. He's over the top, dressed in army fatigues, a green beret, and combat boots! Does he realize he's only in a hospital on Second Avenue? He leads me around the separate wards and day room. The sight of so many slow moving, silent men locked in cages, wearing brown jump suits, is a testament to prison population-management through Thorazine.

This is a tutorial for me, enabling me later to detect among inmates the results of different medications. As I leave the hospital, I know that I'll never underestimate the powers of mental illness and the sorrows it leaves in its wake.

My memo to my supervisor after the visit reads as follows:

"Interview with Captain Ellis who is administering the prison ward in the absence of the Warden who is on holiday:

He describes to me unique security measures for this inmate and definitely conveys the feeling that they expect an incident from an outsider.

Chapman is being kept in a cell which normally houses 3 to 4 people. The cell has an enormous bolted steel door with a window in it for observation. It is not padded. There is an officer (B officer) stationed outside the door who records in a ledger his activities every 15 minutes...I saw the ledger. He does not stand up and stare at the inmate 24 hours. I am told that along with the B officer there is nursing observation as the facility is in joint custody with health and hospitals. There is no toilet or sink in the cell. When Chapman needs the bath facilities he is escorted. When he goes to the clinic (which appears to be on a regular basis...perhaps for medication) he is escorted by two officers and a Captain.

In addition, his cell window was frosted yesterday and then painted black. This was all done with his knowledge and approval for his safety. He was told by Captain Ellis where his bed should be placed and that if he positioned his head at a certain end it would be safer. Also, Capt. Ellis has made a cell (similar) on the opposite side of the ward available and he moves him (plans to) from cell to cell. We took a walk outside and he pointed out from both sides of the building the window of his cells. Clearly, if this is known, it could be a security problem. As he described the security it appears not to be so much of a breach of security from within but rather and attack from outside. He states that TV's Chris Borgen had been there last night filming and after that he decided on the further security measures. He takes his meals in his cell, they are served by the CO's...he does not have any contact whatever with other inmates. Ellis feels that in time he will wish to. When taking him out of his cell, they cleared the hall of other inmates, put him in a gated hall area, had me wait on the other side of the bars, searched me, then commenced my visit with him.

The visit was a face to face. The Capt. stayed in the area along with a person from the hospital. Capt. Described to Chapman the interest of the Board and introduced me. I then described in what areas he may wish our services. He thanked me and assured me that he is confident they are taking good care of him (remember, he comes from a security job himself).

Ellis was waiting today to see if his request for outside surveillance on a 4-12, 12-8 basis is being approved. He wishes to have a CO parked in a car observing the area. His rationale for not having a foot officer is that it is cold and that the man would go inside to warm up. He'd rather he be comfortable and alert.

Chapman is on the second floor and the architecture is such that there are terraces and window ledges. Ellis claims that in years past, he would have been able to easily get to Chapman from outside. He is ultimately security minded, 21 year veteran (knew Willie Sutton) and is taking no chances with the security system."

In the ensuing months and years, much is written about Chapman: Born in 1955, growing up in Georgia a very unhappy and bullied kid. He was fearful of his father and protected himself from his peers by fantasizing that he was a king to Little People who idolized him. When angry, he would blow his people up in his mind, but they would always forgive him. He began a rebellious period and some drug use at age 14 until he became a born-again Christian in his teens. Amazingly in his late teens he carried out his earlier fantasy by becoming a real hero to little people; real kids he counseled at summer camp. Throughout all this time he was a fan of John Lennon. After high school he dabbled in stand-up comedy but ultimately worked with Vietnamese refugee children through the YMCA. They loved him and it made him think he was somebody. Once this 'resettlement' job ended, his downward spiral began. He had suicidal ideations, depression, dropped out of college, had a failed engagement and says himself that this was the beginning of a period where he "fell down a dark hole."

In 1977, his dreams of Hawaii propelled him there for a fling. He lived high on the hog briefly in Honolulu before homesickness brought him back to Atlanta. In Georgia, things didn't go well and he again returned to his

Hawaiian paradise where he was hospitalized after a failed attempt at suicide. Once discharged, he flourished as a result of involvement through volunteerism with senior citizens. When he was thought of as a hero, he functioned well. But this attention was always short term and his temper and depression caught up with him. He took a whirlwind trip around the world and was on such good terms with the travel agent that they eventually married in Hawaii. It was a tumultuous marriage interrupted by his obsessions and traumas.

After a succession of jobs, he took one as a security guard, but drank heavily. He made his wife miserable and wrote to a friend that he was going nuts. Perhaps as early as September, he talked about going to New York and killing John Lennon. His see-saw moods and travels between Hawaii and New York ultimately found him in New York on December 8th, with a purchased weapon from a Honolulu gun store, some money and a plan to shoot John Lennon.

At the same time I was meeting my date for an evening of fun on the town, Mark David Chapman was spending his time talking to his demons and a doorman at the Dakota, and autograph seeking. If anyone had really paid attention, they could have seen that he snaked through his day like a moving violation, until John Lennon got out of his limo and was met four times by Mark David Chapman's five bullets.

Chapman got to Attica before I did. He moved there in 1981. I didn't get there on the job until 1984. I was a regular there until 1996 when my twelve years as a member of the New York State Parole Board ended. It was Attica, after and before all, that was the engine of my interest in criminal justice and became my profession. It had been those riots in 1971, through which I saw and judged the system, as I was ripping and reading news reports in the *Newsday* wire room. And it was Attica, until a year ago when he was transferred to Wende, where Chapman had been living in segregated housing for his protection, serving his twenty-to-life sentence for Murder II as number 81A3860 since August 25th, 1981, thirty-three years ago.

As for my entrance on the Attica campus, it was accompanied by twelve years of wrestling with the question of justice; of traveling 33,000 miles per year to the state's 72 prisons to decide on liberty issues in the public's best interests; of being tossed around in the air in a 'puddle-jumper' aircraft; of checking into orange-colored, shag-carpeted motel rooms stinking of cigarette smoke on the road; of arguing with colleagues; of eating fast food; of missing my family and friends; but most of all, of often being alone on the other side of a decision on my side of the table.

Attica was one of my first stops on the circuit as I began this new job. This dungeon opened in 1931 as the state's fifth prison in order to accommodate the growing inmate population with this place alone warehousing over two thousand human lives. When I enter to review cases for possible parole, I'm reminded that there were approximately 77,000 people living in these institutions in 1984 in New York (today down to 56,000), all with personal stories. As I travel from a Batavia motel to this midway point in Wyoming County between Buffalo and

Rochester to work at betting on people's freedom and public safety, I'm always jolted by the sight of the fortress with the gun towers. The place where famous inmates have and do live, inmates like Willie Sutton and Mark David Chapman, and where the 1971 riot defined prison life.

There is nothing that can prepare a neophyte for the specter that is Attica. Its reputation precedes it. The walls are haunted by the blood of the uprising that took 39 lives; 29 inmates and 10 prison employees on September 9 of 1971. In the five-day riot, Attica was the site of "the bloodiest one-day encounter between Americans since the Civil War." The uprising of 1,000 inmates happened spontaneously over conditions within the prison that were racist and inhumane and too long ignored. Some demands could have been easily remedied, such as the inmates request for more toilet paper, decent medical attention, fruit occasionally with meals, and a shower more than once weekly. But instead, four days into the riot Governor Nelson Rockefeller, who was requested by the inmates to come and negotiate, refused. What he did was to send helicopters early in the morning over the prison and 'blanket it with tear gas.' Once the inmates and hostages collapsed, 500 state troopers burst through spraying thousands of bullets randomly into the scene in the yard. Within 6 minutes, 2200 lethal missiles were discharged, making Attica infamous in the annals of history and human degradation. It was in this context during the actual days of this riot, when I stood working in a newspaper wire room, 'ripping and reading' about this unspeakable savagery on the part of the authorities, preparing for a life in journalism, that I redirected my career and some thirteen years later found myself entering the bowels of Attica.

As you know, I left my position before Chapman reached his twenty-year minimum necessary before parole consideration. He became eligible for his first parole interview in 2000, a nice round number. Every two years he has interviews; this is because it's the maximum time allowable for a denial (hold). Surprisingly Supreme Court Justice Warren Burger, who held very conservative views on criminal justice matters, including belief in the death penalty and stringent sentencing said that "the parole decision turns on primarily what a man is and what he may become rather than simply what he has done." But as my colleagues knew and said, it was possible to hold a ham sandwich! It's pretty clear that the political heat for letting out the shooter of an international icon would not be survivable. Considering public safety and public opinion, while acting as an independent arbiter of the facts, is tricky. I must own up to the numerous impressive interviews I've had with reasonable candidates who, despite their sincere remorse, were denied their freedom. These denials of mine included a member of the Manson family and several other players of notorious doings. Was I rating the value of the victim? Public disapproval? Enough time served? I would hope none of the above. Sometimes the crimes are so deviant that one wonders whether in spite of perfect institutional behavior, the person could ever be trusted. The key to writing a denial of one's freedom is to write those real reasons that make you wonder if the person will be a community risk— within a legal framework, to tell the truth. This doesn't always happen on the board and as such, inmates are sent away shaking their heads and not understanding reasons for denial. They are held accountable for programs they can't participate in, future planning that is beyond their reach, misinterpreted details of their behavior, etc. But in the end, it's because of the magnitude of the crime. Inmates regularly feel that parole is a setup, that the decisions are made before the board meets them (not true). They are often instructed to complete certain programs before consideration however, once accomplishing that, they continue to be denied liberty. The anxiety and frustration over parole expectations for inmates and their families is a valid catch-22. For many of the less notorious cases who are denied parole and left warehoused, there could be more legal challenges based on their inadequate interviews and poorly-reasoned denials. As it is, the many appeals take up most of the time of parole's legal counsel. In Mark Chapman's case there are no advocates to argue his parole denials and the probability is that he will remain incarcerated throughout his years on Earth.

Each time Chapman's been before a board his folder has been replete with petitions against his release. The media has been tuned in to each of the seven hearings over the last fourteen years. Much of the content is similar. He talks about his state of mind then and now, his motives, his contacts, his relationship with his god and his everyday life. He has lived in the special housing unit for the past thirty-three years for his protection, where he works as a porter, mopping and sweeping, and as a law library clerk helping others in the unit, and contemplates his life in his seclusion.

The following is his third hearing transcript held on October 5th, 2004, which tells his story and is representative of his other presentations before and since. He met before the New York State Parole Board comprised of Commissioners William Smith, Jr., Vernon Manley, and Livio Lazzari. I've included also the denial of his last appearance on August 22, 2012. Had I been around for any of his boards, I would have had to recuse myself, as the sympathetic figure he painted so many years ago walking the 'Thorazine shuffle' down the corridor of Bellevue Hospital still stays with me. Read into it what you will but know that more than half of the prisoners in the United States, according to the 2006 Justice Department Study has a mental health problem. Among female inmates, almost three-quarters have a mental disorder. Forty percent of them never received treatment during incarceration (due to Chapman's keep lock status, he becomes part of this 40% as he can't his leave housing area to get services.) And, also in the year 2000, 20 years after John Lennon's murder and 30 years after the group disbanded, the Beatles sold more records than any other performer. Chapman will be facing his eighth parole hearing in August, 2014.

Commissioner Smith:

Q. Come in and have a seat. Are you Mark D. Chapman?

A. Yes.

Q. Okay. My name is Commissioner Smith. With me today on my right is Commissioner Manley.

A. Hello Mr. Manley

Q. And on my left is Commissioner Lazzari.

A. Hello

Q. You are reappearing before the Parole Board. You are Mark Chapman. Is that correct?

A. Yes, sir.

Q. Mr. Chapman, I don't know if you remember, I was on the panel, I was not the main interviewer on a prior board, which was your first board. I do not believe any of my associates, the other two commissioners, were on any panel that you were involved in. And so we may be going over some of the information that you've talked about before.

A. Okay.

Q. Certainly, there's also new information that we have that we'll take a look at. You were found guilty by verdict and are serving a twenty to life sentence for murder in the second degree, is that correct?

A. Yes, sir.

Q. Again, you were seen in October of 2000 and October of 2002. You are housed currently, I think, in the SHU. Is that correct?

A. Yes sir. Second floor.

Q. It's not because of disciplinary activity. It's because basically, of protective custody

A. Yes, sir.

Q. A matter of protective custody, correct?

A. Yes, sir.

Q. Okay. What are you doing, what have you been involved in doing in the last two years since the Board last saw you?

A. Well, I'm still the law clerk up there. I handle the law for both floors. I'm still married, still participating in family reunion program. My mom passed away in February.

Q. Okay.

A. That's basically it. It's basically the same.

Q. Okay. And you had contact with her; had she ever been to the facility?

A. My mom?

Q. Yes.

A. Sure.

Q. So certainly that's an area that we are sorry to hear about. A lot to consider as we look at the record.

A. *Yes, sir.*

Q. *I know that your criminal history is limited. This is your only crime of conviction. This is your only time in State prison. You have discussed the instant offense in the past. Do you have any hesitation talking about it at this point?*

A. *None at all.*

Q. *And certainly we can read through what was discussed in the past or with past panels. There are some questions though that I have. The description, in the past you've talked about thinking of committing this act over a significant period of time; is that correct?*

A. *Yes, sir.*

Q. *And apparently had planned to commit the murder of Mr. Lennon several months prior to when it occurred; is that right?*

A. *Approximately three months.*

Q. *Okay. The description immediately after the shooting according to the presentence report, indicates that you had fired, it appears, five times, and had struck Mr. Lennon four times with those bullets; is that right?*

A. *Yes, sir.*

Q. *Now, so you had the weapon beforehand. How did you happen to have the weapon on you? I mean, you were there all day long. Where was the weapon on you?*

A. *It was in my coat pocket, my right side.*

Q. *Okay. And during the course of the day, you had talked to a number of individuals; is that right?*

A. *Yes, sir.*

Q. *There is some description here that you may have even, in some convoluted way, made mention that Mr. Lennon might not be long, not have a long time remaining in his life; is that true?*

A. *I don't remember that, sir.*

Q. *Did you ever talk to anybody?*

A. *The only thing I remember that would have predated the crime was when I signed out of work, I signed my name John Lennon to the ledger.*

Q. *I believe that happened in, it was October, a couple of* *months prior, right?*

A. I do remember, sir, at lunch that day I spoke to a woman and I said, you never know where he might be. He might be in Spain tomorrow or something like that. In other words, I don't know how long he's going to be in the building. I think I alluded to something like that. I don't know if I alluded directly to his death or not. I don't remember.

Q. Okay. Now you had the gun in your pocket. You had seen him earlier in the day. Is that true?

A. Yes, sir. He came out of the building, and he signed an album that I was holding.

Q. Was anybody with him when he came out that time?

A. Mrs. Lennon was.

Q. Yes.

A. They both got in the limousine to go to a record studio, I believe.

Q. Okay. Once you fired the weapon, is it true that you dropped it?

A. No. sir. I didn't drop it. I stood there and held it in my hand. And the doorman, Jose, came over and he said, what have you done, what have you done? He grabbed my hand and shook it, and he shook the weapon out of my hand, and he kicked it across the asphalt about twenty, thirty feet away. Pretty brave man to do that. But that's what he did.

Q. It describes you taking off your coat and jacket, folded and piled on the street beside him, where you stood quietly. Is that basically what you did?

A. I don't remember folding them but I took them off and put them to the side, inside the alcove building. Not on the street, inside the alcove, whatever you call it. And I did that because I knew the police officers would come, and I knew they would probably have their weapons drawn. And I put my hands on top of my head as soon as I saw them, so there was nothing, any weapons for them to see, and things like that. That's why I did that.

Q. So you had concealed it in your coat and jacket. Did you have a coat and a jacket?

A. I believe I had a sweater on and then a long London Fog *blue jacket, knee length.*

Q. *Okay. And that's where you concealed the weapon. You took it off, and it was for what reason; so the officer wouldn't what, wouldn't think that you had anything remaining on you?*

A. Wouldn't think that I would be harm to them I guess is what I'm trying to say. That they wouldn't see a weapon on me, you and plain clothes, because—without a dark coat, I think that's why I did that.

Q. *Why did you want them to have that thought?*

A. *Well, I probably didn't want to be shot by them.*

Q. *Okay.*

A. The first thing I said was, I'm alone, I acted alone. Something to that effect. Because they came in, and they were looking. And looking all around at me and everywhere else. And I wanted to assure them that there's nobody else to worry about here. It's just me.

Q. *So you didn't want to get shot?*

A. *That's right. I had the weapon pointed at me and, you know, that's not a good feeling.*

Q. *If you didn't want to be shot, then you were thinking at that time of what may occur?*

A. *Yes.*

Q. *Why do you think you committed this act?*

A. *I committed this act for attention.*

Q. *Yes.*

A. To in a sense, steal John Lennon's fame and put it on myself, thinking I was nobody at the time. And that's basically it.

Q. *Okay. I know that in the first interview that you had, there was some discussion of other individuals who were considered.*

A. *Yes.*

Q. *---to be possible targets by you. Is that true?*

A. *Yes.*

Q. *And you remained with that understanding; is that right?*

A. *Yes, sir.*

Q. *Was there anything, or any contact that you had with any of these individuals that you had that kind of thought about, any personal contact that was ever negative in any way?*

A. Just what I perceived at that time to be phonies, to be somebody that—I didn't think they were being who they really were, and that angered me. Of course, I'm just mirroring myself on them. And I would say that's it. Maybe a sense of phoniness.

Q. And they were certainly all famous people?

A. Yes.

Q. And as you have said today, maybe some sort of transferring of fame from them to you?

A. It wasn't the guy down the street.

Q. Right.

A. Exactly.

Q. Right. And you've accomplished that goal, probably, one could say

A. In a twisted sense, yes. In some ways I'm a bigger nobody than I was before, because, you know, people hate me now instead of, you know, for something positive. So that's a worse state.

Q. But in the same sense the accomplishment of some sort of notoriety if you will.

A. Yes, sir.

Q. You've accomplished that?

A. Yes sir.

Q. Okay. One of the difficulties that we have looking at a case like this is there's certainly, and it isn't just this case, it's any case where there's a homicide, is that it's a serious matter. There's no coming back from the brink.

A. That's right.

Q. And certainly society and legislators have created sentences which are significant in time, and the amount of time that is necessary or is given to serve. You've now served about twenty-four years. Is that right?

A. Yes, sir.

Q. That's approximately, we look at a number of factors, some of which we've talked about, some of which we'll still be taking a look at in terms of our decision today. One of the factors that our statute talks about is, in terms of release, is will a release deprecate of diminish or belittle in some way, if you will, respect for the law. As far as reviewing your case, there's no incident beforehand that would have anger or resentment in terms of real— it may be something you perceived, but no direct contact that created any fright or flight, it didn't create a situation where rational individuals would commit such a violent act. Would you agree?

A. *Yes, sir.*

Q. *And, again, in terms of your behavior, you've continued to do well. I know that's been discussed before. There's no Tier II's or Tier III disciplinary reports since we saw you last time. Is that still the case?*

A. *I believe so, sir, yes.*

Q. *And over the course of time, you've had just a few. I think it's three Tier II's. No keep lock or SHU time directly related to any discipline, correct?*

A. *Earlier in the day— I mean earlier in the years, yes. But not in the last fifteen years or so or more.*

Q. *So your discipline has been good. The section of our law talks about discretionary release on parole shall not be granted as a reward, merely as a reward for good conduct or efficient performance of duties. It goes on to talk about will you live and remain at liberty without violating the law. That certainly is something we are looking to see. Can you live a law-abiding life and will your release, you know— that your release is not compatible with the welfare of society. That's another consideration we will have. And, again, one I talked about— and will not so deprecate the seriousness of the crime as to undermine the respect to the law. I know those actual words were used in your two decisions.*

A. *Certainly understandable.*

Q. *I'm sorry go ahead.*

A. *Certainly understandable.*

Q. *When one looks at it, I guess I'm looking for you to comment on it, because it's a consideration we have and rightfully I'm looking for your input because this is an important factor. You set out on a plan—and correct me if I say anything that's wrong— you set out on a plan which included killing this individual, correct?*

A. *Yes, sir.*

Q. Part of that was gaining notoriety. Is that correct?

A. Yes, sir.

Q. There was some discussion in the past as well in that you may have felt that he doesn't act appropriately as it relates to maybe his, the wealth that he had. Is that correct?

A. At the time that's what I perceived, yes. It angered me. Now I realize it was bad judgment.

Q. Now with any homicide, we also, as a panel, the three of us have to look at it and say if we release, in this case, Mark Chapman, will it diminish, will it belittle, will it deprecate the seriousness, and as a result of that will it undermine respect for the law, which is important, respect for the law.

A. Yes

Q. Will it be undermined in some way? And in the past that's been looked at and found certainly to be a factor. What are your thoughts about that?

A. I deserve nothing…Because of the pain and suffering I caused. I deserve exactly what I've gotten right now. Those are my feelings.

Q. Okay. The first panel talked about among other things…and I don't believe that I specifically spoke to this…But I think that some of the other Commissioners may have talked about your continued contact, in terms of let's say your continued contact with the media. You did this for, you did this for some notoriety and you have continued that. In last two years have you had any other contact?

A. In the last four years, nothing.

Q. Okay. And I mentioned that because, again, it was something that came up before. And I think it's important. During all of these events that led up to the shooting, why didn't you stop? You are an intelligent person, the record shows that. As a matter of fact, there's some testing that would tend to make one believe that you have greater than average intelligence.

A. Thank you.

Q. Why did you not stop?

A. I went back and spent another two, three weeks there in Hawaii, it started building again. It was just a tremendous *compulsion of just feeling this big hole, of being where I thought was. At one point I tried. I had flown to New York once. And then called my wife. And after seeing a movie, "Ordinary People", I guess it struck a chord with me. And I called her and said, "your love has saved me, and I'm coming back." And she said what are you thinking about? And I told her on the phone what my plans were. And I did try to, at one point, stop what was building inside me. But then when I came as a big nobody, a big nothing, and I couldn't let it go. And it just kept going very strongly, and I couldn't stop it.*

Commissioner Manley

Q. *How long had you planned this, I mean over what period of time, for the record? We didn't get to that.*

A. *I would say in 1980 I was wandering around when I wasn't working in the museums and libraries, and I went to the Honolulu Public Library and I had this grandiose plan of looking through all the books and maybe reading them all. And I came upon a biography section.*

Q. *Yes?*

A. *With a book called* One Day at a Time.

Q. *Yes.*

A. *I believe that was the title. And I picked it up, and I opened it up, and Mr. Lennon was there being photographed on the roof of his building in the Dakota, and it just angered me. You know, here I was with these struggles.*

Commissioner Smith

Q. *But your struggles were just every day, you know, how to put food on the table?*

A. *In one sense, yes. In another sense, no. I was drinking. Nothing I couldn't have gotten out of. I'm not going to use that as an excuse. I could have pulled myself out, but I chose not to.*

Q. *Well.*

A. *Yes.*

Q. *Certainly what I'm looking at is why did you not stop yourself? And that was kind of the question I had, you had options.*

A. Absolutely.

Q. You had your wife. Did you confide in her that you were desiring to do this?

A. Not initially. No. I didn't tell anyone.

Q. Did you eventually tell her?

A. Yes. In New York on the phone the first time I did. She said, come home right away. And she was frightened.

Q. And she never went anywhere to inform authorities?

A. No. I convinced her, quite thoroughly that I was fine and that it had come out of me and, you know, I was going to be okay.

Q. When you were then going back to New York, did she again fear that you might have these thoughts?

A. I don't know what she feared. I told her I was going to go to New York to write a book, write a children's book. I used that phony excuse for her and she believed me. I told her that I had thrown the gun in the bay, and that it was over, and I was going to go try to make something of my life. And that was a lie.

Commissioner Manley

Q. Did she always believe when you were younger that you would obtain fame?

A. Absolutely. When I was a young man, I thought something was going to happen to me. I thought I was going to be famous.

Q. And why? Because you are bright.

A. I didn't know what it was specifically. I certainly didn't think it was going to be murdering John Lennon. But I thought something was going to happen to me. Maybe that was an attempt to make up for low self-esteem problems at a young age, I don't know. But it sounds pretty much it.

Commissioner Smith

Q. So you mentioned it to your wife. You did not, obviously talk to the police authorities. It appears that when you ---one of the questions that I had. The first time that I was on the panel had to do with the weapon. And it does appear that when you came – just sort of clarification – when you came to New York State, you had talked with the airline authorities on how to transport that weapon.

Is that true?

    A. *I probably called about the bullets.*

    Q. *Okay.*

    A. *But I knew, from having experience as an airport security guard, that bags are not checked. At least they weren't then. And you could probably put a weapon in a bag in the cargo department, not in the passenger area of the plane.*

    Q. *Okay it was not –*

    *..***A.** *And it could get through. I knew it probably would get through. I don't remember calling. If I did, I don't remember doing it. But I could have.*

    Q. *So it was your intention then to have it in the baggage so it wouldn't be discovered is that what you're saying.*

    A. *Yes, sir. Absolutely.*

    Q. *Okay. And I was not totally clear on that after having read some later information in the record. In terms of what occurred after the crime, did you say anything after you shot Mr. Lennon?*

    A. *To the police officers? I dropped my book, a copy of the* Catcher in the Rye, *and I told him to get my book for me. It was on the ground. They escorted me to the back of the police cruiser.*

    Q. *Yes*

    A. *I believe Mrs. Lennon came over at the time, looked in. That was a very traumatic thing that I locked out of my memory for several months. I couldn't remember that for a while.*

Commissioner Manley

    Q. *She didn't say anything to you?*

    A. *No. Just through the glass.*

Commissioner Smith

    Q. *Okay. Now I'm sorry.*

    A. *And they asked me what did I do. And I said, "I just shot John Lennon."*

    Q. *---been reviewed as well. Because of the nature of your crime, with any murder second we have to…... At this point it appears that…...Is that right?*

    A. *---------*

Q. And we know, we talked to you a little bit and the record reflects...

A. ----------

Q. And you understand that if we release you,------

A. Yes, I do.

Q. I had reviewed your record. There was a friend that you hoped to live with, if release, and he lived, I believe, in----

A. --------

Q. --------

A. Yes, sir.

Q. Is that still where you intend to live?

A. If released, yes, sir.

Q. And there was some indication of farm work; is that right?

A. He was a friend that owns and runs a farm and he asked him, would you be willing to let Mark work? And I believe he said, yes.

Q. Okay. What type of farm?

A. I don't know what type of friend.

Q. Farm.

A. What type of farm? I don't know.

Q. Have you ever worked on a farm?

A. No, sir.

Q. I do see there was also some indication about skills and what you might do. Including--I think you had some printing skills.

A. Yes, sir.

Q. You worked on presses before?

A. Yes, sir.

Q. Was that at a hospital?

A. Yes

Q. Okay. On a color press?

A. It was just black and white. We could have run color, but you had to run one color at a time. So we just basically ran forms black over white.

Q. That's a good skill. It's kind of sometimes maybe more art than science.

A. It's all computer now.

Q. It's changed a lot. I was going to mention it

A. *Yeah, that machine is probably long gone.*

Q. *Well, they still have some work like that in smaller press set ups. And although a lot of it is tied directly into whatever program might be appropriate, it's a skill that you have. I know you talked a little bit about what you are doing now. Have there been any particular programs, whether it's therapeutic or vocational, that you felt have been positive to you while serving this time?*

A. *Nothing official. I enjoy reading short stories. I am soon to start a ministry with my wife again. We are going to start it up again, where I want to distribute a short story I've written called* The Prisoner's Letter *to Prison ministry and also a testimony to prison ministries. We are just about to do that now.*

Q. *Okay. Now you had talked about doing some sort of work in that area at all.*

A. *Yes.*

Q. *Is there any desires or any plans---what are your plans in that area?*

A. *Well, if release, I'd like to tell people about what happened to me. About Christ, about what he's done for me. Without him, I don't think I could have made it this far. And that's a very serious concern for me to be able to tell people that, which I'm doing now with the brochure, but that's in a limited sense.*

Q. *Okay. And you understand also if released, in terms of geography—*

A. *Yes.*

Q. *Your ability to move would probably be highly restricted.*

A. *Yes. Yes, I understand.*

Q. *And that's for a number of reasons. And so it's important, it's important that you have an understanding of that as well. When you saw the victim and his wife the first time--*

A. *Yes.*

Q. *—why didn't you commit the act then?*

A. *I guess I was just so awed, and it was daylight, and Mrs. Lennon was right with him and it just happened too quickly, has been my understanding of why I didn't do that then.*

Q. *And how close were you when you actually shot him?*

A. *I would say ten to fifteen feet.*

Q. Were you the distance we are apart?

A. Farther away.

Q. I've asked you a lot of questions. Is there anything else you want to tell us as we look at this decision?

A. No. What I said earlier about me being in this situation is about what I wanted to say.

Q. Okay. Have you had other contacts? I know you had a sister.

A. Yes.

Q. Any other contacts? I know that there's been some contacts with your records with I think some clergy as well. Is that right?

A. Yes

Q. Any other support in the community that you have that you've---

A. Not locally. Not too many people local.

Q. Well, again, we thank you for coming in today.

Commissioner Smith

Q. Commissioner Manley or Commissioner Lazzari, any questions?

Commissioner Manley

Q. Do you have contact with other – you are in protective custody, right?

A. Yes.

Q. And how many people do you interact with?

A. I work with one other fellow.

Q. One fellow?

A. He's another porter. That's it.

Q. of work – you read and you told us that you can do a little bit of writing – what other things can you do in protective custody?

A. I play the guitar. I have access to a television set, I watch about one hour a night. I work two shifts seven days a week. In addition to being the law clerk, I'm also the porter. We do the kitchen work. We just did the meal now. Keep pretty busy.

Commissioner Smith

Q. Have you done any violence or anger programs on this

term?

A. *No, sir*

Q. *Okay. And that's because you're restricted?*

A. *Yes, sir. I tried years ago to get down to Cephas Attica program, but they said no.*

Q. *Okay.*

A. *But they used to come and talk to me. Harold Smith, when he was still alive, he used to come and talk to me. But not officially.*

Q. *Whether inside or outside, that would also be something we would like. Thank you for coming in today, sir.*

A. *Thank you.*

Q. *We'll give you our decision in writing.*

Decision;

"Hold twenty-four months. Parole denied, next appearance October, 2006. Following a personal interview, a review of your records, and deliberation, your release to parole at this time is denied. This is based upon the extreme malicious intent you exhibited during the instant offense where you fired a handgun multiple times, striking your intended target, John Lennon.

Your course of conduct over a lengthy period of time shows a clear lack of respect for life, and subjected the wife of the victim to monumental suffering by her witnessing the crime.

Your limited violence and anger programming due to your housing status, as well as your positive disciplinary record have been considered.

During the interview, your statements for motivation acknowledge the attention you felt this murder would generate. Although proven true, such rationale is bizarre and morally corrupt. To release you on parole at this time would significantly undermine respect for the law."

Decision of August 22, 2012

"Denied 24 to 8/14. Despite issuance of an Earned Eligibility Certificate, parole is denied for the following reasons: After a careful review of your record and this interview, it is the determination of this panel that, if released at this time, there is a *reasonable probability that you would not live and remain at liberty without again violating the law and your release at this time is incompatible with the welfare and safety of the community.*

This decision is based on the following factors: the instant offense of murder in the second degree, wherein you shot and killed an innocent victim, an international music star. Your action clearly demonstrates a callous disregard for the sanctity of human life. Your record does not show any prior convictions.

The panel notes your prison record, good conduct, program achievements, educational accomplishments, positive presentation, remorse, risk and needs assessment, letters of support, significant opposition to your release and all other statutory factors were considered. However, parole should not be granted for good conduct and program completion alone. Therefore, despite your positive efforts while incarcerated, your release at this time would greatly undermine respect for the law and tend to trivialize the tragic loss of life which you caused as a result of this heinous, unprovoked, violent, cold and calculated crime."

When I left my appointment, I left Attica behind. But I will never leave behind the lasting impression of its image: the atrocities, the bloodletting, the injustices carved indelibly in our history. In some crazy way it's the rally cry of Attica that continues to reignite my work for justice and reinforce my belief that a person goes to prison *as* punishment, not *for* punishment.

Mark David Chapman continues to live within the boundaries of his cell and his imagination and until last May, when he was transferred to Wende Correctional

Facility, a prison outside of Buffalo, has spent all these years at Attica Correctional Facility.

There are different ways to get to Attica: the state can send you, you can visit or you can work there. But everyone has to travel on (I-90) West to Exit 48, to Route 98S, to Route 238S. Turn right at Exchange Street traffic light. Facility is on left. There's no U-turn if the state sends you.

2| Teddy Boy... 'She's just a woman.'

Life after high school proceeded according to plan with my entry into an all girls' school, Mt. Ida Junior College. It was made for me. The social life was imported to campus by boys from Boston's many colleges. The scholastic demands were never too great and the emphasis was definitely on one's social skills. No student here had any illusions, or desires, about her future becoming more than a traditional housewife, the norm of the times. It never occurred to us that we would need (much less want) careers, not jobs. Nobody thought or was told that she could be a doctor, a lawyer or any kind of life-sustaining chief. Our goals didn't go beyond the day we were in. We were a happy bunch.

When we weren't involved in some actual hijinks, we reveled in the afterglow of the last one or planned the next one. There was the party where we pushed the signature carriage from in front of the Red Coach Grill restaurant on the Cape to another location (not found 'til days later and resulting in the corporation cementing them all in place); the planning of the 'spontaneous' elopements of girls out the second-story dorm window by ladder; the house party my parents forbade me to have that was advertised on the trolley ending in the burglaries of guests' purses; pilgrimages of carloads filled with kids to the house in Maine; underage drinking; and the familiar annoying behavior for parents and school administrators. Fortunately, none of our activities led to disastrous consequences. Mostly, we were good kids taking these two years to figure out the next step. Revolutionary causes or political consciousness was not the vogue in my crowd... then. The question we all asked ourselves was would the next guy be our forever? It was serious business and we lived the search subconsciously and full time. This was our future after all.

Although my parents were relentless in their watchfulness, I still managed to get in harm's way. In the fall of my second year at school, the imaginable happened. I was introduced to a beautiful blue-eyed, blond-haired sailor at a high school football homecoming game. I was pinned at the time to a very appropriate Bowdoin pre-med student but meeting Dean Hanson put an end to that. He was at the game with my friend, a Boston College dropout, who was in the navy and who became our best man the following year. I could not have married a person more different from me. Opposites indeed attract: he was intellectual, introspective, cool and stoic. I thought he was a perfect anchor to my extraverted and emotional self. Beware of gorgeous men you believe are the strong, silent type. You may discover they really have nothing to say. And so, with my heart on my sleeve, I continued my last year at school secure in the belief that the rest of my life would be filled with tow-haired children and my sensitive sailor man.

At this little college I met friends who'd last me a lifetime. One in particular became a touchstone throughout my days, my friend Annette. She was my confidante and she also was in love. She had left Brooklyn to come to this campus in Newton, Mass., that was the former estate of Lady Aster, leaving her high school boyfriend back home. I could never figure out why she was a student here as she was on full academic scholarship and was the token brainiac. Among the many other differences between us as Brooklyn and Brookline girls were the clothes. She came equipped with the requisite motorcycle jacket (with studs) and I had the more conservative suede fringe. We were different on the surface, but beneath it all were both square pegs trying out the round holes. We shared our dreams, our likes and dislikes, all our thoughts. Under all the immaturity we were very solid and serious people. You wouldn't know that side of us as we squealed while watching Dick Clark and American Bandstand on TV, borrowing the lives of the instant celebrities that the show made of the dancing teens. We kept up with their romances while Annette's guy Ted was back on Avenue U in Brooklyn in a matching leather jacket and my boyfriend was part of the Destroyer Atlantic Fleet in the Pacific. It was a safe way to date…in absentia.

Annette and Ted beat me to the altar after graduation, but were at my own wedding just months later. They made their life in New York while Dean and I got to postpone any permanent decisions as he was still hitched to the navy out of Newport. We got a large but cheap apartment on the back side of Beacon Hill, 14 Anderson Street. This was home when his ship was in. Our friendships expanded to half the fleet as we figured that his shipmates could share the rent and the apartment when they rotated in and out of port. It was wonderful to play house and be den mother for all these vagabonds in this duplex apartment…basement and sub-basement (I've seen these digs recently; incredibly upscale and pricey.) I had a meaningless job at an insurance company to help pay our share but it lasted not very long when early on I became pregnant.

My debut into serious living happened dramatically a year later. During the later stages of my complicated pregnancy, it was evident to the navy doctors that I'd be in better hands with a private obstetrician affiliated with a Boston hospital. And so it was that we gave up our group apartment and I bounced back to my parents, both because it was free and it still was really home. Not much had changed in my lifestyle since marriage. Living with my folks during those months consisted of keeping up with friends and seeing doctors. I remained a child. Dean came home as often as possible from the base in Rhode Island and but for the sixty pounds I gained, our marriage was one long date. Other than my dad, no one commented that I was as big as a grand piano until the week before delivery when an exam showed that I was about to have multiple births. This was a rarity in 1960 before any need or notion of fertility drugs. After several false labors, my son and daughter finally saw their way out, three weeks late. My father was my designated driver to the hospital as the navy gave up giving Dean leave-time for all the bogus anticipated delivery dates. The babies arrived when they were ready despite doses of castor oil and tips about Chinese food inducing labor. They were big and healthy and the main attractions in the hospital nursery throughout our nine (!) day stay. It fell to the proud new grandfather who had driven us to the hospital to bring us home to the newly furnished nursery in their dream house in Swampscott. With my father driving, my mother in the passenger seat with a baby in her lap, and me in the back with the other, I was on a one-way trip to my permanent adult life.

The details of the next day can never be properly shared with anyone, written or told. As long as it takes to exhale, my life changed and would never be the same. The death of my father from a massive heart attack as he left my crib-filled bedroom after playing with the babies was surreal. It happened instantaneously but felt like slow motion lasting forever. I had adored my dad and felt his unconditional love every single moment. I knew with him around, that everything about my marriage and parenthood would be okay. I also knew that my folks never approved of my marriage and that while they were thrilled with these grandchildren, we had no more right than the man in the moon to have children: no money, no job, no housing, no experience. It was too late for me to tell him I knew this and it was too early for him to leave us. In a heartbeat (his) my entire life would change.

The beautiful home they had moved into six months earlier, trading in the house in Maine and the city apartment was filled with people coming and going during the mourning period. My mother was a pillar of courage showing little outward emotion but questioning if we thought that the many stairs had been too much for him. Out of town relatives, friends, business people all showed up; he was a beloved man. We made decisions about our future during the midnight feedings while my mother, my sister and I lay across a king-sized bed with 3 newborns (the twins and a nephew one week older) as we watched Jack Paar. After the public and ceremonial grieving finished, we all faced a very different future. While my sister was on steady footing returning home to her family in Toronto, my mother left Boston to live and work back in her hometown of New York City, and my plan of moving to Long Island materialized three months later when Dean separated from the navy. It was supposed to be a one-year plan only so that my mom could be near the babies. Overnight I had a full-time husband, a widowed mother, a son and a daughter. Responsibility had found me.

My wonderful friends Annette and Ted from my college days are living in an affordable development on Long Island. It is the quintessential Pete Seeger 'ticky-tacky little boxes all in a row' place. It answers the needs of thousands of young families and it looks good to us. So we follow our friends' lead and settle in amidst other couples who have the same style house, the same income, the same age kids, the same hopes and even the same looks. It would be easy to take a wrong turn and at the end of the day wind up sitting in some other family's kitchen. But it's comfortable and for a little while I even feel that I fit in. Instead of returning to Boston after a year, our plan to go home is shelved and we've blossomed where we're planted, here as refugees to the burbs.

But the bloom is off my marriage within nine years. We were a mismatch from the beginning with that 'passive men/wild women' formula. Nature has done its job well enough with chemistry working its charm and producing those tow-haired offspring as a result. But I was learning there needed to be more in order to spend my life with someone. I have ambitions that make my marriage feel it's crowding me. My husband, who is at most a silent partner, doesn't share my curiosity about the world beyond March Lane. When my kids, who are eight, are gently told the concept of a separation, Heidi decides she needs to get a new dress in order to walk backward down the aisle for a divorce ceremony and Jimmy begs me to be more like the other mothers on the block. Despite shock and disapproval from friends and family, and protests from Dean, I go ahead with a separation. In New York, two years of a legal separation qualifies as grounds for divorce. I thought this would be the friendliest way for us to negotiate and the least guilt-provoking for me. People can't believe that a marriage without arguments and betrayals doesn't satisfy me. But I believe that a marriage without conversation and interests will deliver a deadening future. And so I am the first on my block to become a single working mom. This, in 1968, puts me on the other side of everyone's table in this community of sameness.

Still the house has acted like bones for me; it's held together all my personal change. It's given me stability and security as I've worked hard on my way to 'becoming.' The safety of its familiarity has allowed me the freedom to take risks over time; risks with relationships, risks with a career. And here I am, 26 years later on the same street. Everything but the address has changed in my life through sheer will and determination which leads me now to being a Commissioner on the New York State Parole Board.

It's Thursday and I repeat my usual routine. It's the day I get home from the road after leaving on Monday to begin my assignment at one of the state's prisons to interview over 100 inmates for parole. It's late afternoon and I've just dragged my luggage in from the car. I collect my mail and hum to myself as I begin my homecoming rituals. I check phone messages and look at new growth on early April spring plants left without the benefit of water while I'm away. Throughout my chores my mind drifts to the prison I was at just hours ago; of the sorrows I've left behind, of the wasted souls, the dead-end for so much promise. And I never cease to marvel that I have this job, how much I love it and how fairly I think I do it, and just how hard it is. I run the bathtub.

The phone rings. I pick up the antique wall phone with the long cord that reaches throughout the tiny kitchen allowing me to continue my fiddling. On the other end is my friend Ted and the call is not about 'catching up.' No time for pleasantries in his tone. I know something is wrong. This is an S.O.S. While they've traded up their house to a fancier neighborhood, our friendship has remained a constant. Life, I thought, has been good for them. I've been very wrong. The truth of it is that their youngest of three children, Teddy, a 20-year-old son, has been going through more than his share of grief. Stricken with a genetic, life-threatening Mediterranean disease, he is slow to mature but has been quick to experiment with wild living.

Wrong doesn't begin to cover it. With intensity Ted says, "I need your help. Teddy-Boy is shackled to a bed in the jail wing of Meadowbrook Hospital. He's going to be reviewed for conditional release and we have no idea what that is."

"Oh my God! Why is he there? What's happened?"

He'd been arrested for taking a red pickup truck for a joy ride. He may never have been noticed but for the fact that due to his Cooley's Anemia condition, he's very small. The police think they're looking at a child behind the wheel and pull him over. His parents, who are stern disciplinarians, decide to play hardball on this one and believe that facing the consequences will serve him well...this time. He's been testing their limits for a while. And so with shame big enough to keep this a secret from me, their close friend, they walk through this alone. Who could have foretold that he'd need emergency hospitalization several months into his local jail 'bid' and who would think that Nassau's county hospital was not equipped to care for this man-child?

I tell him, "I'll help in every possible way. Conditional Release is the name for local parole consideration. If you get a year in county you do eight months (a third off for good behavior), but if you get approved for 'CR,' you do six months, getting two months off in exchange for a year on parole supervision. I'll write a letter to the folder and support the release".

I've always thought this kind of release is a good deal. The Division has leverage with the supervision, the taxpayer saves money having the offender at home and the punishment has been meted out. It's impossible to release egregious cases. If they were serious to begin with, they'd be serving state time, not locked up in the County Jail. However, the prevailing attitude of the paroling commissioners is that few of these cases pass muster and they are routinely denied. They believe it's already a 'favor' to get jail rather than prison time. Never mind that the courts have determined that the punishment fits the crime. Never mind that the crime is a pickup truck, not an armed bank robbery. But I don't tell Ted this. I want to get off the phone as quickly as possible and start pushing this rock uphill.

I'm not confident that this can actually happen because

of who I am. And 'who I am' is a woman who brings an added dimension of understanding to the table and resultantly is always second-guessed and distrusted. It's seemed to me that "getting tough on crime" talk is code for 'men only.' In this culture in 1986, women in any part of the criminal justice system mystifies the boys. Whether the woman is an inmate, a defendant, a professional, a victim or a commissioner; the odds are that we are seen as manipulative and emotional. Indeed, the good ole' boys have always been the face of my workplace with the exception of one female colleague of mine who basks in being called 'Dragon Lady' by the inmates. These folks believe that fair paroling practices mean insults, revenge and denials to inmates. There's no looking around the edges of the crime during the interview to figure out the behavior. No aggravating or mitigating circumstances considered by this bunch. It's pretty one-dimensional in their eyes and the 'stay' or 'go' decision-making seems to depend on the severity of the crime, regardless of what the law says about the elements to be factored. And my decisions, be they stay or go, are usually challenged by colleagues who exercise their power and control over me by their majority, the only white 'girl' and youngest member at this time. I make a habit of writing in shorthand all my reasons for my decisions ready to defend myself without letting my outrage get in the way. For all these challenges have little to do with the inmates but more to do with my not going along with the easiest job security trend, to deny parole. In years to come a judge has ordered the board to consider in its opinion the rehabilitation of the offender and not refuse based solely on the crime.

I sit with this queasy unsettling feeling of tentativeness as I think about my plan for Teddy. I've been an advocate of fairness for so long and here comes a chance to finally get the system to do something right. Teddy's file sits just a few miles away on a desk in the Long Island office. It would be so easy for me to say that I want to go into that office tomorrow and review these local cases. But I know that my 'sitting' on this case is ethically verboten. All twelve commissioners are alternately cycled monthly through the county regional offices for local parole cases and the decision can be made by one person. They're called 'paper cases' as the inmate isn't interviewed personally but the file is reviewed. This is different from the card shuffle that brings every one of us, in twos or threes, to all the prisons to talk to state felons. So one of us is assigned to go to the Hempstead office tomorrow….and it isn't me! It's Joe Mulholland, a guy I've got a political bond with and a guy viewed as my friend. I consider him compassionate, almost to a fault. I know that he's a deeply spiritual person but often trades his good judgment for a 'snow job' from an inmate. And there's no predicting which way he'll go.

The stories about Joe are legion. He's been on the Board about a year longer than me; a friend of the Governor with a background in education. He's been an activist for the underdog all his days and a fighter for himself. Stricken by polio as a youth, he was told by the church that they couldn't accept him for the priesthood with his handicap (God doesn't think he's perfect?). And his second choice as a probation officer resulted in their rejecting him due to his disability. He successfully sued probation and won which helped lay the groundwork leading to the

Americans with Disabilities Act. And so, Big Joe, as he is known to his friends, is a hero of sorts. He's a short, round guy with the elfin face of a five-year-old and the booming persona of a limping sumo wrestler. Joe and common sense are often strangers. Once, when we were driving the Thruway together coming home from hearings, we were pulled over by an alert trooper. Our car, with Joe behind the wheel, was weaving from side to side as he was gesticulating broadly about a domestic violence case we had disagreed about...in fact the trooper could probably hear him screaming as he screeched down the road at 80 mph. I'd just denied release to a guy in the prison. He was a man who repeatedly over years had abused his wife until the day he fractured her rib cage and her skull, and while hospitalized, she finally pressed charges. The guy was a model inmate, had served the three years, had no prior record, but during the interview said that she always started the fights so was responsible for the assault. Joe didn't believe that he was a 'risk to public safety' and thought he should go home. He thought he was a standup guy who was only a threat to his wife, not the greater community. His belief system stemmed from back in the day when family matters were private and arguments were never viewed as crimes. So this woman, were the guy to be released, didn't translate as the 'public.' As I saw it, this guy definitely had unfinished business with the now ex-wife.

Joe wanted to clear up the matter with me as we drove home. The cop wasn't taking chances and when we were pulled over he saw two business people arguing about their day at the office. But one was red-faced, still in the midst of the argument, and then there was me. I was relieved for the interruption because I had no words left to explain to Joe how wrong he was and explain the cycle and complexity of domestic violence. The trooper waved us on and Joe continued his rant without the car swerving. I tell him the familiar example of the guy who comes up to a strange woman standing on a corner and assaults her. In response to this Joe says, "What's wrong with this guy?" Then I tell him about the guy who belts his wife standing in the kitchen and Joe says, "What'd she do to provoke him?" There were many of these conflicts when we worked together but essentially he was a fine man who believed that some good resided in every person. But he stood his ground as a macho man in believing that he had to show me the error of my ways…and decisions.

Should I bump him for duty tomorrow? Is this courage or cowardliness on my part?

Knowing this is a life and death decision for Teddy and for my ethics, I get all the information I need on the phone and tell Ted Sr. I'll be back in touch. I immediately call back to speak to my girlfriend, his wife, and hear how she's doing. I'm horrified to learn of the agony this family has been secretly suffering for a while. While I know of Teddy-Boy's health issues, I have no idea my friends have also been fighting the consequences of a rebellious teen for a while.

I slam down the phone, bolt out the door and take a run around the block. All the while I'm forming what should be a decision that on the face of it doesn't need a Rhodes Scholar to know the shortest distance between two points is a straight line. But in this system there's no reality, only perception. I decide to write a personal letter to the file and get it faxed to the office in the morning in time for review. I don't dare be in touch with my colleague personally. I definitely want a paper trail here. I want to trust that this system works and I know what an ethics violation looks like. This intuitive nagging sense tells me the memo needs to be deliberately unemotional but factual about the circumstances. After all, I don't want to get 'punished' for being totally knowledgeable and passionate about this case and have the decision boomerang.

After two years I know the distrust with which my judgment is viewed in this business of revenge. There are three dirty words here that seem to taint my opinions: female, advocate and emotional. Funny thing about this process that's done in the absence of the inmate: one person's signature can start the ball rolling for release with two more names required for sign-off. But, only one is needed to keep someone in jail. Clearly, there's much more of a safeguard to let someone out than there is to keep someone in. I wonder how the framers of this policy would feel if it were their kid. The stakes are high.

I write:

To: Reviewing Commissioner

From: Commissioner Barbara H. Treen

RE: Ted Martucci – Nassau County Correctional Facility

Date: April 11, 1986

As a close personal friend of the Martucci family for 30 years, I would like to profile for you the character and background of Teddy and his parents.

As the youngest of three children, born with Cooley's

anemia, Teddy has never had an easy time. His life expectancy as medically described, is limited which I feel has been the causal factor in his low self-esteem, bid for attention and criminal activity. I can say without qualification that his parents have provided the healthiest support system possible including their 'tough love' attitude at the time of his arrest.

At this time, his first incarceration, my belief is that this 20-year-old would be served far better as would the community, to be released with strict supervision and haste. Due to his medical infirmity, his time is spent in the hospital unit with no opportunity to program, limited family visits and certainly no incentive for more positive community reintegration.

His family has plans to remain firm and watchful of Teddy as well as considering an independent small business venture for him upon release.

I hope my reflections shed further light on reviewing this pathetic case and that you are in agreement with a release recommendation."

I learn that as the letter is being read by Joe during the review along with the rest of the file, the Parole Officer's editorial comments accompany it. He suggests that the kid is spoiled, that his parents are enablers and that if he serves his whole time inside it will probably save his life. And so during this macho bonding between these two men over Teddy's case, early release which will allow him to get proper medical attention is denied by Joe, while Teddy is handcuffed to a bed in need of a blood transfusion that Nassau Medical Center can't give. This is a death sentence.

It's Friday night. The family is informed of this decision immediately. Ted calls to tell me the outcome. The problem is not only that he has to spend more time in jail but that this hospital can't treat his condition. I feel so responsible I can hardly breathe. I question if this is even the right job for me. I don't seem to be able to pull anything off. How could I have done this differently? I know I've got to find out what's happened during the review and if my recommendation carried any weight. There has to be a reconsideration put in place. I've been up all night debating with myself and rather than taking twists and turns as if there's some particular strategy or reason for guilt, I go for the simple truth of it and follow that straight line.

I'm so mindful of possible spins here that I'm making it harder than it needs to be. I ask Ted to get me the new medical documentation that's in the folder and on Saturday morning I call the Chairman of the Board of Parole at his home and describe the circumstances. Not wanting to invite any appearance of impropriety, I go right to the top asking for advice. He advises me to call the reviewing commissioner (Big Joe) directly and impress the medical implications on him to see what his thoughts were when he made his decision. I immediately call Joe. I remind him of the case and of my concern. I read him the following letter that he should have seen as part of the file that Ted has delivered to me. I wonder if he's read it or galloped through the file and listened instead to the parole officer drone on about these suburban kids and my connection.

The letter's dated April 4, 1986, and it's from NYU

Medical Center Department of Pediatrics for parole information.

"Dear Sir,

Teddy Martucci is a 20-year-old white male with Thalassemia Major, who has been followed by the Pediatric Hematology Division at NYU-Bellevue Hospital since the disease was diagnosed in infancy. This letter is to summarize his history and current medical problem.

Thalassemia is a severe congenital anemia that is fatal in early childhood if not treated with transfusions. In recent years, patients with Thalassemia have been treated with super-transfusions, which maintains the hematocrit above 35% in order to shut off production of abnormal blood by the bone marrow; this reduces their blood volume and energy requirements and extends their lives. Multiple transfusions, however, have numerous complications and patients with Thalassemia are prey to all of these. Most severe is hemochromatosis, which is a the medical term for disposition in the body of excess iron from the transfused blood; this causes loss of function in some organs, most commonly the hormone secreting glands, liver and heart, and is the most common cause of death and major medical problems in Thalassemics. Daily subcutaneous injections of Desferal, a chemical that binds iron and allows it to be excreted in the urine, has been shown to delay onset of this problem.

Teddy has been maintained on a hyper transfusion protocol since early childhood and so does not have skeletal deformities typical of the untreated disease. He has had his spleen removed in childhood to decrease his transfusion requirement. Desferal therapy was started late in childhood; for a time he complied with treatment, but in recent years he has not done so, probably due to substance abuse and psychological factors, and his hemochromatosis has worsened. Tests now show that Teddy has severe iron overload and his medical condition reflects this fact.

Short stature and delayed puberty are common complications of iron overload and Teddy has both; he has been successfully treated for delayed puberty with injections of testosterone. Impairment of the adrenal glands is also evident. His liver is massively enlarged and liver function tests show chronic dysfunction.

Since admission to Nassau County Medical Center in January 1986, more problems have developed. Gallstones which were known to be present began causing severe pain and inflammation of the pancreas, necessitating surgical removal of the gallbladder. Diabetes mellitus, another feared complication of Hemochromatosis, was diagnosed after 2-3 weeks of weight loss and extreme thirst. It is now being treated with insulin injections, but Teddy's general condition makes this treatment difficult. The most serious development is evidence of poor pumping function of the heart. Heart disease is the commonest cause of death in people with Thalassemia; the vast majority die within a year of its diagnosis. The condition of Teddy's heart as reflected in the most recent test results make it likely that overt heart disease will be detected soon.

The medical regimen to which Teddy is subject (in addition to the testosterone and insulin mentioned above) is as follows:

Transfusion with red blood cells every two weeks

Penicillin and Vitamin C by mouth daily

Desferal injection under the skin daily for a total of eight hours

In summary, Teddy Martucci is a young man with severe congenital anemia, who has several of the worst complications of the disease and its treatment. His life at best is restricted by his medical condition and requires treatment, and is likely to be progressively more restricted. It is likely that development of more complications will prove fatal within the next few years or sooner.

If I can be of further assistance in this matter, please do not hesitate to contact me.

David Martin, M.D.

Fellow, Pediatric Hematology

Frances Flug, M.D.

Attending, Pediatric Hematology"

There's a short silence at the other end of the phone as I read this to Joe. His concern is that he's offended me, his friend, rather than that he's made the wrong decision. He tells me that he's going to call the Chair of the Parole Board and get some input from him as to protocol. I tell him that I already spoke to him and that the ball's in Joe's court. Politics being what they are, I understand that he wants to cover himself and check it out. I explain that if there's information he may not have been aware (the medical), he can reopen the case and reverse the decision. Before he hangs up he says, "Yes, I know about your memo but the PO and I decided to remove it from the file. Ya' know Barb, we're trying to protect you. You don't want to leave a paper trail about your connection and get in trouble."

I feel immediately the kind of rage the guys inside describe to me when they tell me about their crimes and the disrespect they felt that lead them back to the bar with a gun to get even with the thug who dissed them! This undercutting of me, though it's done in a manner of paternalism, is impossible to get Joe to understand. I absolutely and intentionally want this paper trail! It's also hard to blow up at him because it's such a politically thorny situation. He has no problem telling me what they've done believing it absolutely right; they're on my side. I could almost hear them asking each other what could be wrong with me in my naiveté. They are so misguided. I had hoped I'd be wrong but I knew going into this that he was going to be a problem. He's clearly troubled by the situation but his patronizing attitude wins out over the facts of the case. After he makes a call to the Board Chairman, he reports back to me. He tells me he was told, "You can do what you want, but if I were you, I wouldn't change the decision." Then says to me, "You're very close to the case and you're an emotional woman." I'm certain he's echoing his conversation with the Chair who I'm quite mindful that, while he gave me direction about a remedy, is giving Joe a different spin that serves as cautious job security.

My next call is to Bill McMann, the Chair of The Commission on Correction (the state oversight agency) who compassionately hears the story. He has no authority to release this boy but does say that he will have his agency medical staff speak to the hospital and confirm the diagnosis. He understands that we're not just looking at more time; we're looking at time spent in a place that can't medically treat him. This man has a deep belief that the people in prison are our children, our parents, our friends, our neighbors. He takes action immediately.

He tells me that he will see if he can arrange a custody transfer to New York City Department of Correction so if he does remain in inmate status, he can be treated at his own hospital in the city. It's Saturday night. There are no more calls I can make now. I sit and wait and wait and hope for a callback. I hope I've put some wheels in motion.

On Sunday the calls come. One of them is from the Division's Executive Director who tells me that I should get new updated medical documentation and bring it to the full board review meeting tomorrow morning in Albany. And a call from Commissioner McMann comes telling me great news: that Jackie McMickens, who is the Commissioner of the New City Department of Corrections, will accept custody of Teddy in her jurisdiction and that they will have an ambulance at the back door of the Nassau County Medical Center and transfer him to NYU Medical Center on the City's inmate 'count.' This will happen as soon as all the kinks are ironed out.

And so the Martuccis are updated and they are able to immediately get me new information from the doctors to take to the meeting and at the same time we're hoping to transfer him to another hospital ASAP. I'm doing the best I can in spite of the resistance of my own agency. Either the full board can vote to reverse the decision and his parents take him to the hospital as a parolee, or New York

City Corrections will take custody and transfer him to NYU Medical Center as an inmate. We're racing the clock. This sounds pretty foolproof if the system weren't as broken as I know it is. Sometimes, I think, if you're sitting at the family table your opinions are discounted. Your family calls in a specialist instead of listening to you...too close.

I'm armed with the new letter for tomorrow morning's meeting in Albany.

Dear Sir:

This letter is intended as an addendum to my letter of my previous letter describing the medical condition of Teddy Martucci. Since that letter was written Teddy has continued to reside in the Nassau County Medical Center (NCMC); I have been in contact with the physicians treating him there.

Teddy now has congestive heart failure (CHF), a condition in which the heart is unable to pump blood to the tissues efficiently. CHF can be treated with medication, but it is eventually fatal. People with thalassemia, who have CHF because of iron overload, have a severe and rapidly progressive form of this condition. Half of them die within three months of its diagnosis, and the vast majority does not live more than a year from that time. The rapid deterioration in Teddy's cardiac function in the past few months makes it likely that he will not survive much longer without intensive treatment.

Options for treatment of CHF in thalassemic patients, aside from the standard medical treatment, are limited. At present, the only other treatment known to be of benefit is high-dose chelation (Desferal) therapy given continuously by intravenous transfusion through a surgically implanted line for an indefinite time. This regimen is experimental and requires close supervision by an experienced pediatric hematologist and a cardiologist familiar with the problems of thalassemic patients. We intend to start it as soon as possible, but he must be in this medical center for treatment to commence.

At this point, we think that it's very important that Teddy be released from his jail sentence. It is likely that he has only a few months to live and that his health will continue to be poor. If he is to survive longer than that, he needs to be under the care of a team of physicians and nurses experienced in the management of thalassemia and its complications, and to receive the intensive treatment described above. Such a team exists here where Teddy has been a patient virtually all his life and we feel that it would be unfair to deny him the benefit of its expertise at this critical point. At the NCMS, Teddy is managed by physicians with no experience of this very complex disorder, who cannot be expected to provide him with the best available care.

We will be happy to provide further information to the court should it be required.

Sincerely,

It is signed by Drs. David Martin, a Fellow of Pediatric Hematology and Margaret Karpatkin, Professor and

Barbara Hanson Treen

Director of Pediatric Hematology at NYU Medical Center.

It's Monday. I'm packed, prepared to beat the traffic for the three hour trip.

I have the letter. I've got all the documents and have rehearsed the story in the least emotional way possible so as not to be accused of mixing feeling with fact (quite a crime). The phone rings at 6:30 a.m. It's Bill McMann, telling me that Teddy has died earlier this morning. No one reads the letter.

I'm now really an emotional woman!

I've thought before about leaving this job. I'm thinking more seriously now. The three hours of driving has helped put things in perspective though; I'm no calmer but I'm definitely not going to run from these guys. The consequence of their sexism is murder! I think I'm feeling those twin outrages, victimization and revenge, those things that injustice creates. My arrival in Albany later this morning is greeted like the sound of one hand clapping. No one in my agency even offers condolences or suggests that perhaps the decision rendered was folly.

I not only mourn the death of my friends' child but will always feel responsible. When I get home from the road, I go to the wake. I didn't attend the funeral but have been to the cemetery since, where my friend Annette, his mom, had her ashes buried in his grave upon her death five years ago. My friend Ted left the neighborhood and moved to Florida where two years ago he died of loneliness. I am certain that Teddy Boy's death hastened their premature demise. But then I'm only an emotional woman in this male bastion.

3 | Attica and Other Riots

During my nine year 'practice marriage' I tinkered with work as the Religious Education Director of our Unitarian Church. This was the Boston church in which we married as a 'mixed' couple and this was our NY church once we moved when the children came along. While the job scarcely paid any bills, it did get me out of the neighborhood and introduce me to a broader agenda of social justice of the time: anti-war and civil rights activities. It was also in this church that I became an accessory to a heist when men came to the door telling me that the minister had agreed to lend the grand piano to the neighboring parish for the holidays. I cheerily led the way, accompanying the men and the piano to their pickup truck. This accomplice status unwittingly occurred again at another job and it was but one in a series of being witness to the wrong side of the law. And also in this church, Jesus Christ was never mentioned except when someone fell down the stairs. The nine years of quiet boredom in an increasingly platonic marriage paled in comparison with feeling part of the real world at work. What I would have given for this 'quiet boredom' so often in the chaotic years of the future.

I think it's luck if a couple stays together after marrying at 20 years of age. Infatuation and hormones served as the starter kit of my marriage. Although we agreed about the big issues, our personalities were so different that it was almost impossible to get a conversation going. He flourished around the advent of the babies but dealt himself out of adult relationships. And in this Leavitt house, coffee-klatsching community, I found myself lonely and different. It didn't help that I gave a sermon entitled "Ticky-Tacky Little Boxes" with Pete Seeger music in the background instead of hymns, directed at the error of homogenous neighborhoods. We lost several of the congregation's more influential but conservative members after that morning. Although I had all I thought I wanted - a family, a home - it still didn't seem to be enough. I wanted passion and went looking for it in the political issues of the day. I cared deeply about the mess in Vietnam and the red-lining going on in housing and I lent my support as a not-too-well informed housewife. My mother argued with me about taking the twins in their stroller to protests. Funny, I never thought of this as a risky practice as it went beyond politics, it was a social trend of the time --- until I was arrested and clubbed in the same day but luckily without my children.

The arrest was for soliciting prostitution! At 5 AM on a Saturday, I was the designated 'team leader' for the planned march in Washington to protest the war. My job was boarding people on the northern line of the LIRR from Hempstead, LI, to Penn Station…easy. Only due to a real communication gap, when I herded people on the pre-arranged last car of the train after asking if they were with SANE (Sane Nuclear Policy organization), the uninformed conductor immediately became suspicious. Further complicating the matter, he'd seen me wandering around the station asking men if they were Steve (an unknown I was instructed to pair with.) Plus telling him the train car was my private party once he came to collect tickets didn't help my credibility. Much to my surprise, I was dragged off the train at Penn Station, taken to the bowels of the place and booked, until friends from the southern line train, hearing of the commotion, came to my rescue. And so began a day on Amtrak to D.C.; plotting, meeting people, feeling connected, making a difference. The rhythm of the march only intensified what I knew was missing in my life: a sense of purpose. And then Wham! I was clubbed by a cop riding a horse clearing out this crowd of do-gooders on the streets of Washington. I was definitely on the right path here, I thought.

Every time I left the house on another world-saving mission, I felt conflicted. While I was totally free to do as I wished, I knew that the deterioration of my marriage was what was making it possible. After all, there is such a thing as giving one so much 'space' that they fall into a new place. And I did. My husband didn't seem to notice my absences and while this may have been someone else's ideal love affair, to me it meant indifference on his part. There was no negotiation, no mediation, no arguing, and no need for it. I merely announced that I wanted a divorce one morning and my husband Dean's world fell apart in surprise! How unaware he was demonstrated how different we were.

I felt guilt for years after. I got the house and the kids. And he got a broken heart. The kids seemed resilient and never really voiced worries in the beginning. Trying to appease myself with the decision, I did everything I could for him not to hate me. He found an apartment in the bachelor's mecca of Long Beach and my mother made him curtains. I made him my 'friend' by sharing stories of my dating dilemmas....O.M.G! And I requested no alimony although we didn't have so much as a plug nickel to begin with. We opted for a divorce based on a two-year legal separation. It seemed safer, more of a test, and cheaper. We had nothing to divide except the care and custody of the kids and for several years this went well. He, a reliable and devoted weekend father, and me frantically searching for work and purpose.

Life as a single parent could not have happened as seamlessly as it did on the home front had it not been for a neighbor. If one of the primary reasons for leaving a marriage is for the good of the children, it follows that there has to be a plan for them while I'm at work. In my case, it didn't take exactly a village to raise my kids, but pretty close. Enter Anna Russin, who we called Nana. Anna was an older woman who lived with a family on our block that had five teenagers. In her childhood she was raised along with the mother of that family. Nana never married and had no family of her own. She was overjoyed at becoming totally in charge of my little house with Heidi and Jimmy in it. They were in the third grade. If she was overjoyed, I was over the moon with the arrangement. Although she was hired just to be there after school until I got home from work, the hours became longer and longer. She'd appear at 7AM if anyone was sick, she stayed if I was late at the office, and I soon learned that she loved to iron and cook! Nana's salary was $20 per week. This was 1968. I was a woman ahead of her time.

Nana didn't have an easy job. Jimmy was a little boy with a quick temper and a short fuse. He'd asked me one evening why I couldn't be home for him after school like the other mothers. He'd had every reason to feel betrayed as he interpreted this new life as one in which he was the only male and was outvoted. We were lucky to have all kinds of weekend support from my mother whom, while he saw her as his ally, presented for him an unwelcome and domineering addition to this imbalanced family of three women and him. His father was on board seeing him each weekend but his male bonding skills couldn't balance the unhappiness Jimmy felt. Boys need the support of strong role models and his father was slipping away. And Heidi was an acute asthmatic who since infancy had experienced hospitalizations including cardiac arrest as a result and had to be carefully watched by an experienced eye. I was riddled with concern about them but convinced that raising them in a household bereft of emotion and conversation would be more damaging. The dance of juggling appointments and using lunch hours for teachers conferences and errands was the easiest part of running our lives while I worked. The hardest part was short changing our time together. This is a reality I will always regret.

My first interview responding to a want ad landed me a job with the very less-than glamorous Boy Scouts of America as a clerical something that paid $85 a week, and with child support of $25, I was certain I could manage. It was a time that was driven by my absolute determination. I never had any doubt that I'd make it. Shortly into this new life, a neighbor I slightly knew asked if I'd be interested in a job at *Newsday*, the Long Island newspaper. She worked there in some secretarial capacity and seemed certain that I too would have a shot at it. The paper was less than a half mile of home. *Newsday* was a household word. It covered the Island; fashion, food, national news, local murders, politics -- to borrow the motto of a better known paper, 'all the news fit to print.' The names that graced the by-lines rolled off the tongue like celebrities. I never envisioned the white low-rise marble-like building down the road I regularly passed would become my employer, nor did I ever consider a future in journalism. I just needed a paycheck and was positively certain that any gofer task they had, I could do. Neither my neighbor nor I knew if there was indeed a job opening, but her enthusiasm told me it was in the bag and prompted an interview. And it was bagged. It was as if they hired people (young women) they liked and then found spots to fill. It was a veritable Playboy Club of journalism. My first interview was with an editor of some renown who approved of me. He was an older and kindly guy reminiscent of an uncle, anyone's uncle, and he listened as I stumbled over the fact that I had children. One never knew if parenting was a liability requiring time out from work when 'Johnny' sneezed or if you were seen as working constantly for the need of money. I took the honest route and as it turned out, found that I was to be one of many working in a stable of single moms....hmm. He passed me along to the managing editor who I more than made points with; this guy's interest in me was not journalistic. The code words and attitudes that added up to sexism, which was treating people differently based on gender, was an invisible language well-known to all of us. The gender gap posed inequities for me in almost everything I needed; from credit for installing a phone in my name to unfair and condescending treatment wherever I went. But sexism didn't always treat me badly. And now it was responsible for my getting hired. I had no compunctions about accepting. It's the way things were and in this case it worked okay for me. I was assigned as the editorial assistant to the dayside City Desk.

In so many ways I came of age at the paper. It was no place for a 29-year-old Gibson Girl. I was the chief gofer-girl on the day-side. There were clones on the night-side when the paper was put to bed and on the 'lobster shift' when they printed the paper. The work was demanding with my name on every editor's lips yelling for something, everything. It could have been research, telexing messages to far away worlds, a run to the pressroom, food, a note delivered to someone too far to yell to, fetching from the morgue, etc. The real job description was to make the guys (and they were all guys) on the city desk happy and guard the gateway between the paper and the public. I took all the news tips by phone and walk-ins and doled out the info to the Desk, differentiating between the nut-jobs and the real news …sometimes it was hard to tell. I sat at the nerve center of this vintage news room at the head of the Desk. It was a huge horseshoe shaped table that wrapped around a room the size of a gymnasium. At the Desk were the editors; national, city, local and rewrite. Filling the rest of the room were the reporters' desks where they waited for assignments from these editors. It was still the days of the typewriter, carbon paper, news spikes. The newsroom hummed; pencils were thrown, people tapped, conversations were yelled from 50 yards away, everyone was on a phone, most of the desk drawers were filled with supplies including bottles of bourbon and scotch, and the UP wire room behind glass backing up to the Desk droned. Ideas went around the room like electric currents! The petty jealousies, creativity and huge egos made it a combustible place to work and I loved it.

My recollections from my school days were that all

those students aiming for serious writing careers were dorky. This newsroom was not where those people had ended up obviously. It was mostly filled with beautiful people! If they weren't beautiful, they were part of some family dynasty or another. I learned early on that one of my most important tasks was to keep the social score; who was dating who and it rotated very quickly. If I had to reach people at home, it was important to know whose home to find them in. People in this news room seemed not to notice that there was a world of available people beyond the office at 550 Stewart Avenue in Garden City to socialize with. Their dating lives were confined to the cast of characters in the building and thankfully I was included in this game. Not only was I available to date but my short half-mile commute to work made my home an attractive hangout for long distance reporters after hours, for take-out and talk. And my children were always included in these gatherings. I was perceived as everybody's buddy and a damsel in distress. The pressure cooker of getting out a fine daily paper, amazingly and successfully coexisted with three martini lunches, fist fights in the newsroom, hangovers, smoking dope in the elevator and romantic hijinks. Every depiction of Spencer Tracy and Katherine Hepburn in newsrooms was true!

During a time that I was dating a sports writer (a super guy who gave me the guts to be a bit of a maverick with great confidence), I manufactured an editor whose name popped up often. Part of my job was to prepare the 'night budget.' At the end of the day when the shift was changing and people were 'up,' a list of stories and follow-ups had to be communicated to the next crew. It'd been a slow news day so I added some humor by writing, "Art Bascombe (totally fictitious) called in sick. Get mid-east writer fill in." No one ever questioned who Art was even though he would appear often and no one ever called a fill-in to cover. No one it seemed wanted to risk owning up to not knowing him. Instead, the sports department headlined him in a bowling tournament, taking bets on his winning as they had heard of his notoriety but couldn't exactly place him. Bascombe (posed by me) lost the match of course. My boyfriend and I won the purse and the jig was up. Bascombe (always with an "e") became one of the legends. Another not so ridiculous adventure but equally as memorable, was accompanying two 'visitors' in the lobby to the accounting department. Once there, their guns came out and a holdup ensued. Remarkably, when taken to the police station, I couldn't identify them. I should have learned my lesson back at the piano in the church. Although the paper dealt with fact, fantastical flights and humor were de rigueur. One of the more publicly celebrated events was a book written and published with each chapter written by a different reporter. Some chapters were pure fiction and some autobiographical. The reader was left to decide. It was a grand episode!

Even though the job gained access for me to many events -- a week at the Mets spring training camp, box seats at basketball games, a story that sent me to Puerto Rico, and the general envy of the neighborhood -- my ego was beginning to shrink as reporters filed stories I believed I was capable of writing. Although I spoke to the editors, they flatly refused to run my pieces. My jealousy was mostly reserved for the female writers who were outnumbered by the men. They sat in a grouping that looked more like a sorority as they were assigned to what was called "Part II": a home style section. It wasn't quite their time yet to question legally why they weren't assigned to hard news stories but it was still a time when I felt they lorded their status over me. To test my abilities, I wrote a few pieces using my latest editor/boyfriend's byline which got accepted. I never got my name out there but at least I knew I could do the job. There existed a very real barrier that left me frozen in place even though I recognized I didn't have a professional resume. The women's movement was on its way inside me!

One typical news day two years down the pike, a call comes in for me on the Desk. It's my husband. We're still living in the amorphous legal separation status zone where you can date yet cling to the cushion of your marriage on hold. He's calling from his bedside phone in a hospital. He's been in an accident, is in traction and is going to be fine but perhaps will have a limp. He requires care once discharged and wants me to come to the hospital in Washington Heights, upper Manhattan. I leave work and throughout my hour-long drive to the hospital, I'm rehearsing my options, thinking I am so sure why he wants to see me. He needs help, he'll say, and wants to come back to the house and stay for a while until he heals. I've gone so far in my thinking that I will have to explain to the kids not to get too comfortable and that Daddy isn't really coming home for good. I rearrange the furniture in my mind making the den into a bedroom for him. Clearly, under the circumstances I'm prepared to have Dean in the house. He is an incredibly sympathetic figure after all. He's even more forlorn once I get to the hospital room. He's in traction, his leg in a sling, his head bandaged, and suffering. Had I made a mistake, I ask myself. Should there be reconciliation? He seems not to do well without me. And then he starts to talk. He tells me of the auto accident and how this will change his life. And by the way, once he's discharged he's planning to live with his girlfriend at her apartment ...but not before marrying her. She's a nurse and perfectly suited for his needs and not incidentally, very virtuous. Therefore, they've arranged a ticket for me to go to Mexico immediately and get that divorce based on the separation. It has been more than a couple of years. I am speechless! I've been so used to being in charge and suddenly I feel like the one who is being left behind. And in the room walks the bride-to-be, all very civilized. I figure the shock waves serve me right and I have no reason to complain. I mentally move the furniture back in the den.

In order to accomplish this two-year 'quickie' divorce, they'd researched what has to be done. Tucked in her hand is the plane ticket, a check for travel expenses and documents to be signed by the hospital notary. This is a Catholic hospital and the notary is a nun. Dean gets in a wheelchair and we push him down the corridors to the administrative offices. There's much pleasantry all around until the Sister-Notary reads what she's signing: my request to divorce this patient. She looks at him, then at me and never speaks another word. I too find it pathetic. There's an agreement with the Tijuana courts for this rushed divorce and after making arrangements for the children's care and my two-day absence from work, I board what's known as the 'Freedom Flight.'

The about-to-be singles on the plane are a mixed bunch. One couple is there together cashing in on this divorce as a last holiday in Mexico! Others are in various degrees of heartache to jubilation. And still others are planning immediate weddings in a different part of the court house once these divorce decrees are signed with a stroke of the pen for both. A lawyer meets us all in a limo at the airport and deposits us at a dingy motel in a Texas border town. We are told to be ready early in the morning for the trip to 'Freedom-land.' I have a roommate who sobs the entire night while I phone Dean at the assigned hour to tell him I'm safe and on schedule. We seemed so chummy it's a shame, the roommate says, that he can't join me. And so with a group of strangers, I answer questions posed in Spanish in a Mexican courtroom expunging the first part of my life. After the hospital visit, I never lay eyes on the second Mrs. Hanson again. Unhappily, the children do.

I return to work a new woman. I needn't have worried. I discover that I don't need the safety net of the separation. I'm a new category of person, divorcee, and it makes me feel as though I've taken the pains to stand for something! I feel almost defiant. My veil of guilt is lifted now that somebody else is taking care of Dean. The remarriage of their father also makes a difference to Jimmy and Heidi, but not in a good way. Their eagerness to visit their dad is fading as their stepmother presents them with a list of chores each weekend. Unfortunately their father's passivity allows this to continue. I don't think these kids who are used to weekends playing with their dad should suddenly be enlisted as little worker bees. Jimmy is particularly angry with this turn of events. Another woman added to his already crowded world of authority figures: sister, mother, grandmother. It's not what he wanted or needed. And this newest woman is a particularly strident one. My reports to Dean about this disenchantment falls on deaf ears and his wife's treatment of Jimmy creates the beginning of what is to become a lifelong estrangement between father and son.

Meanwhile, back at the newsroom, it's a veritable tide of reporters; they go out to cover their stories and come back to file them. There should be a revolving door. It isn't unusual for them to ask for tips from me regarding stories or profiling me in relevant stories. One of the people I become friendly with is a talented guy who I steer to interview a friend. The story is about separated couples who continue affairs with one another. After she's interviewed by him, she tells me of her dislike for him and his grilling her about me. This is indeed a surprise to me. His name is Joe Treen and he's, in my estimation, totally off limits to me in the romance department. He's the personification of a 'golden boy'; charismatic, well liked, mid-western preppy with Hollywood looks, and let's not forget, married! At 6'3" he has a loping walk, a thick mop of beautiful hair, huge brown eyes and holds back what often seems like howling laughter using a slow smirk instead. He invented 'boyish charm.' Oh no, he is definitely not interested in this suburban divorcee with two kids from around the corner.

If I were to identify the two driving and lasting forces in my life, it would be my passion for justice and for Joe Treen. I think he came into my life at a vulnerable point in his. As I was to soon discover through sordid involvement, he was separating from his wife. As I was the person charged with reaching reporters, I was one day given a change of phone number by Joe's closest friend. It was Joe's number! Wow! What's this? Has Brian moved in with the Treens? A few days later, a change in Joe's number, moving in with another reporter (male). This musical apartment syndrome is not unheard of. My personal situation at the time is filled with the drama I seem to attract; I'm trying to break up with someone at the paper who's started stalking me. It happens to be one of Joe's bosses although no one has knowledge of this. Joe and I continue a cool friendship which includes lunching together sometimes in the upstairs cafeteria. Seeing me as 'safe' I'm certain gives him permission to confide in me. I counsel him, listen to him, empathize with him…whatever it takes, for he is dazzling. His personal affairs straighten out quickly with a fast divorce as the continual buzz of other people's scandals make his old news. He has moved his desk far across the news room and away from Brian.

My romantic intrigue, long kept secret and known by only my stalker and me, continues with on again and off again predictability. This femme fatal stuff could be very heady until it's unwanted and happens to you; then it's just scary. Finally, in a fix of mental health he accepts a position at *The New York Times*. I am so relieved and happy not to be ogled at work daily. I'm certain most of the staff knows but who would really care? Everyone else is carrying on and their stories beat mine by a long shot! But his absence from 'my' newsroom doesn't last so long. Short of a year into my friendship with Joe, he asks me out on a real date. Of course I accept, still in disbelief that this isn't all rebound. I don't kid myself that I could be more than 'one of the girls in the newsroom' to him. The date is to be a trip into the city with dinner waiting at the other end. Very soon into the drive he notices that we're being followed. I feign ignorance while I am horrified that he'll find out who's following us making this the shortest date on record. We go to Joe's apartment to dodge the car following us when the phone calls begin and hang up when he answers. I ultimately fess up, telling him my story. The truth and the guy's ID come tumbling out. It feels pretty tawdry to me in the retelling and puts me in the same league as the many others at the paper. But his reaction takes away my shame and I'm suddenly the victim. He becomes my knight in shining armor and in this moment I fall head over heels in love with Joe Treen...and the other guy exits from my life.

The newsroom at this time is as public as social media is today. All the private lives that inhabit it became instantly exposed. I don't know anyone working here who doesn't love being here. Folks come in early to their shift and stick around long after. While the business of news is to tell others' stories, the storytellers reveal themselves in so doing. Discussions among reporters and editors as to the shape a story will take solidify before me throughout the days. Missing babies, far away wars, local elections all become the threads of borrowed reality. The human interest stories all are much more personal; except for the older secretarial support staff, almost everyone is paired with or mooning about a colleague du jour, despite their marital status. It's hard to differentiate an affair from the real thing. I have no idea how to define my own romance with Joe, which has bloomed for me into obsession. I still have no illusions that he could really be serious about me.

But I have abandoned the notion that I need to be part of a couple to count and certainly there isn't need for rescue. I've been managing happily with family and work and dating so I worry little about anything but the present and protect my feelings by telling this to myself. Still, this guy is different and his ardor feels great. Just how different he is, I'll find out.

We are secretive at work about our relationship. Just a couple of Joe's close friends know. And I have no real women friends here. There is that caste system between the reporters and the assistants (I would have been known as the 'copy boy' if I looked different) and I don't fit into any clear clique. We feel very safe and smug keeping us a secret and pass notes to one another placing them in our mailboxes which surround the back of the room. This privacy that we've decided upon for dignities sake makes me begin to feel that we are really serious. When Joe is anywhere within range, my pulse races. We go out of our way to ignore each another so as not to arouse suspicion. It becomes a game of risk and brings on bouts of jealousy for both of us as we banter with the beautiful other people in the room. But after only a couple of weeks it is the birth of a real relationship; one that I trust. And we begin playing house almost immediately. I rush home from work settling into my real job as mother and begin dinner. After Joe finishes with his story, he shows up and we carry on as though we'd always been a family of four.

Joe was overly solicitous of the twins which I loved. At 28 there was only a 17 year difference between him and the kids. He'd not been around children before and treads very lightly initially. He seemed to be as much enamored of my package deal - the house in the burbs, the kids, the dog - as he was of me. I had always, on the other hand, been apologetic about my regular-ness. Oh, how I wanted to be viewed as a sophisticated city woman! I never felt I was the suburban stereotype but for Joe it became part of my appeal. He seemed so compatible that it was as if he was searching for his identity in my ordinary reflection. Our newly acquired togetherness had him waking up in the mornings on the living room couch. All the experts these years later will say that to expose kids to a relationship until it is permanent is the wrong thing. But at the time I found that honesty and showing affection was a plus for them and didn't worry about the appropriateness of the man in the house. However, Joe was quite Victorian and embarrassed to find himself ducking from two adolescents. Not willing to live apart and not willing to 'live in sin,' his solution was that we marry. After a blissful six weeks of romance, we married on May 7, 1971. The day was a Friday. It was decided two days earlier on Wednesday. In looking back, I think the real engine in his rush for marriage was his insecurity.

To attest that we had pulled off our secretive romance, when I came to work on Thursday, the morning after the proposal, I was asked out on a date by one of the writers. I said I couldn't because I was busy getting married that Friday! We were both stupefied by my pronouncement but it took these words for me to believe it was true. That was convincing enough to legitimize us, I'd say. The guy felt like a fool and I felt that I had tempted fate. The wedding was not hailed by many, most of all, my friend Pam who had so disliked him that she refused to be my witness. His parents showed disapproval from as far away as Milwaukee. My mother knew him and was thrilled as long as I was. And, there was that call from a city desk assistant on the wedding day telling us that my stalker, back at the paper, had planned on disrupting the ceremony. This didn't bother Joe at all but I still felt the whole thing so entirely extraordinary for me that I waited for the other shoe to drop. It was as though I was peeking into someone else's life. There were eight of us there at the Ethical Culture Society; the bride and groom (a lapsed Episcopalian WASP and me), Heidi and Jimmy, my mother, two friends from the paper as witnesses and the Leader who performed the service. Joe resisted inviting anyone else to the ceremony which seemed appropriate in that it was a second marriage for each. But was this just a private experiment? I recall my nervousness asking if I could sit through the ceremony. The impulsiveness of this wedding left my knees shaking: it was too good to be true. Indeed! We left immediately for a honeymoon in Montreal with an eye toward checking out relocation. Not long after the vows, Joe's dark side surfaced.

Joe moved into my ranch house. We continued our work half a mile away at the paper. In general we took great pleasure from planning dinners and PTA meetings through notes to one another. I would leave him a note on the kitchen table when I left for the office while he was still asleep; he would leave a note for me in the same place greeting me when I came home in his absence and in between we wrote each other at work. The notes were filled with plans for the future, as needed apologies, clarifications of conversations and swooning. Had we confined our marriage to the written word, it may have worked better. One of the more typical notes found in my mail box when I got to work : "I just thought you would like to know that we are together both here and at home and that I love you, back you, worship you, adore you, dig you, believe in you, and want to stay together with you for our lifetime. Joe."

Step-parenting is the second hardest job in the world (the first being parenting) but he acted like an old hand at being a stepdad and in the beginning this worked. We had agreed that remaining at my house should be temporary and that in order for a marriage to work it needed 'our' house. He assumed that those digs would be a brownstone in the city - not a setting I could easily endorse for two suburban preadolescents. But it was all very early to rearrange our living. We'd barely had time to change the linens. And almost as soon as we'd returned from the honeymoon, he announced that we should have a baby. I was atwitter with the romance of it but as with making a move, I thought it premature. I wanted to concentrate on bonding as a family in this marriage, at least for a year. A new husband, a stepfather and a baby? When the baby issue was set aside for the time being, he decided that he'd legally adopt Heidi and Jimmy. This notion was also rejected as they had a full time dad, just living in another house. When he finally accepted this fact, he decided to hold the purse strings of the meager child support; who needed sneakers and when. I worked hard to bring harmony to this collision course. He didn't appreciate my resistance and his resentment began to show itself. He wanted equal time.

During our first summer together I tried to fulfill social obligations that he seemed to be ducking: meeting relatives and friends on both sides. Unless he was at work, he was ill at ease with others who he thought believed he was going to flunk some kind of test. Over time he became an increasingly tough disciplinarian with my son, reflecting his own childhood experience and he allowed for no mistakes. He made no bones about his rarified life as the son of demanding Wisconsinites who he claimed put their kids second to the kennels of dogs they judged. The daily battle with Jimmy took on legs leading to his criticism of my indulgences and parenting. There was never any wiggle room allowed. And so as his decisions to move, to have a baby and to adopt the kids were formed, so too was his decision to send my son away to a military boarding school. This latest one was a deal breaker for me that carried a silence with it that lasted much of the summer and Jimmy was not the one who ultimately was sent away. Heidi on the other hand had a huge crush on her stepfather and was overheard telling a friend that "all her mother's husbands were beautiful." She was in agreement with anything Joe wanted.

Then came the day that did change everything in my life. It was September 9th, 1971, while I was working in the wire room 'ripping and reading' that I learned about Attica, along with the rest of the world. I read the accounts of the riot that had been fomenting for a while because inmates wanted to have more than one roll of toilet paper per month and more than one shower a week, and reasonable non-racist work assignments, among other fair demands. The reports came to me in stereo, as while I read the wires, I talked by phone to Joe who was covering the story, circling the prison battlefield in a helicopter. By the next day, 1,281 inmates held 43 hostages and took control of cellblocks and buildings trying to get the officials' attention. After four days of repeated attempts at negotiations by the inmates and standoffs by the authorities, the machismo of Governor Rockefeller trying to be in power rather than right, resulted in his sending in between 500 to one thousand state troopers spraying the population in the yard with bullets after they were felled by tear gas from the sky making Attica's grounds "the bloodiest one-day encounter between Americans since the Civil War." It cost 39 human lives and made an indelible imprint in the annals of history; a cautionary tale of injustice.

I set the bar for the achievements I wanted for the rest of my life in the wire room on that day. There are no words to describe my reaction to this inhumanity. It triggered a shift in my consciousness that would change me forever. And it did. It became a calling for me in the way the ministry and the arts call their recruits. It gave new dimension to my soul. My personal problems became insignificant and dwarfed by the events happening in Attica. While my job was envied by many and I was never at a loss for conversation in talking of it, I was not setting the world on fire. I had no byline and my ideas were often trivialized. I needed work that was as important as Joe felt his was. I was not unaware that my husband and I were hugely competitive. He seemed to thrive on my disappointments. He was flirtatious to a fault with others while in my company, critical of me regularly, screened my phone calls, humiliated me publicly, was personally moody and withholding yet unfailingly supportive and loving at my low points. Still, I adored him. How could this be, I asked myself. I told myself that all this was fueled by his insecurity, that living in my house and parenting my kids was an uneven playing field for him. And I acceded more and more to his demands, whatever they were. One of the more violent arguments found me whisking my kids in my VW and driving in the night off to my sister's five hours away. Within a day he found me and appeared on the doorstep pleading for me to come home. I did. And as a birthday present to him the following November, my gift to him, even as I was promoted at the paper, was to leave my job at *Newsday.*

I continued to resurrect my dreams as my marital disappointments grew. I knew that I wanted to pursue criminal justice as my career. One in which I could support myself, should my Sir Galahad fail me in the end. I was only 32 and there still was time. But I had no credentials, zero contacts and my marriage still took precedence over everything else. Certainly there wasn't work in that field available to me yet so I took a job that I knew as the continuity director at a local radio station. It was okay but not very demanding. I definitely couldn't luxuriate at home as our financial setup was crazy where we shared the bills 50/50 while he made three times my salary. And then I became pregnant. Upon hearing this Joe said that I had two choices: I could have the baby and get a divorce or get an abortion and have a marriage. I was in no position to have a baby alone leaving me with the decision to do both…an abortion and a divorce.

The abortion happened immediately. Joe unwillingly left the house but thanks to his many friends for whom his charisma had not faded, he was able to stay with another one, displaced from another marriage. The idea of a divorce sat dormant for a while. He reckoned that many people who adored each other successfully lived apart and those he knew who were married living together were in trouble. Why didn't we try this? It was cockamamie thinking. But each time we got together to talk about divorce, we ended up on a date...that charm was irresistible. And then he was sent to the Mideast on assignment and his suspicions proved right. His absence brought us closer together. When he sent for me to meet him in Rome, I jumped at the chance. I thought this could be the time for me to redeem myself; to be smarter, more understanding, become a more beguiling person. All through Italy, his dark moods kept me in the shadows. Until he attempted to choke me in a Venice restaurant. People describe their rage sometimes as a white heat. This is what I felt as I left the table, the restaurant, Venice and Joe...all within an hour. I ran for fear of losing my better judgment and of living a life filled with emotional muggings. No longer did I think about his approval of me; I didn't approve of him. I took a train from Venice to Munich where he followed me and accompanied me to the airport. In his contrition, he tried to convince me to stay on for a trip with him to Dachau (!) and then time in England. It was in the minute of this insensitive invitation that I decided on the life ahead of me, without Joe.

Almost immediately upon my surprise return to my home and my children, I did two things. I enrolled in a full time undergraduate college program at Hofstra University and contacted a lawyer. My depression was balanced by my will to get a degree in order to start my overdue career because as it turned out, I needed to rescue myself from the man I thought was my rescuer. The divorce part was more difficult as, 1) I needed the money to pay for it before I ever got to a lawyer, 2) the lawyer I wanted was involved in a class action suit on behalf of the women at Newsday (finally) and Joe was handling it for the paper and 3) last but not least, Joe wasn't agreeable to a divorce. He also said, "I don't want a divorce. What if I want to get a mortgage some day and they refuse me because of two divorces?" It translated to me that he was so apathetic about me that he didn't even need to legally close the chapter. It was a devastating experience for me. I was crazy about him but he was bad for my health. I borrowed the money…all that was in her account, from my friend Pam. I found a fabulous attorney who had me come to her home so that the coldness of Lafayette Street didn't totally terrify me and she convinced Joe that his worries were wasted and that two divorces would not mean that in the future a bank would refuse him a mortgage due to instability. On the day of the divorce he was busy in the next courthouse covering Martha Mitchell and never showed up. I asked for nothing but I kept his name which is as close as I would ever get to him.

Family violence wasn't a term known in the mid-70s, let alone used to describe the marriage of people who loved one another, a Jewish, middle-class, young mother and a beautiful, well-liked, Midwestern, Episcopalian, successful writer. In the decades that have followed, I became an expert in the field, each time feeling the flashback. My marriage lasted for just four years but left a lifetime of unfinished business in its wake. The best of times were absolute ecstasy. The worst of times were panicked heart-stopping misery. What went so wrong?

4 | Rikers Island, The Wonder Years

My first trip over the bridge to Rikers Island was preceded by a night of wakefulness. I am finally on my way to where I want to be professionally. I'm working as a court diversion social worker for the Salvation Army. It's been quite a journey, like a cat with multiple lives, but this is the one I've been waiting for.

This incarnation had been on its way since I was back on the terra firma of Long Island from Italy. My depression and wound licking was overcome only by taking action on the divorce and beginning an education that I knew would be necessary for the work I wanted. Taking my cues from my friend Pam, I followed her lead applying to neighboring Hofstra University. I was extremely lucky in that it was a time that welcomed single impoverished moms with incomplete educations. They gave me a full scholarship and credit for my associates degree earned fifteen years earlier in socializing. This time I aimed for sociology. I entered that first semester feeling extremely ancient at 35 sitting in classes with college students but soon became an insider in the evening student's affiliations. I did well enough taking 24 credits in the evening while working all day. And when this degree was finished, I went on to receive a Masters in criminal justice…and the hunt for meaningful work was on. I had something to prove I felt, to Joe, but really it was to me where it mattered.

Thank heavens that Nana hadn't given up on us yet and was 'minding the store' and the teenagers at home. This was my second or third adolescence and I wanted to get this one right! I was working by day and in classes at night. I was far from alone with this schedule as I was to discover, viewing all of the other campus coeds who had kids. My clean slate returning from Venice without any income or hope was beginning to fill in. Since returning to school, I'd been researching every single possible angle for work in criminal justice; internships, volunteerism, anything that could get me closer to the field of criminal justice. With sheer determination I made appointments with not-for-profit agencies, corrections officials, attorneys, researchers. I became a one woman promotional agent for myself. I was running out of time and money, though, and needed to be working so I took a job as the public relations director of a 160-store shopping mall. I still viewed any job as temporary until I got where I wanted to be. My audience of customers couldn't have been farther apart; shoppers were what I had and inmates were what I wanted. The picture in my head of Attica replayed regularly giving me ammunition to keep believing I'd get there. It's a good thing I had the newspaper experience behind me and was used to workplace nonsense. The shenanigans at this job came from only one person: he was the manager, and I was soon to find out, a cocaine user. He was wired and expected everyone else to function at his speed. It was impossible for me. His demands were beyond my abilities. He issued daily proclamations with deadlines; PR, promotional events, merchants meetings, signing new leases, enforcing mall policies, tenants complaints, customer advertising…even garbage removal. One particularly colorful gimmick was the showing of the Star Wars movie with a Disney partnership where Mickey Mouse and Santa were to land by helicopter on the traditional day after Thanksgiving, outside the theater at the premier. I rented the android robot R2-D2 (one of the movie's leading characters) to stand on the movie line. I controlled this battery-operated tin man by remote control. I thought this whole production a little iffy at the outset when the idea was concocted. When we got the call that Mickey Mouse was sick and that Santa would be landing without him I thought we were sunk. The contract said that no one else could don Mickey's suit so I beefed up the performance of R2-D2. I gave him a bigger part, walking around, shaking hands, being friendly. As luck would have it, he leapt a bit out of character with me at the controls and knocked over two small children. This was my undoing and after a couple of years at the job, I gave notice. The other staff became my cheering section and my leave-taking became a spectator sport. I was doing what they all wished they could do. I told the hopped up boss that I would usually give two weeks' notice but in this case it was two hours! He told me I had no guts but it seemed gutsy to me to give notice with two children to support. I did depend on unemployment benefits as I was certain he was as glad to see me go as I was to be gone. And so it was. And with all the pressure that had been building up between school, working for a maniac, looking for my next job and running the family, I decided to give myself a grace period before taking any new job. I paused.

I'd been needing some minor surgery that I let go for a while for lack of time. Now looked like the time. With my medical insurance in a state of grace for a bit longer from the mall, I checked into Booth Memorial Hospital. I had a routine procedure and recouped during the four days of hospitalization. I had a roommate. She was an elderly and indigent cancer patient whom the hospital could not fix. The doctors ceased visiting her but the discharge plan was not one that the social worker approved so she wasn't going anywhere. She needed an advocate and here I was in the next bed. On my mother's visits, she brought ices and sweets for both of us. And throughout my second and third days, I called downstairs to the social worker begging her to let the lady go to her home (a poorly-appointed garage with her son) or else she would die in the hospital of a broken heart. On day four, the social worker asked what agency I worked for. I told her I was her roommate on the 5th floor, a job-seeking criminologist. She said she'd be right up.

This was a Salvation Army hospital of which I was unaware. The social worker was a chatty woman whom I had pictured accurately by phone. After interviewing my roommate she sort of interviewed me but not about my health. Then she told me of a job opening as a prison social worker at their half-way house for women on 16th St. The Stuyvesant Treatment Center. Oh, heaven! She put me in touch with them and I left the hospital on my way to an interview. Boy did my medical insurance pay off. My roommate went home.

And now through a surgical procedure I've landed exactly where I want to be! The job itself is to provide jail alternatives for women at the 'front end' of their sentence and screen those at the 'back end' finishing their time, for entrance into the residence at the halfway house. It requires meeting them at arrest at Rikers Island and near parole at the state prison, Bedford Hills Correctional Facility. I pretty much run my own schedule; weekly in court, jail and prison. Each Thursday I present a social-diagnostic to the therapy team hoping my candidates will be acceptable to the Army and the court and live at the residence instead of in jail. The smell of the brownstone is a combination of pot-roast and Lysol. Those who live here have to adhere not only to probation and parole stipulations but also to the Captain and the Major. These two are lifelong soldiers, both single and very rigid. If the venetian blinds don't pass the white glove test, the women are threatened that their parole will be revoked...never mind that they managed to stay drug-free. We are a tiny staff of five, agreeing more often with the clients than the Army. I have a weekly meeting with my supervisor, Florence. On one particular Friday into my second year of this work, I enter her office breathlessly telling her of my two attacks that week; one on a Tuesday evening walking cross town in tandem with a date. Blocks ahead I sense trouble in the form of a strange man accompanied by a collie dog headed my way. He gets up to me, begins to punch my arm whilst yelling, "Susan, you bitch!" Unhanding me, my date says as the stranger takes his leave, "Oh, I see you know him?" I leave the date and go home alone. And then the next day, a day off, I take an aunt and my mom for a cemetery visit where while they are out of the car at tombstones, I am molested in the car! I am really shook up. And here I am on Friday telling Florence that I'm a magnet for this trouble. She chides me for looking at people too directly and tells me to whistle if I need help. Whereupon after our conference I leave for lunch and on the corner of Third Ave and 16th Street, a business man takes me over his knee and kisses me smack on the lips! And I've never been able to whistle. So much for the notion of a liberal being a person who's not been mugged. I still don't seek vengeance. I also don't seek eye contact. My job evaluation cited that I overly identify with the clients. I take this as a compliment. It is not meant to be.

I did side with the women. Their stories of street life, abuse, and poverty put them on the fast track to prison. The job has taken me to alleys where I've removed needles from arms, to pawn shops to recover lost treasures, into drug houses and homeless shelters, all to save a woman. They survive by grabbing on to most anyone who'd have them and end up holding the bag. I learned everything from them: that women worry about their kids after arrest and that men worry about their cases; that women curl around visit rooms waiting to see their men in jail and that women don't have many visits; that they are shackled to their beds as they give birth in the jail hospital; that these are our sisters, mothers, daughters and friends. I spend endless hours with clients in detox, some of them not making it. I never give up on them. But I've laughed behind the stern face I've had to keep. One particular resident, Mary B., had a vendetta against the Major and acted on it by taking her trombone and pawning it. This at Christmas time! It was the mystery of the house but with the help of a friend I recovered it and no one was any the wiser. And one day I found myself claiming a stripper's life possessions at Show World (an infamous club on 8th Ave). As I introduced myself and affiliation, the crew poured out of the peep show to have a look at what they thought would be a soldier in a bonnet with tambourine.

When one goes over the bridge to Rikers Island in East

Elmhurst, Queens, you can't help but notice the drama. The island is half the size of Central Park. Families are doing their time on the outside and waiting on long quays to see their loved ones. The self-contained island stretches before you and every six hours the stench of low tide adds to the surreal colony that sits between Queens and Bronx Counties with 15,000 people living here classified in ten different buildings. This is also the flight path and within reach of LaGuardia Airport. It's so close that the jets blow off fuel as you round the ring road to the first staging point. Before crossing the bridge over the East River you're stopped by officers and must show your clearance. I watch the families who are dropped off at this 'first base' and who have to wait outdoors in all weather for buses to take them across to the Island. They are mostly the faces of women and children; the mothers, the wives, the girlfriends, their kids. You feel the intimidating and arrogant attitude of the officers who so hate their work and are serving their own time counting their days until retirement. Once over the bridge if you're in a private car, you find a place in the huge parking lot before entering the 'control building' where the ordinary visitor signs in, gets searched and puts jewelry, purses, possessions in lockers before stepping on yet another bus to the individual jails. No ordinary visitor me, I drive my car to the parking area in front of 'C-73' avoiding the bus that goes throughout the complex. This is where the women are housed. I draw in a huge breath and pray this goes well, my first of thousands of times.

Shallow though this seems, I'm very self-conscious about outward appearances. I want to dress appropriately as a professional without being too austere or too flashy for my first introduction to women in prison; just the right amount of cool. (And by the way, these women know fashion - they don't boost anything but the best!) Jails are strange lockups. You might say they're the original in mixed housing. They house people who have been convicted of a crime and are awaiting transfer to state prisons, they house people who are held without bail or people who can't make bail awaiting trial, they house people who have been convicted of crimes that carry only jail time of up to one year and they house people who have never even jaywalked in their lives. The emphasis here is on security, designating separate housing for the different classifications. Ultimately, all kinds of women over 21 live here, guilty and not guilty. I show my credentials in a heavily deodorized hall to a CO behind a teller's window (a bubble) and the first gate opens. I sign several different visitors' books before an escort guides me through the labyrinth of halls and bars to a place that will become my office on Tuesdays and Thursdays.

I soon find that it takes diplomacy to endear myself to the officer on duty in this social services area in order to get to see the inmates. She is ultimately responsible for finding and calling the clients for my interviews in this jail. The whole process depends upon her. Infrequently are women sitting in their cells and housing areas; they could be working, in the visit room, out to court, at sick call, in school or in some program, or the count could just be 'frozen' when no one can go anywhere. The frozen count happens in every institution about four times a day to check the census. And when there's an unusual incident. Such mayhem! It serves me well to become an ally of the duty officer. Before I earn my 'creds' I'm sure

I'm seen as another bleeding heart social worker who's about to be used by every inmate and believes every story she hears. And, most important believes no one is guilty. The inmates, upon reception, are told about programs they can sign up for and if they're interested they 'drop a slip' in their housing areas to be seen by that worker. So I have a list of women requesting the help of the Stuyvesant Treatment Center. Among professionals in the field (even the women), women are thought the least desirable population to work with. We are considered to be manipulative, noisy, and overly dramatic. This has always seemed like a betrayal to me coming from my own gender. I'm swamped by the requests that come from the inmates. Finding yourself in jail is a come as you are party and the women have left children at home and are loathe to tell anyone for fear of losing custody of them. My phone is the most popular spot in the jail as I overhear the pleas on my side of the cord. The needs are overwhelming! The histories of abuse and anguish know no limits. I am perhaps naïve at this stage of professional development but no less compassionate. All of my best efforts and hopes are not enough to change some lives. How could these particular people reinvent themselves with no money and no friends; how could anyone? Where we decide to go has a lot to do with where we come from.

The society in which many female offenders live is neither peaceful nor safe. In the years ahead I meet many of the same women as older, sick and frail inmates waiting for parole after serving lengthy sentences. But happily, and statistics back this up, the greater percentage of people formerly incarcerated live their lives uneventfully ever after. One of the more remarkable exceptions is the story of Olivia Hart. Olivia left Bedford Hills after serving a very long bid. She had been released after 15 years a few months earlier when she pops up sitting outside the steel wired rolling entrance gates of the state prison. Soon after release she decided things are too tough on the outside so wants to check back in. A correction office finds her waiting on the pavement hoping to persuade someone to let her in. Once the Superintendent gets wind of this strangest of all requests, parole is informed. Little (and she was) Olivia was told that unlike a hotel, in order for her to get back in, she'd have to commit a crime. Olivia found a way by breaking into a car so once again she was separated from the community. This (in 1984) at the cost of $33,000 a year per person ($60,000 in 2013). In parole, this is called 'gate fever.' Olivia's fever came late. Usually it shows up just before the parole board sees you and when you walk into the hearing with years of a clean record, botched by a recent outburst, you're not going anywhere. What is this challenge at freedom thing? "The devil you know...." I think its fear.

The work I do constantly begs for me to look at myself and think of my choices. I've seen the cases of people dragged into court after drug raids at parties and now I'm really careful about where I go and who I go with. I no longer drive after just one drink. I've seen much that causes me to say, "There but for the grace of God go I." This is serious business and perhaps a bit of paranoia at work but I'm a quick study. We are all living perilously close to the edge and drug activity doesn't confine itself to one class. We're all pretty lucky in this late '70s social world in Manhattan that more of us don't get bumped off.

Much of the gossip among the jail employees is passed

around in the huge parking lot on Rikers: the scandal du jour, who's leaving, who's coming, who's in trouble, new policies, etc. And of course always the disbelief of the uneven romances; a tale of a lawyer plotting her client's escape, or a scantily dressed health worker inside carrying on with an inmate or the more ordinary story of a woman marrying her incarcerated pen pal. But really, who could hope for a more romantic marriage? You've got a common enemy, fidelity, fantasies, no monetary problems and a place to visit all the time. This could continue forever, or at least until you get to live together. This tarred swamp on the East River is also ground zero for the social life that enfolds among workers. I'm very aware that many of the most successful program employees are those who've served time. Who could be a better mentor on how to stay clean and sober and how to negotiate the system than one who's been there? Some of these same people don't make it over the long run causing an unfortunate chill over the effectiveness of the programs. After a few dates with one of the many people I meet in this alternate social universe, I leave behind for good the lure of the bad boy! I'm thinking that maybe I should wear a Salvation Army bonnet. I must say, though, that among the luminaries I befriend in the parking lot, there is one who plays a huge role in my future. She works for the NYC Board of Correction, the watchdogs of the industry that is corrections, and suggests I talk to her boss about working there. A very nice compliment, but I'm still pretty new at this gig.

I feel privileged to have met some amazing people through my work, both professionals in the field and people who've been through the system. As I'm often reminded, we're more alike than different. Among these friends of mine there's a code of behavior that's fueled by the knowledge that life is not a dress rehearsal and that we should live on purpose with honesty and accountability. One of my earliest lessons of real compassion and friendship is the example of Sister Elaine Roulet, a Sister of St. Joseph. She worked as a chaplain/counselor at Bedford Hills which is where I met her on probably my first trip there.

I can think of no better way to describe Elaine to you than to quote a *New York Times* article written by Francis X Clines in 2005:

NY: Bedford Hills--A Tough Life All About Drugs & Sister Elaine

December 31, 2005, The City Life: Well-Spent Prison Time

by FRANCIS X. CLINES

A two-time loser nicknamed Sexy - so dubbed in her earliest years at the Bedford Hills Correctional Facility for women - was dying in the prison ward. Old friends, both inmates and keepers, were stopping by, anguished that radiation treatments had taken Sexy's beautiful head of hair. "What really upset her was she lost her teeth, not her hair, and she would die that way on the inside," recalled her chaplain, Sister Elaine Roulet. The nun smiled, singling out Sexy to make a point about the thousands of women convicts - murderers, drug addicts and courier "mules," prostitutes and thieves - she grew close to in 47 years of service at Bedford Hills, a New York prison.

"A tough life for Sexy - all about drugs," the nun

recalled, speaking from her supposed retirement at one of the nine homey shelters she created across the city over 25 years for the women she regards as her larger community of sisters: Bedford Hills prison alumnae who have done their time. "But Sexy was always elegant, and she wanted to die that way."

Vanity behind bars is more than an acceptable vice in the subversive catechism of Sister Elaine, who broke out of parochial school teaching early in her career to become a reading teacher for imprisoned women. From there, things took off: she discovered that maternity, not literacy, was the big problem. She focused on programs that allowed felons to mother their infants on the inside for the first year, to stay close to their children through creative visitor programs in the years that followed, and eventually to find a year's shelter with their children at one of her Providence House shelters in converted convents and rectories. She is so busy in retirement that she could not resist starting another program, called Our Journey, for quick spiritual retreats in the city where the women encourage one another and watch their children grow. "Something new - there's nothing worse than old ritual," the nun warned, digging through piles of family prison pictures she keeps in a lockbox she got from a longtime friend, Ruth Brown. "'Ma' Brown - the last woman to escape the electric chair," Sister Elaine said. "She died inside." Sexy's last rites turned out to be special. "The very kind prison dentist said, 'Look, we can't make her false teeth - she'll be dead soon,' "Sister Elaine said. "But he made a plaster mold on his own, and we ran around to dentists, begging them, and one directed me to this guy, some kind of dental mechanic, who finally laughed and made a set for nothing." Sexy loved her new teeth, smiling as much as possible with them before her death, her chaplain recounted. "And the point of this story is you don't do anything alone, in prison or outside: look at all the people who got Sexy her teeth," the nun said, enumerating the half-dozen who had nudged the search along to the final touch of ritual elegance for Sexy. —FRANCIS X. CLINES

It is safe to say that if you know Elaine, your life will never be the same. I became very close to her as we conspired about housing for homeless women being released. The Salvation Army advanced payment for women coming out of prison for housing at $35 per night. These were women who were not coming into the Stuyvesant Center. The only clearance they needed for this was mine. No one else needed to meet them. If they were on my caseload I knew their needs and release date and they were directed to report to one of the city's numerous SROs (single room occupancy). The only other requirement was that they continue follow up counseling with me in the office. This plan always looked ideal from the inside looking out, but the reality was that their SRO housing was filthy, dingy, cold and dangerous in the city's worst properties where landlords were reimbursed great sums to shelter the city's poorest. I'd heard often of the threats and intimidation the woman suffered if they didn't agree to the management's seedy plans. It was awful until the day that Sister came to me with her form of salvation. There was an underused convent in Brooklyn where she was certain her community of nuns would put up a few women. It was no secret that she and the Major had very different philosophies so there was no reason to see this plan as anything other than safe housing for the vulnerable women if asked. The meager stipend went to defray the costs. Now 35 years later, Providence House is a network of nine homes for women and children in all the city boroughs, fully staffed and life changing for untold numbers of families. I was honored to be a board member for many years. It's safe to say that the only sadness for women leaving long term institutionalization is leaving the families they've created inside behind...and Sister Elaine. But when she retired the women didn't let her get away and she now hosts women who are 'out' at her home and the journey continues. At last count 64 women visited her on a Sunday. If we really wanted to overcome criminal activity, we would subscribe to the Sister Elaine Roulet School of Decency. If there is a God, her face is Elaine.

Prisons are small cities and the people who inhabit them are as different from one another as the people in your city: there are people who are convicted of crime as a result of intentions gone awry, there are people guilty of deliberate acts of violence thoughtlessly committed, there are the selfish crimes of opportunity, and then there are white collar criminals who are the world class schemers and manipulators. And then to round out the neighborhood, there are the sociopaths; it's these crimes of unspeakable cruelty that we remember and that make us wince but they are in the vast minority in prison. And in this total population the Justice Department statistics tell us that 56% of state prisoners, 45% of federal prisoners and 64% of jail inmates suffer from mental illness. Indeed, crime is a national health problem that has become toxic with vigilantism in the revenge business, continuing the incivilities. What I aim to do in my work is stop the violence, one person at a time. This takes advocacy ...a word that brings a sneer to people's faces when discussing crime. But how better to heal the victim, to make a safer community and to stop the violence?

One of the finest professionals in the field who made 'advocacy' a clean word is Ellen Schall. I brokered an introduction between her and a woman just released from state prison. Ellen was then Deputy Commissioner for Programs for the City of New York's Department of Correction. The idea was to put together an orientation handbook for the state-ready women at Rikers on their way to Bedford Hills. The former offender had obviously served her time and had compiled a wonderful resource guide. This pamphlet would go far in allaying the fear of the unknown for a jail inmate about to be sent to state prison... and her family. A small thing such as this can change much of the stress that contributes to eruptions in jail. We wanted the city to be a partner in the project: print it, pay for it and distribute it. The meeting took place in the Commissioner's office, in the criminal courthouse. The introduction was easy, almost as if they knew each other. Turns out, they did. After a short conversation, Ellen broke the ice by telling Sally (not her true name) that she knew her from college. They had gone to Swarthmore together. In typical women's fashion, we stopped standing on ceremony and took the conversation down to the greasy spoon luncheonette on the first floor. I was the fly on the wall listening to the route to justice that they each took: both exceptional students and both advocates, one decided that change would come from working within and joined the system. The other decided that social and political change would come only from outside and she became part of the radical Weathermen group. The conversation over grilled cheeses was fascinating as they each outlined their path. The merits of each of their choices showed itself over time: Ms. Schall became Dean of the Robert Wagner Graduate School of Public Service at NYU and while Sally ultimately became an educator and family person, the members of the former Weather Underground group ended up vilified and incarcerated ...some still to this day, 40-plus years later, and the systems are still in turmoil. As I left the luncheonette with Sally, I couldn't help make the obvious comparisons. They had the same motivations and educational resumes, except for their different decision on how to implement their beliefs.

As I approach year three at this job, I've become more entrenched than ever in issues surrounding women in prison. I've been part of a class action lawsuit that successfully argued for a nursery in jail for new nursing mothers; making speedy trials necessary for pregnant women, we'd successfully removed the handcuffs from the delivery rooms at Elmhurst Hospital. I'd started a women's group for the female corrections staff as a place to air and honor their perceived unfair working conditions, but there remains so much more to accomplish. I decide it's the right time to move on and be able to do more and I get in touch with my connection at the Board of Correction from the Rikers' parking lot and happily am hired. My jump in pay goes from $12,000 to $16,000!

Much excitement and satisfaction will come with this position. This is the place that makes the buck stop at the Department of Corrections for the conditions of confinement for city prisoners; from the size of their cells to how they're treated and what they eat. I am a Standards Review Specialist. In plain English, it means that I work for the watchdog agency over the NYC Department of Correction monitoring their jail policies and practices. The Department is legally bound to adhere strictly to the court mandated conditions of confinement in the jails. And it's up to us to decide its being done right. The Board has a pretty large staff assigned to each jail in the city plus a few more back at the office opposite city hall. Our analyses are heard by a volunteer board appointed by the Mayor who exerts its authority. My work is to examine programmatic projects. But for now I'm settling in and have to get to know my way around. There are eight jails plus Bronx and Queens that I've never been to and I best step on it. I have been at the job for about two weeks when I start setting up interviews and tours of all the jails.

On this historic day in my memory, I have an appointment with the warden of ARDC (Adolescent Remand Reception Center) in his office in the jail on the Island. The 15,000 inmates held daily within the detention jails on the Island is more than seven times the population of Maine's entire state prison system and more than the size of entire prison systems in 35 other states. The building called for short, C-74, holds males under 21. These are some of the toughest and most troubled kids in the city. These are the muggers and the gangbangers.

They are detained here either awaiting trial or are sentenced to a year or less on minor charges.

I am to meet Warden Perry, get a tour of the jail, a tour of the jail's vegetable garden and probably a vetting by this personable head of C-74... a show and tell kind of meeting. What to wear (again)! I think about dark suits. I think about loose dresses. This is before pant suits are acceptable and in vogue. I remind myself that in fact I want to bring in a new and fresh woman's dimension. And typically, that woman would dress in a colorful, feminine and appropriate dress. When I think feminine, I think ruffles. Indeed, I had just the dress for the job. And so, a bit nervous, I head east over the bridge in a Laura Ashley powder-blue pleated smock dress, keenly aware that I will probably be the only female in this testosterone-filled institution. The dress I decide is fine; definitely flattering, definitely traditional, definitely appropriate, and definitely in contrast to the stark grays and greens that the inmates and officers wear. It screams, "Watch me. I can do this job."

I take the already described route to the jail. I walk to the foreboding front door of the institution and go in through the gate to the lobby. As with all institutions, the smell of antiseptic cleaners and the din of noise take over the senses. I show all the necessary ID and the Warden comes out and gallantly ushers me through the locked gates that are electronically controlled by an officer inside the Plexiglas bubble.

The Warden (Patrick Perry) takes exceptional pride in 'his' jail and the spell he thinks he has the inmates under. The orderliness in a jail is judged by the number of 'unusual incidents' reported. They range from fights to suicides, to stabbings, etc. Warden Perry's reign of power seems to bear out that he has a pretty good rapport with the 'boys' and the incidents are down. He's curious to meet me, a new employee of the Board of Correction, and in reality I am a quality control officer of his jail. I later realize that every uniformed personnel out in this great restricted no-man's land that dangles yards from the runway of LaGuardia Airport would be happy to check out any visitor, if just to break up the monotony.

After the tour, which impresses me as Warden Perry greets many inmates by name that pass in single file along the yellow-arrowed floor painted on either side of the corridors, we go into his office. An ordinary office, not different from others and not sending any signals that this is a maximum security lock-up; books, photos, a plant or two. I'm invited to stay for lunch and informed that we are to be joined in our meeting by a well-known lawyer, Dan Pachoda.

Coming into this job as an advocate for alternatives, Dan's name is legion. I know him through my chairing a not-for-profit board for an agency that supports inmates' families, Prison Families Anonymous. This is a support group for families modeled loosely after Al-Anon. I greatly respect Dan's work and opinions. As Warden Perry and I wait for him, we talk about 'his' jail and the upcoming lunch that will include fresh vegetables from the inmates' farm. When Dan arrives there are of course introductions until the warden realizes that he needn't choreograph this trio because our paths have crossed before. He sits back and listens as we go over the usual catching up; "How's so and so," and "Whatever happened to?" In fact, the chatting between the two of us is so lively that I never hear the warden's voice again that morning. Our conversation races along with my words falling out of my mouth way before my thoughts have refined them.

When I tell Dan exactly how my transition between jobs is going, it sounds something like this: "Oh, I love this work at the Board but I'm still wrapping up work with old clients who I'm trying to get into drug treatment and so I'm going to court with them in between learning all about the jails, meeting the personnel, being introduced to city officials, getting to know some of the investigations and problems, learning the minimum standards and I'm up until the wee small hours of the morning. In fact, I'm so busy I'm balling a fart!"

The echo of that malapropism seemed to be louder than the jail din in my mind. Both the warden and Dan look down, look at each other, and seem to stifle grins. There isn't a sound. I think, "Why don't they just laugh out loud? Why don't I correct myself? In fact any fool can see how I really am falling apart. Maybe they think *they* misheard. Oh, my God!" And so, with newly found aplomb, I look at my watch, inform them I can't stay for the tomato lunch and race out as fast as the maximum security gates will allow. Wait! Is that laughter I hear as I escape....can there even be laughter in such a place? I sure demonstrated my sophistication and I'm certain my career's over before it ever gets traction.

5 | The Men Who Got Away

Each day I go to work thinking about what new surprises can possibly be awaiting. I listen to the news nonstop to hear the inflated media-hyped crime beat which could be a heads up for something or somebody I'll be assigned to. There's been enough excitement exacted from this job already and I figure that soon things will become ordinary or at least I'll become inured to them. But in truth, there's no such thing as an ordinary day. After all, the definition of this job at the Board of Correction is to investigate unusual incidents in the jails and get them corrected. We're paid to uncover trouble.

As I put together this next caper, I have no inkling of what its ripple effect will be: at the agency we get a million and one complaints about the visiting process at the jails. The policies' priority is security and they mostly make sense. But with 15,000 inmates, there's more than enough room for many flubs. With the background din in all jails and the chaos that reigns on both sides of the visiting room's doors, it's a miracle that visits go as smoothly as they do. But the reasons for dissatisfaction are many; such as, inmates who can't be found (are they out to court, transferred?), long waits until inmates are produced requiring the visit to be cut short, favoritism toward some visitors, confusion around rules, varying regulations by different offices, etc. So I've decided to make this my next project, so I make plans to become an anonymous visitor myself. I have hopes that by doing this I'll perhaps experience firsthand the often-heard gripe of preferential treatment by the corrections staff to youthful white female visitors.

There are designated days of visits at each of the jails on Rikers applied alphabetically using the inmate's last name. This works and cuts down the sheer numbers and crowding. I've suggested they put a counselor in the visiting rooms to provide an ombudsman of sorts to hear and help with the many problems. It's during the visits that bad news is often shared between the inmate and family: illness, breakups, the status of the case, and other real life issues which become magnified when you're sitting in jail. The visiting rooms are like Grand Central Station, crossroads of a million private lives with every personal thing happening publicly. There are often problems in the jail after visits; cut-ups, fights, attempted suicides. Surely we could streamline this.

But I've got to find a prisoner to visit in one of the five Rikers Island jails (today there are ten), one where the staff won't recognize me. Fifteen thousand inmates; you'd think it'd be easy. This has to be a personal visit for me. Not an interview with someone about their visit. Aha, I've got it. I mentioned that I've been a board member of PFA (Prison Families Anonymous.) This jewel of a self-help organization that emotionally supports and educates families about the system was founded by an astonishing woman, Barbara Allan. She came to the world of crime as a married, middle-class woman, teacher of the second grade, wife and mother of two toddler daughters, when her husband shoots his father to death in their kitchen. Her struggle with shame and anonymity has long ago ended but she's made her life one that serves as an example for others finding themselves in similar places.

Her sidekick in this venture is a woman who is presently very familiar with the visit process; her husband Bill is in detention at the House of Detention for Men, HDM. And get this, his name starts with an 'A' so I can get a visit with him tomorrow. I've met him in between his lock-ups when he was PFA's Santa two years in a row for the kids. All I know is that he was great with the kids, extremely personable, forty something, and whom I suppose has a nefarious background but that's none of my business...yet. And so I call Joan to see if I can bump her from her time so that I can visit tomorrow. "Of course," she says and she'll tell Bill to expect me in her next phone call with him that night.

Believe it or not, as a visitor I'm really nervous. I fear authority. Don't interpret this as anything that's motivated me into this authority business. I do well in it, just not with it (because I really don't trust the consistency of these authoritarians.) In fact, I like to think that I use my weight in a more constructive way than many I've seen. But personally, I'm mortified at being admonished and blister at put-downs. I start my journey for the visit on the corner of 2nd Ave and 59th St, at the ramp way of the Queensboro Bridge. This is where the Q101 bus to Rikers Island begins. It's 10 in the morning, late June, so no problem standing on the corner waiting for the bus. The other people boarding are mostly going to the same place but for a few who will hop off at the Queens Plaza stop before we wind through Astoria along Steinway Street to Hazen Street and over the bridge to these sprawling orange bricked buildings that warehouse 15,000 lives and are so quiet on the outside. Some of these folks getting on the bus seem to know one another and exchange some gruff pleasantries. There are a few young women dragging children and babies who I smile at. Only two of the people waiting are men. One is with an elderly woman and the other alone. The bus comes and we get on and away we all go. The conversation on the bus gets louder with excitement, maybe even cheerful, as we get closer and I remember that I'm the one who's different on this bus, not them. But I question how one could ever get used to this. We pull in the dirt lot before the main bridge to the complex, but instead of the usual transfer to get off only to load onto the next bus that will go to the control building we're told to stay on because the K-9 officer is coming through to do a drug sweep with his dog. Oy. What if there's something under my seat? What if I wind up in some kind of unknown pickle? As my identity has melded with the rest of the visitors and we're in this together, I think it's hard to believe that any of my fellow passengers are bringing drugs in. But as a professional, I know better, much better! The dog has done her job and it seems okay to assume we're all drug-free, but it's hard to tell as there are no clues on the officer's face and there could be a surprise at the end of the line with one of us being pulled off. We're waved through the check point and are at the control building minutes later. As I get off, I make no eye contact with the COs for fear I'll be recognized. After signing in, checking possessions in a locker for a quarter, and getting a visitor tag, I hustle on the next waiting bus inside the jail walls that will stop at HDM. I started out in Queens at 10:30 this morning and now it's a little after 1 P.M. The distance at most is a dozen miles. This is definitely an all-day affair for an hour's visit.

Although I know the drill by heart (in fact I'll have a

hand at writing a new and improved visit policy if I do my job right), I need to be told what comes next; where to stand, where to sit, what book to sign, etc. This is not only because I've traded places but because I've done it so well I don't really remember what to do or where to do it and so I follow obediently like a lamb in the clutches of "the man." I pass through each test and advance to the next like a board game until I'm finally in a huge ugly room with tables overseen by an officer who watches from a chair on stilts, like a lifeguard, making certain there's no physical contact. And I sit and wait for my borrowed guy, Joan's hubby, Bill, to come through the door. We all watch this door as if staring at a TV hoping our guys will come to life after such a long time imagining them. What we don't see is that on the other side of the door he is strip searched, as he will be again when the visit is over. And I sit and wait for my guy, Bill. Will he recognize me? Will I recognize him? I wait for Bill for a long twenty-five minutes. I finally see a man come through the door and he approaches the duty officer asking what table his visit is at. Right. He's much smarter than I am.

We don't use the full hour for the visit. We really don't know one another. I thank him. We talk about his kids, his family and the usual small talk. Most of the chit chat is what I came for, finding out anything he can tell me about the visit process and his experience with it. So far I think I'm having a text book visit. There's been nothing out of order; no reckless officer, no discrimination, no rules broken. Kind of disappointing, actually. I don't talk about my work to him and he doesn't talk about his line of work to me. I could be seeing him in any other setting having this same conversation except for the visit query. He's a polite, good guy and we do know a number of people in common. The visit's over and I get up from what in another world would be a picnic table and he's left sitting until the officer allows him to exit that door in the opposite direction and is subjected to another strip search on the other side of the door to resume his life at Rikers Island while I give him a reassuring wave and a smile. But what I don't know is that he's not going to be there for too much longer.

I don't get back at the base of the 59th Street Bridge until after 4:30. It's too late to go down to my office on Chambers Street, so I go to Penn Station and get a train home to Westbury. I'm tired even though I've really done nothing but flex my anxiety throughout the day. I reflect on the lives of others, hardships and happiness. I have to think what I'll report about today. I love this job!

I'm in the office bright and early in the morning doing the usual debriefing. I described to you my journey to this job that started with a friendship formed in a Rikers parking lot but haven't told you about my coworkers whom I've bonded with this past year. We are a young, tight bunch of idealists who believe in the rights of all individuals and think we can make change by being part of the criminal justice system rather than advocating from the outside. Most of my colleagues see themselves as being in the bull pen warming up for a bigger job. I think I've died and gone to heaven even though I've arrived here so much later in my life than the others who are just out of school. And I believe I am in a place where I can make that difference, even though I'm more or less an underling doing reports, program development and investigations at a very negligible salary. This is 1980. The seven Standards Specialists go to Rikers jails every day to monitor the conditions of confinement of the prisoners. They spend all their time out there reviewing reports, speaking to personnel and prisoners, observing conditions being the watchdogs. I get to keep my own schedule and turn out reports and ideas for policy improvements. I also act partly as a den mother for this crowd when they file back downtown. I have a sunny, paneled office in an antique city building facing the hubbub of City Hall. The field workers share a huge marble room that resembles a dance hall.

Actually mentioning a dance hall brings to mind my first experience at Sing Sing, way back as a volunteer doing outreach for PFA. It was a weekend some years ago when Barbara Allan and I spoke to the men in general population about our program and how it could help their families. It was my first time in such a setting and it was held in a rotunda used now as a gym or meeting room. It had formerly been the death house where the electric chair did its job, executing people. In fact a total of 614 people were put to death here. And as we looked in vain for an electric outlet in order to play our video, we were told by our audience of prisoners about the days in which the inmate was walked through this room that played music to calm the nerves before his state sponsored murder! This was 'The Dance Room of the Death House.' How bizarre as I found the plug while wearing a poker face.

Anyway, not to be confused, it's in this other but beautiful dance-like room at 51 Chambers, that the phone calls begin to come in telling us there'd been an escape out on the Island yesterday, only discovered early this morning!

The New York Times
June 29th, 1980
"Three prisoners, including one being held on a charge of attempted murder stemming from the robbery attempt at the Spritzer & Fuhrmann jewelry concern in Manhattan last December, escaped from a cellblock on Rikers Island yesterday after using a hacksaw to cut through a barred corridor window, according to the Correction Department.

"Two of the men were picked up in an abandoned building in Astoria, Queens, last evening, but the search continued for the man arrested in the robbery attempt at the jewelry firm, William Arico, a convicted bank robber.

"The escape was detected shortly after 9 *A*.M. at the island's main jail building.

"The inmates were identified as Mr. Arico, 43 years old, of Valley Stream, L.I. who was being held on charges of kidnapping, bank robbery and attempted murder…."

My heart stops. This is *my* Bill Arico. None other than my borrowed visit honey! And I was his last visit yesterday.

It seems to me that I've just begun to relax about the hugely embarrassing faux pas in Warden Perry's office last year. As far as I know, that never got around. But this? This I know will launch a huge investigation and even if I'm cleared it will stick to me forever. It could cost me my job.

For this story's sake I wish I could write a dramatic follow-up to what looks like a doomed professional life, but there's happily no such story to tell. After a brief interview with internal affairs, it's clear that I'm no accessory to the escape. I am more curious though than ever before about the life and times of Bill Arico.

So let's take a look. After I leave the visit with Bill at HDM, little do I know as I ride the bus and train home considering my day, Bill's putting finishing touches to his long worked-on plan to swim away from his current charges of attempted murder and kidnapping in the jewelry heist but more important than that charge, he's facing extradition to Italy where he's wanted as the international hit man for the murder of Giorgio Ambrosoli. Ambrosoli was an Italian lawyer who was shot in Milan on the evening of July 11, 1979 as he came home from his work of liquidating and investigating the malpractice of banker Michele Sindona. Sindona is responsible for the collapse of the Italian banking empire and the Franklin National Bank in 1974. Ambrosoli is about to discover that the entry point of the bank's money is from mafia heroin-dealing and Sindona orders the hit. Michele Sindona is a self-made international financier and master swindler who is responsible for what was, to date, the largest bank failure in United States history. He moved huge monies for the Gambino crime family, managing their heroin profits. He is allegedly the guy who hires Bill to knock off the lawyer commissioned to investigate this murderous business. He ultimately surrenders to U.S. authorities and is convicted in 1980 and held at the federal Metropolitan Correctional Center, downtown.

We find Bill the morning after the hit in Milan, in Credit Suisse in Geneva, depositing one hundred thousand dollars to his account. He's then out of Switzerland and back to life in Valley Stream, Long Island,

with the wife and kids. He's made one stop along the way
(that we know of) at the jewelry store, and that hold up
gets him arrested and put in this place where I can visit
him. His life is all about risks. I'll never know how long
he'd been working on sawing those bars and how
convenient the timing of my visit may have been for him.
Much of my information comes from the statements of
Henry Hill, made famous by the Lufthansa heist and
portrayed by Ray Liotta in the film 'Goodfellas.' Hill says
that he had given someone (maybe Bill's wife?) a jeweler's
saw to get to Bill. But Henry doesn't have a credible track
record and besides, I like Joan.

In between his gigs as Santa Claus, Arico has been
characterized as a bank robber and partners in drug
trafficking with Henry Hill. One of his past pranks
occurred when he was serving time at Lewisburg, a federal
prison. His capers certainly earned him his stripes, his
reputation and connections, and enhanced his resume for
bigger and better jobs. In the yard at Lewisburg, in the
guise of a serious bocce ball player, in whites yet, he gets
the drugs he distributes inside by arranging to have them
lobbed over the wall as bocce balls gone astray!
Authorities never question this. Books and film have
documented life in the mob and Peter Maas and other
authors have been responsible for the lion's share of
investigations. Hill was rewarded for 'turning' and then
banished to the witness protection program where his
activities had been closely followed up until he's tossed
out of witness protection as he's not helping his hidden
identity with numerous drug arrests, divorce from his
great love in 2002, and living a generally seedy existence.

But Bill? Excusing himself after meeting me from

Rikers Island, he remained in the wind in Pennsylvania for two years. My information tells me that he was captured as a result of a phone tap traced when his daughter phoned to complain to him about a family argument. When he's returned we find him taken into federal custody in lower Manhattan. Once he's in MCC, he's not only serving the four years for false statements (and forget the jewelry heist), he's appealing the Justice Department's attempt to extradite him to Italy for the open murder case….along with Michele Sindona.

They both lose their appeal. Bill waits until the day before his extradition to take another risk, deciding upon what he thinks will be the lesser of two evils; being tried and held in Italy or attempting another escape. Bill meets his maker with his familiar pattern of escape. On February 21st, 1984, three and a half years after visiting with me and taking a dive in the East River, and sitting in MCC for a year and a half of that time, he cuts through a cell window and while lowering himself by rope-tied bed sheets he falls to his death squashed by an overweight Cuban drug dealer who follows him down. On this day I am sitting behind a table as a parole commissioner deciding upon a man's freedom.

Michele Sindona is extradited to Italy but not before he is sentenced in the U.S. to 25 years for 65 counts of bank fraud. On March 27th, one month later he's sentenced to another 25-year sentence. Mr. Sindona died four days after a court in Milan convicted and sentenced him to life imprisonment for contracting Bill for the Ambrosoli assassination in 1979. He was poisoned in his cell by cyanide in his coffee on March 18th, 1986.

And our infamous and more local Henry Hill died at a

L.A. hospital on June 12, 2012, a day after his 69th birthday of heart failure.

These lives were a tangle of criminal manipulations and complicated stories of intrigue and murder. I'm told that the mob holds on tight, even after these players are gone.

Another escapade that finds me involves a different kind of working man, much better known to an adoring public: the famous fashion designer Oscar de la Renta. Nonetheless a man entirely unknown to me but a man that this oddest of jobs puts in my range. And a man when needed, while being sought after by an unhinged woman, is unavailable. Enter me to run interference as directed by my boss, his lawyer. I seemed to be the only one not protected during the four months that I lived through this intriguing nightmare. The truth here never interfered with the events.

Again, pressed into service by a ringing phone in my hallowed office. It's the chairman of the Board of Correction, my boss. His is an appointed position by the Mayor and carries no salary but holds influence in New York City jail's system. Seventy-five percent of the Board members are lawyers, as is this guy; his firm represents American business royalty and the social elite. Among them is Oscar, his friend and client.

Seems there's a bit of an unwelcome nuisance involving a woman who has landed in New York from Spain. She is attempting to get in touch with Oscar. Hence a call from his lawyer to me to take care of this, the least likely of all people to get involved. But I do. I'm thought of in the agency as a 'social worker' but I seem to be mostly the trouble shooter and that qualifies me as the one to solve this short term problem. I guess I'm flattered, Superwoman! When I got my degree in administering criminal justice I never imagined it would entail keeping paparazzi or others away from the rich and famous.

I'm told the unfortunate circumstances and required secrecy of this predicament. The woman named Maria von Somebody needs a place to stay over the long holiday weekend, Memorial Day, until help in the form of Oscar arrives from The Dominican Republic and it can all be sorted out. I have no idea what connection there is between the two but understand that public figures are targets for scandal. He tells me I'll find her at a walk-in shelter on Madison Avenue in the 50s. She's come there after staying a stint on the Bowery in the women's shelter where she was supposedly raped. A hotel is out of the question. This is a pathetic story and I am after all a sucker for pathos.

I arrive at the church shelter and introduce myself to the case worker. I can't tell her who's sent me or much about the odd circumstances but she either trusts me enough to take charge of this Maria or is happy to get rid of Maria. Either way I'm introduced to a red-haired, fairly attractive, slim woman in her late 30s, slightly hunched over and wearing a red print silk sheath dress under her mink coat. An unusual site in a shelter. Maria meets me hospitably, asking no questions and hearing that I'm going to attempt to find her a place to stay. I get on the phone and call every convent and halfway house that I know in town. It's Friday of the unofficial start of summer and typically a day when services are overburdened; when accidents happen, vacancies are filled, and the professionals are headed out the door for their summers.

Bingo. I get a referral to a parish house in the Village and we're told to come right down. I come to an immediate conclusion that something is wrong with this woman to venture out with me but what're her choices?

Once we hop a cab she begins her story of claiming her rightful share of the Dupont fortune. Anything is possible! It doesn't matter if this is so or not, it's her story and she's sticking to it. I just have to get her housing but it does make for a riveting story. We arrive at the parish house and she's read the rules by a Sister in charge which include being awake and out by 6 AM! This lady is clearly not used to this lifestyle but I have hopes that we'll both be rescued by tomorrow. It's scarcely supper time and Maria hasn't had anything to eat all day. We walk around the corner to a deli where with my $12 we get her a supply of candy, chips and soda for the night. Her story becomes more astonishing by the moment as she continues! Her mother, she says, is Princess von Somebody and knew Oscar as a young designer when Maria was a small girl. She needs help now and has decided to reconnect with him while claiming her fortune from other sources. She had been banished to Spain from the States somehow after sustaining a head injury many years earlier. She says she's now well and ready to face the legal battles of reclaiming her rightful life!

My head is swimming. We exchange phone numbers in the hall of the convent and I beg her to stay there just for the night until we see what the next day will bring. Once home I call my friend and ally in strange circumstances, the very same Barbara Alan of PFA. She's, as I've explained, a woman with deep compassion (too much for her own good) and as a result a Calamity Jane of sorts. Yes.

She'll drive back in the city with me in the morning, fetch Maria von Somebody and let her stay at her house. Before we have a chance to head into town, Maria's on the phone with me threatening dire outcomes if she has to stay any longer with the nuns. Frankly, I don't disagree. I've briefed Barbara on the alleged tale as we drive in to the city to collect her. I did expect that this bail out would come from the powers that be, not from my friend and I'm incredibly beholden to Barbara. I don't want Maria at my house but also feel that since she's a 'professional' charge of mine, she can't also be a roommate. Did I mention also that after these seven years since my divorce, I'm finally involved with a great guy? Maria is already cramping my style. Throughout the hour's drive back to Long Island and Barbara's home, we hear more details of Maria's story. Barbara has prepared the guest room for her and it looks like it should be a cozy evening.

Saturday comes and goes with phone calls back and forth between our two houses. If she were an ordinary houseguest, hearing that she went shopping with the family and was making lasagna for dinner wouldn't seem strange. But this Rockwell-like picture that she paints seems way out of kilter. Then Sunday rolls around. By phone I hear that Maria's been up most of the night complaining of exquisite back pain. Had there ever been a checkup after the rape or a police report? She's started life, she tells us, with scoliosis and seems she's now without any medication. By the time evening rolls around, we're very concerned about her health; both physical and mental. Her stories just could not be true; they are beyond anyone's belief. However I'm assured that Oscar's on the way so there must be something to this, right? We review the need for secrecy, and the scarcity of any funds which neither Barbara or I has to bankroll her. We decide that we'll take her to the county hospital in the morning.

Monday dawns bright and sunny (the unofficial beginning of summer) and I hope this is a harbinger of good things to come; Maria, the season, my new romance. I arrive at Barbara's late morning and hear the complaints from Maria myself. It occurs to me that perhaps she'd been addicted to more than prescription drugs and that we're seeing a meltdown that needs medical intervention. For a growing number of reasons, I feel confident that taking her to Meadowbrook Hospital is the only thing to do. Once she hears that her pain might be alleviated she agrees to let us take her to the hospital. As local residents living within the shadow of this hospital, neither Barbara nor I are thrilled to go there. It's a typical county hospital, notorious for screw-ups and poor practices, according to the press. Its reputation casts a gloomy physical pall to the neighborhood but we've arrived at the emergency entrance and here we go.

To my surprise I have a fairly easy time explaining sketchily the very anonymous background and the problem to the admissions gatekeeper. She sees fit without records, history or insurance to pass Maria on to a doctor. There's of course a fair amount of sitting and waiting, but I feel finally that I'm not in this alone and that responsible physicians will do the right thing. For the first time I call the boss, to inform him as well as to find out from him what's going on. Getting him on the phone takes a series of forwarding calls until I find him on a boat off the Southampton shore. I'm lowly enough personnel to feel that approval from him is enough to clear my doubts about what I'm doing. He tells me that I'm in charge and that whatever I think is necessary is more than fine with him. Another person probably would be mad as a hatter under the circumstances. Speaking of 'mad as a hatter,' the doctors have called me in after their examination is finished. They're not as concerned about her back pain as her irrational behavior and want to commit her to the psychiatric ward for observation. As I recall this, my throat tightens these many years later! This is a devastating responsibility for me, totally unfair and I'm way out of my league. I again call the boss and the vision of him sopping up margaritas on his yacht while I'm here sends me appropriately into orbit. But I still don't know what I could have done differently. I'm sure as 'lawyer to the stars', he's also acting in a no-fault style. I'm left to translate to Maria all that the doctors have recommended. I tell her that if she voluntarily agrees to the commitment, the observation time will be brief, ten days. If they commit her, it could be more than a month. I beg her to check in willingly, reminding her that it will relieve her pain and get her the help that I can't give her. As I tell her all the benefits of this, I'm really telling myself. I'm concerned that I may be doing this commitment for my own convenience. This is an appalling event for me, and for Barbara. Maria, kicking and screaming throughout, signs the necessary admission paper. As two nurses prepare her for the trip on the elevator to the psyche ward just short of a straight jacket, she tells me that I've always reminded her of her mother, Princess von Somebody, "both as horrible and deadly." I shudder at my own deed. I sign papers not as next of kin but as the person to be notified at time of discharge. This could never happen in today's medical world. Barbara and I leave the hospital and stand outside the car in the light of the full moon. We are speechless after the enormity of what we have done. Where the hell is Oscar?

The next day it's Barbara who hears by phone from Maria. Could she please deliver shampoo and nail polish to her at the hospital? Amazing! But my friend Calamity Jane cannot say 'no' to anything, and I'm in no position to judge in this case. She does deliver all kinds of Revlon products and they both feel much better. I, on the other hand, believe that they both may be crazy.

While these beauty treatments are going on in the psyche ward I'm back to my usual job downtown. I reveal nothing to my colleagues who're aware that I'm on some kind of special assignment. Then the dreaded call comes in at the end of almost ten days. The hospital decides that Maria can go 'home.' She's not a danger to herself or others and they tell me to come get her. Now what? Another call to the boss is in order and he asks if there's any kind of motel/hotel that may be in the area until the 'problem' goes away. The only possibility of such an oasis in this desert of suburbia with its big box stores, malls and commuters, is a well-known bar/restaurant/motel for out-of-town business men, after-work regulars and men hoping to get lucky (and by the way, it's my watering hole). I see that there's no help on the way; no one is coming to pick her up and there's no sign of Oscar. Of course I'll be using my credit card until I get reimbursed. Before we hang up we agree on my meeting him tomorrow at his office to transfer the billing information to him and settle whatever else is outstanding. I'm thankful for small favors.

And so I check Maria out of the hospital, and a mere three miles down the road, check her into the Island Inn. It's surprisingly effortless. This is, for her, not a bad situation. The motel has a restaurant, a bar and a pool, and is within walking distance to a large shopping mall. In fact, for some it's considered upscale. She shows me the medication she's prescribed from the hospital and clearly she'll need refills. I get her settled with her sparse belongings (her silks and furs are at Barbara's) and instruct her to order room service and leave her with some cash.

As I leave the lobby I know that until she leaves New York, I will not be having dinner or drinks here. This is where I've met my current heartthrob who seems to be filling the Joe Treen void left so many years ago. He's very aware of Maria and that what started as a fleeting caper two weeks back has turned into a steady stream of conversation between us with no hope of her going away. He passes my test for being supportive and accepting of my less than conventional job. And along with him, I've shared the secret with my mother and an aunt. It's become a veritable soap opera. My aunt can't seem to forgive Mr. de la Renta for imposing his personal life on me but in reality he has turned to his trusted lawyer who has it all under control. And I'm really questioning whether he's been told any of this update. Each time I speak to my aunt, all she can say is, "You'd think he'd at least give you a bottle of perfume".

If I thought that Maria would be quietly hidden at the motel, I was wrong. Not more than an hour after she's checked in, she's acquainted herself with the bartender, the manager and the maitre'd. She's felt this necessary to order up the best champagne and dinner possible as she's invited Barbara and her two daughters for dinner. And Barbara accepts...still on my credit card!

The next day my finances are settled with me properly and I suspect there are many more settlements that don't pass through me since Maria, still at the hotel and having become one of the regulars, seems to have a limitless shopping and medicine budget. Sometime in June in what seemed an endless summer with humidity draped like a curtain, I receive the first of three phone calls from Oscar; an inquiry as to my diagnosis of Maria and gratitude for my work; the second call, much further along the calendar, is one in which he tells me his intension to come to the hotel to convince her to return to Spain; and the last comes in August, asking me to arrange a meeting between them. I do. And they have a visit in the lounge where she's given a ticket home which she accepts. And after each call, my aunt asks about the perfume!

In early September arrangements are made for Dave Johnson, a Board staffer, to take a city car and, with me, pick up Maria finally and get her to the airport. We do but it's not a direct trip. She must get her wardrobe which was left at a friend's apartment in Manhattan, where she lived upon arrival from Madrid before it seems she wore out her welcome and then moved to the Seville Hotel until she ran out of money, which forced her into the women's shelter and before the last stop at the Madison Avenue walk-in where I found her. She asks now, with the car full of her fabulous de la Renta furs and fashions, that we take her to the shelter where she distributes her worldly goods among the women.

Although I've finally traced Maria's many moves since

landing in New York, I never learned about her family tree or her truth. It was sad to watch Maria board the plane; she gave a smile and a feeble wave. Somehow, she looked smaller. My boss and I never spoke of the matter again during my employ. I never did meet Oscar nor receive that bottle of perfume.

Two Christmases ago I went to a Board of Correction reunion. It's been twenty-nine years! I'd know these folks anywhere. They all look great and it's true they'd been in the bull pen warming up for the big time. The staff has grown into commissioners, and judges, and notable foundation and agency heads, and even an ambassador floated by. It was my former boss who stood still when I laughingly reminded him of the Maria Incident. It was clear that I still felt put upon all these years later, he smiled amused at the story, not one bit apologetic for being in the Hamptons while I was in the psych ward and said, "Oh, yes. She was an imposter!"

6 | The Star Chamber

I got a phone call in the fall of 1983, in my office at the Board of Correction from a program officer working in Governor Mario Cuomo's Division for Women. This bureau is dedicated to advancing women in governmental roles. They're interested now in looking at how women are treated in the criminal justice system. And they need a tutorial. Jail is usually the last stop for women who the system has failed and worse, while incarcerated they become all but invisible while their problems grow. I'm referred to the program officer as a person who can give the Division a primer on women in prison. Interestingly, this reference comes from a woman with firsthand experience in prison, Dr. Sandra Brown - a savvy inmate who holds a Ph.D., and has insinuated herself in many issues (both in and outside the wall.) I can thank this woman, a world-class swindler, for my invitation to have this conversation about women who have been on the fast track to prison for years through abuse, drugs, and poverty. Since Dr. Brown's release from Bedford Hills, I see her now and then at criminal justice conferences, often as a panelist (if you can't beat them, join them.) I owe her a huge debt of gratitude as this introduction becomes my passport to the Women's Division and to my future as a parole commissioner.

It's my fourth year working here at the Board of Correction and I'm pleased with my involvement in affecting some change for incarcerated women. I've been a sympathetic caseworker throughout both jobs at the women's prisons now since 1976. I'd been part of a lawsuit allowing women with newborns to nurse their babies, leading to the creation of nursery programs for city and state inmates and speedy trials for pregnant defendants. Finally there's attention being paid to the connection between violence against women and their subsequent addictions and criminality. I believe highlighting these early abuses in pre-sentencing reports will lead to fairer sentencing outcomes and urge implementation of expanded background reports. Also, I've started after hours grousing sessions among the women who work in the system. Their complaints about their male counterparts and their view of their pampered female charges in prison as malingerers are legion. I don't intend to broker friendships but I do think that the traditional style of yelling and ordering female inmates around leads to a management style that further infantilizes and promotes poor choices. This is true for the jailed and the jailers. I feel good about my work.

The program officer on the phone asks if I'd be interested in meeting with her. I certainly am. This woman, Linda Loffredo, aka The Ear, becomes a lifelong friend and I become professionally affiliated with the Division as we all develop a sort of road show, touring conditions in prisons and speaking with the women. It's headed by Ronnie Eldridge who found her way through the 'glass ceiling' before it was ever defined. Her intuition and brilliance cracked the codes in traditionally male-dominated policies. She's created the agency's role as advocates for women who are caught between the crossfire of domestic violence and their resultant criminality. We all learn that these two issues are directly related to each other as cause and effect. I admire all the people working here. We're a regular think tank that strengthens and supports my belief that our ways of doing business in this male province of crime is not gender exclusive and that woman's common-sense ways are needed. To further bolster my comfort level, they've just hired as their agency counsel the angelic attorney who was my support system throughout the Treen divorce debacle of eight years ago - small world stuff, but boy do I owe her! It's in this safe nest that it's suggested I might be interested in becoming a parole commissioner.

My response is a disbelieving and passive nod, thankful that my skills are even noticed. Typical of an advocate, I go home and call friends to ask if they know anyone who might be a good candidate. I never dream that the job could be mine. After a few days and prompting from friends, and with the recollection of Attica as my drumbeat, *I* go for it. I call to find out what I need to do. It becomes an all-out lobbying campaign...letters, personal appeals to judges, politicos, former employers; anyone who has clout. I've not held an important enough position to make enemies, so this outreach proves quite encouraging, and I really am qualified. No one knows the bottom line of what buttons to press to get appointed. These days it seems that one has to have been a bodyguard or a driver of an official to be in line for any political appointment. In the midst of my lobbying, I understand the discussion about my appointment among people pivots in my favor around the argument that there has never been a white woman or a Long Islander on the parole board. So it's about location and gender. This conversation is promoted by the two immensely capable women who run the Civil Service Commission. Diversity is key here, but in this case it means the inclusion of the first white woman and an acknowledgment of suburban crime. I can never be certain where the big pull comes from as I'm not in the queue for patronage, but I sense it's the endorsement of an important campaign donor doing his former law partner (my date during the Lennon shooting and now close friend) a huge favor. Politics: love it or leave it!

Being a serious candidate means the requisite visit to the capitol take place with the criminal justice czar, Larry Kurlander, the former Rochester DA. A most engaging guy who'd met me at roundtable discussions, but has limited knowledge on which to base a judgment. I'd been at the meeting where he polled the Women's Division about the fairness of female correction officers assigned to male institutions. He is open, candid and approachable. Still, being called to his office makes me particularly tense. My future depends upon his opinion. This is a job interview like no other.

I'm told to arrive in Albany in the late morning and wait for a call at my hotel. This summoning is by no means assurance that the job is a shoe-in. In fact, in the years that I was on the board, there were dozens of people who were mistakenly certain they would be my next colleague and rumors were always swirling. The phone rings at 5:00 pm to come to the capitol. This is December and I soon discover Albany is at least 20 degrees colder than the rest of New York. I walk up the hill that is Washington Avenue where the capitol building sits at the top watching over its people. The winds are whipping around, making the atmosphere for this occasion exactly right. It's pitch dark except for the lights leaking out of the capitol onto the snow. The architecture could be inspired by a European bastion. I'm certain that all capitol buildings are designed to intimidate and I feel dwarfed looking at it. The feeling is akin to the Grand Canyon, standing at the foot of cold marble stairwells and arches reminding me of how unimportant I am in the scheme of things. I guess this is good to remember as I climb the rises to the rich mahogany paneled offices of the 'second floor,' which is a euphemism for the executive chamber. This office is the pulse of all that happens in the criminal justice system.

Mr. Kurlander takes me through a travelogue of the state of New York. My eyes widen as I hear about waterfalls in Livingston County, fishing in Erie, farming in Wyoming, the vistas and great camps of the Adirondacks. I think that what one needs for this job well before an education in law, social work or criminology, is a driver's license! The conversation is very much on the fringe of the actual substance of the work. Mostly I think because no one other than those on the job and inmates had ever witnessed the parole board at work up close and personal. I'd like to think that if they had, the board would operate differently. I think the meeting goes okay enough and frankly, unless I did something unseemly, the political die is cast. Now the long wait.

Waiting is not easy. I rationalize that if I don't get appointed, it's for the best. I do have some misgivings should it come to pass. There are many reasons: living in motels is not appealing in any way; being away from home; and being away from home when I finally have a great guy in my life. My kids, now 22, are fairly independent and pretty much out on their own but we've never really been apart, and my mother, only in her mid-seventies and healthy, still depends on me. I resume my everyday life and work waiting for what feels like judgment day. My personal life has always taken precedence over work which is why this possibility for the first time, has become so important to me. I'd like to at least change the game now that I'll soon be an empty nester. I rely on the anchor of my family and friends to stay in contact with reality. I've kept my private life pretty separate from work. About the most revealing I ever got was on a "Bring Your Daughters to Work Day." Co-workers always seem fascinated to learn about my kids. Most of the women I've worked with have deferred motherhood in lieu of law school or MBAs. And so I've monopolized the spotlight by being the lowest on the totem employee pole with having the oldest kids. It's usually in the ladies' rooms that my colleagues, who are way above me on the T of O as attorneys and execs, ask themselves and me, if they'd done their lives backwards, and while we each envied the other, I never regret (nor could I have changed) my situation. I never let my jobs become my life, until parole.

As I ponder the pros and cons of the appointment, the difficulty of the work is never one of my considerations nor is the thought of camaraderie with the rest of the board. I consider myself a 'people person' and foresee no problems. However the reputations of the Star Chamber-like constellation of the parole board precedes them. Should I get this job, here's the cast of characters: a former corrections worker who has tailored the department's discipline book; several ornery men who rose through the ranks of the Division of Parole beginning as parole officers and thanks to some patronage became board members; the only other woman, who measures her acceptance by the guys on how tough she can be and happily lives with her inmate coined nomenclature, 'Dragon Lady' - this always draws laughter and approval from colleagues; a nerdy kind of grandiose guy who, it's claimed, was appointed by his sheer tenacity and personal appeals to the Appointments Office (appointment by harassment); a controversial black leader from Buffalo who directs inmates to study black history before he'll consider their release; a former upstate Sheriff who'd choreographed the security for the original Woodstock 'happening,' but sadly in my time, is being done in by a brain tumor and consequently is often lost on the road and makes many professional blunders but is protected by his colleagues and allowed to remain on this job that determines people's liberty; a wild and emotional advocate for Hispanic rights; and finally, another man with an academic background who is a radically liberal, truly likeable man but who never met an inmate he didn't like and so grants releases far too often for the public's good. This group, for no other reason than this work, would never have found themselves around a table together.

And as the long wait and hopes continue, I'm bolstered in my personal life by my latest love, and my work out at Rikers is always guaranteed to hold my interest. This new guy is no passing fancy. I met him at my popular watering hole knowing he was different at first blush from his reaction to my telling him I was a penologist (although he may have thought it meant something else!) He seems also to be the antidote for the fantasy I've kept going these many years of the husband that I loved but fought to divorce: Joe. I compare the feelings I had for him with each new man I meet and until Roy, they all fall short. Roy is one of the ping pong men: the kind that go back and forth between a wife they've separated from and with whom they have a bond, and the woman they love but are afraid to risk their future over. I know exactly what this dynamic is about and fully accept the drama, the ups and downs. Sometimes I want things to change and at other times the separateness works well. I've been living alone for a long time now and don't want to lose my 'stuff' ever again. And Roy is sterling in every way in my eyes and adores me. When we are together it's always a honeymoon.

Friends keep me posted on Joe's exploits and I occasionally run into him at old hangouts and various events. And when we speak at these times there's always a flirtatious tension exchanged as if we don't know one another. I keep thinking if we could have a real conversation leaving out this layer of attraction, maybe I could finally detach. But unfinished business is a bitch! Well, the chance comes during this time of waiting for an answer about the appointment. Joe and I speak by phone about trading boxes of letters from each other we've saved. He apparently has some history of his own to take care of. We arrange to meet for a Saturday brunch downtown. This meal is happening almost nine years since the divorce and I have no idea whether my intention is to end this old addiction of him or discover a new romance – again. He's become even more successful as a writer since we're apart. And sadly in my mind I've remained in the demeaned position he held of me – whether true or not. I always saved the indelible impression he had of me when he yelled so long ago, "All you know how to do is to become pregnant." At the time of that showdown, if I could only have foreseen the ironic position he found himself in, when far in the future his third wife writes a book about their experience with infertility and adoption. A book that supposedly details his virtues as a dad but also graphically depicts a guy who never wants children, who fights the adoption, who's tempestuous, inconsistent, tyrannical and immature. A guy, the book says, is jaundiced by his once upon a time step-children! Yep, this is the same person I divorced.

But here and now in this restaurant sitting with this guy I still have a crush on, I continue to feel lowly and apologetic, until my beeper goes off. This is way before cell phones become an appendage. So off I go to find a telephone booth and return the call. It's the Appointments Secretary telling me the date to get to Albany for swearing in. And boom, I return to the table a new confident person! Joe is pretty mute hearing this news that I rub in. I don't think it gets me any points. We leave the restaurant trading the shoeboxes of mixed love and hate letters. I have my doubts he ever knew me. I do think I knew him. Somebody once said, "If the horse is dead, get off!"

And now my coworkers back in the huge marble room

facing City Hall at the Board of Correction are holding a party for me. They're filled with good wishes but all seem fairly mystified as to how I got there and speculate on my hidden influence. I have no answers for them. The more important members of this board are surely dazed. Certainly the chairman, who threw his client Oscar's problems my way, must be surprised. I must admit that this does feed my ego. In a strange way I feel that I'm betraying these colleagues who've become family of sorts (you don't spend time in prison on any side of the bars without becoming closely connected) and here I am casting my allegiance to the other side. I want them to know that I'll carry on the work higher up in the system than I dreamed I could ever get. I was to be part of a Star Chamber, the face of "The Man," what had always been considered the enemy of all prisoners' rights activists.

Even inmates express their opinion on hearing of my appointment: One of the more memorable inmates I met in the early '80s is Macio Ennis, AKA #82A3343. I came to know him when I worked for the Board of Correction investigating prisoner complaints. Macio was a detainee at the Brooklyn House of Detention (BHD). He was, it seems, pretty well-known as a squawker and was able to get more than his share of attention. He had pressed the buttons of Legal Aid attorneys and social workers and his name made eyes roll. This was not because his problems were bogus, but because it meant work. There was after all these regulations called 'the Minimum Standards,' carefully crafted to spell out under what conditions we confine prisoners. Many looked askance at such protections but I for one was thrilled to know they existed.

Macio's complaints dealt with visits and recreation in

his jail, which in Brooklyn happened on this pricey real estate's roof. I met with him twice. I found him to be a savvy, intelligent, manipulative, attractive and articulate guy. He was too friendly and very jail-wise. This was a repeat performance for him as he had been in before. He was a guy in his late 30s so he couldn't blame his crimes on youthful stupidity (although, stupidity doesn't discriminate). I'm sure he viewed me as a dumpling and an easy mark to get a visit with each complaint he filed.

When it came to 'truth,' Macio pushed the envelope to the limit but stayed within the legal definitions. Something I never blamed him for. Experts tell us that when freedom is at stake, thoughts of escape and manipulations are strong survival skills. I believed the experts and went about doing my job. I never knew what his arrest was about, nor was it an interest of mine. I may have had some curiosity but this was not the reason I was at the BHD and certainly not anything that factored into whether he was getting his outdoor recreation. He was, after all, there in detention awaiting trial and not convicted of any crime. When I went to visit him for the last time, I told him that I would probably be moving on to my next job as a Member of the New York State Parole Board. He had a deep and bawdy laugh that resonated through the concrete walls of the counselor's visiting room. I didn't think this was a vote of confidence. Did he think I lacked critical judgment evidenced by my talking with him? He said I better watch out for the 'bad boys' (exactly which side of the table did he mean?). He thought that I could do it for a while but he was afraid I would let the wrong people out! Wow.

In 1986, after two years on the parole board I got his

letter datelined Eastern Correctional Facility.

"Hi Barbara,

"How are you, fine I hope. Well, I am doing pretty fair for an old timer. It's been a long time, but I did try writing you, but received no reply. I guess you received the letter because it never came back to me.

"My lawyer gave me your address, because I asked him to, because there is some information I would like to get from you. Since I have been incarcerated I went back to school and have received a GED, also my Associates Degree and am now working on my BA with 39 credits to finish. Yes, it is a surprise to me also, that I went this far and believe it or not, I really enjoy it.

"Anyway, what I need from you is some information on supervision and the purpose of it, what the board accomplishes by supervision. The reason I need this type of information is because I am doing a thesis on Parole & Probation in one of my classes. The course I am taking is CRJ – Parole & Probation. So it's good that I found you, since you can't (unreadable??), than I can get other help. "smile" I still have my spirit, and look for a better day. However, I have slowed my pace a little.

"So how long have you been in that position and I see it's a higher position. I hope you are able to communicate with prisoners, if not I won't write. So I will take it for granted if you don't reply, but I hope you haven't changed as a person because of the position. Because I thought you were a very good person, that you cared about people.

"I'll say so long for now, and good luck in your position. I guess you could say I need the luck, in a way I do. But I'll be alright, what starts must end. So take care."

Respectfully Yours

Macio Ennis

I went into the inmate locater website in recent time checking on his release (or not). Macio died at Attica in 1995, while serving his convictions for two rapes, a kidnapping and sodomy.

I'm not sworn in alone but with a former director of the Commission on Correction, (the state watchdog over the correction's department) Kevin McNiff. He has a background as an educator for the Department of Correction and comes from the vantage point of fairness, rehabilitation and second chances. He was a priest as a much younger man but chose instead the great love of his life and marriage. His reputation precedes him and I'm thrilled to be 'twinned' with him. We both stand up with some embarrassment as we're sworn into office in the august Senate Chambers. Our backgrounds are so different from the other board members that we think we are mistakes, and if not, imposters. We'd come this far and now we're in it together. Kevin leans over to me and whispers in my ear, "Barb, you only have to do this for one year and then leave." "After all", he might have thought, stereotyping me, "she lives in the suburbs, is a single mother of two children, has a dog, a real life and a monthly commuter ticket on the LIRR. How is she going to negotiate life on the road?" How wrong he would be: I'll never cave. I think I must look like a real lightweight. He thinks he's being gallant and protective for what is to come. There would be no turning back for me!

I needn't have pinched myself to come down from my

'high' after the swearing-in. For as I alight from the train at Grand Central Station, I'm astonished to be met by a friend. She's been dispatched by my mother to tell me that while I was in Albany, my little dog of seventeen years, Pogo, has been hit and killed by a car. If ever I needed to put things in perspective, this is the lesson I remember. This also gives credence to my worries about being away from home. And so starts the next twelve years on the road.

I walk into the board room on a day in February, 1984 (by the way, just days before Bill Arico has been crushed to death at Metropolitan Correctional Center) for my first meeting with the above described body of ten members plus two (me and Kevin). I take my seat at the end of the table in order of seniority and am introduced to my new peers. This is a ritual that repeats itself at least 15 more times during my twelve years on the board. For a group that seems to remain static with the same faces and ideas, it does change over time. During my tenure I come to know 25 different colleagues with the same powers. Most of them, but for a very few in my opinion, are the same people but with varying features and names to tell them apart. This is due to the culture of a board where the majority of members defines itself as community avengers and wrongly interprets parole as forgiveness granting it scarcely.

There are 2.4 million people incarcerated in the United States in spite of a 40% drop in crime and although we have 5% of the world's population, we have 20% of the world's incarcerated. And reflecting the expansion of the prison industry, this board expands from nine to twelve to fifteen, to eventually 19 members in order to carry out its mandate. The job has always been to meet inmates at their minimum eligibility date, review all factors clearly defined by statute to judge their risk to the community if released. It's wrongly been used by most, however, as a resentencing mechanism. In my time I thought the release rate that hovered around 60% was too low. But today there is only a 29% release rate! In my opinion a more fair and impartial board would be one hired through professional qualifications rather than patronage where it is impossible to ignore parole decisions based on political pressures.

Kevin and I are greeted enthusiastically by the team in this smoke-filled board room. They are salivating for replacements to fill the empty seats because it's impacted their work load. I try to look through their posturing. It's tough though, because they're all looking back at me (which I would come to do myself with the introduction of each new member). Over time, my initial opinion of the members is reinforced. These are the people I'm going to be practically living with for the next twelve years. We will sit all day together, we will travel together, and we will eat together until we go to our rooms at night alone. But I'm certain I can escape this fate, be more of a loner and still carry off the job. I know walking into this position that the long-held punitive attitude among the already appointed board is going to be the toughest challenge I face. Their reputation as a star chamber is well-known. My experience around the tables of The Governor's Division for Women discussing feminist practices gives me a running start, and I give myself permission to bring a woman's perspective to this 'get-tough' business. This is going to be a piece of cake, I told myself! How hard could this be? Little do I suspect anything close to the obstacle course it would become.

The Board travels in twos and threes. Each week there are four separate boards at different institutions. This shuffle changes weekly to allow for all 72 prisons to be visited monthly. Our board schedule is put together in Albany a month in advance. There is rarely a change requested and we all march in lock-step, working only sometimes with folks whose opinions are simpatico. There's an attempt to balance the political views of the assigned trios to more fairly impact the release outcomes. At the first publication of the schedule the support staff books travel and accommodations. The work week lasts until the roster of candidates have all been seen – averaging 150 cases a week per board on the road. We usually meet from 50 to 60 candidates in one day! If the interviews move quickly, there's a caravan going on to the next prison. This could consist of up to five cars, including three commissioners and two court reporters. There's a military-like mentality to 'come, to see and to conquer.' Despite the wrath of the 'Weather Gods,' (cars in snow drifts, grounded planes, iced over roads) the Board has never in all its years missed a hearing. They are tough. The rules of the road had its traditions long before I join. As I've said the Board culture has always been one where the 'good ole boys' travel together, share similar criminal justice philosophies, stay in the same motels, eat at the same restaurants and in general, spend more time together than most married couples.

My start-up training is all of a day long. It includes teaching me how to fill out an expense account! Any regard for the actual release or denial decisions is left up to individual discretion, professional philosophy and peer influence. I come to realize that this is a group that practices no collective mission and bumps into one another's opinion to gain power and control. Release statistics can tell who the assigned commissioners are almost without knowing their names. As I hunker down into the job, I experience in varying degrees that I often have to argue each case and my point of view about the decisions made; majority rules here. Coming on as the youngest and the first white woman, I am the minority opinion more often than not. It's not only the difference of my take on criminal behavior and reformation but my colleagues' stereotypical attitude toward me. They do not view me as their equal. I am not macho; things would be so much easier if I were. I fortunately have the same powers. But the free-range nature of the appointment process itself allows the members to scatter like chickens, each making judgments for very different reasons.

In preparation I have read the executive law, I have heard the stories from the other commissioners, I know the rumors and skepticism from the inmate's side of the equation as a legacy from my former jobs. Now I'm armed with the legal language of release denial. It reads: "After careful review of your record by a panel of the Board of Parole, you have been denied release on parole. The members of the board of parole that conducted your release interview have determined that there is a reasonable probability that you will not live and remain at liberty without violating the law and that your release at this time is incompatible with the welfare of society. While your entire record was reviewed, the following are the factors upon which the denial of parole at this time is based..." This terminology is used 75% more of the time than a release where there is nothing in writing required other than the approval of the majority and conditions of release. It's always safer to deny than to parole; it takes no courage and is the best route to job security. One doesn't want to find oneself in the headlines. I realize that we sentence people to more time for what they may do than for what they've done.

The first board I sit on is trial by fire with an assignment to Clinton Correctional Facility in the nether region of upstate to observe a board in action. The state rule is that anything north of Albany allows you to fly. This is a mixed blessing as the planes that fly to regional airports require a belief in immortality or having a good will ready for your heirs. These are the 'puddle jumpers.' It's harrowing! Larger planes are available to get to Syracuse, Rochester, or Buffalo. But Kevin and I fancy ourselves a different kind of public servant who aim to save the state money. So on a bleak snowy Monday in February, en route to Clinton, known as 'Little Siberia,' 320 miles from NYC, we opt for the train from Grand Central Station, rather than fly. The schedules always have us leave home on Monday to travel to any one of New York's upstate prisons. This train is the milk run from NYC to Montreal with our stop in Plattsburgh 30 miles from the Canadian border. It's an eight-hour trip that allows me to imagine what will be waiting up ahead. Kevin is serious about his privacy and his cigar so we don't sit or talk with one another the entire trip (hmmm). And much later on, when we turn in our expenses, no one mentions or cares about our frugality.

Arriving late at night we go right from the train station to the motel, lucky to find a taxi waiting. This night in the Howard Johnson's Motel of Plattsburgh, my sleep is more turbulent than I've experienced in years. My dream hasn't surfaced but its left me uncomfortable...like a secret kept down deep. I'm sure that once I get the routine down this tossing at night will be history.

Walking into Clinton Correctional, named after the county and located in the teeny town of Dannemora up a mountain off Military Turnpike a long way outside Plattsburgh, on my first Tuesday morning on the road, I'm mindful of the history of the facility, the people living inside and the responsibility of dispensing justice. Auburn used the first electric chair in 1890 but then this is the place where the chair was housed, and between 1892 and 1913 twenty-six men were executed before the chair was moved to Sing Sing. In many instances generations of families work in these prisons and mark their time on the inside much the same as the inmates. Looking at the complex from the road, one is overwhelmed by the long shadow this prison casts. The wall borders the main street where the only thing that moves in this town are the people connected to the prison. The two businesses are a motel and a restaurant. Both owned and run by the Ting family, who also have their name on an airplane service. Ting has become code for families who have someone upstate. While building prisons upstate has ensured income and jobs for rural communities, it's made it often impossible for families to visit and transitional services to be nonexistent.

The prison was built in 1845, conceived for using

convicts for iron mining labor on the two hundred acres and a mine that were purchased for $17,500. The first 50 prisoners arrived from Sing Sing and Auburn. They were shackled and wearing stripes having walked the 17 miles from Plattsburgh. Clearly theirs was a worse trip than mine. Over the years the prison has expanded and has been classified variously as needed for tuberculin inmates, criminally insane and other experimental programs. The most interesting fact of Clinton is that it's built on the side of a mountain where separate 'courts' are created by inmate cliques that socialize, cook and play cards together. This has served the facility well in what officials refer to as 'population management' and where inmates develop their own elite social groups. There are approximately 3,000 inmates being 'managed' here.

The Board is favored with special parking at all the facilities, necessary for easy and fast access. At Clinton we park on one of the levels of the tiered lot that abuts the miles of concrete walls. We walk through the outside gatehouse and locked gate into a courtyard, before entering the labyrinth of the inner sanctum. In each facility you get used to showing your ID and signing in, usually several times. The corrections offices know this is board day and there are special 'posts' to escort inmates back and forth from their housing areas to the board room. We start interviewing at 8:30 in the morning and walk into the prison at eight to get a head start on reading the folders and being prepared. This makes for very early morning wake-ups continuing until the calendar for the day is completed. The air is tension-filled as I walk into the board room to begin the day's work. The fear emanates from the inmates who have waited years for this interview.

They sit in most facilities in alphabetical order close to the conference room and ordinarily the first twenty people get to see you walk in at the top of the day. On this morning, I see each face and pair of eyes peering out at me knowing that I'm the new kid on the block. They are nervous for themselves. They are nervous for me. I am nervous. The inmates' grapevine is always more accurate than the professionals'.

At the end of the day, I have not yet interviewed a candidate for parole and have not yet sat in judgment. But I have learned. I watch the body language on both sides of the table, I hear the horrendous and pathetic stories, I know the unalterable pain of the victims, I put myself in the position of all the players. I review again the policy of parole as I interpret it: that inmates who've served the minimum period of their indeterminate sentence are eligible for parole unless one can articulate why that decision would pose a community risk. While the most important factor that brings one to prison is undeniably the crime, he should not in this hearing be defined by that one act of his life alone. We are not voting guilt or no guilt. We are voting risk or no risk. I remember this is a maximum security prison with men who've committed the types of crimes that get them long sentences. At the time of these crimes many of these men were too young to become who they would be. So hasn't the time they've served changed them and why are there so many denials being handed out? I can figure out the differences between behavior gone amuck with criminal consequences letting impulse and stupidity be your guide, but sadism, mindful harm over a long time, repeated patterns of unlawfulness, multiple victims? These would be the ones I don't want to put to the litmus test. For sure there's a huge pool of crimes to choose from here. And after hearing and reading the stories, I'm amazed that with so much working against these men, our communities do as well as they do.

The board I'm observing is personally offended, thinking they're being lied to by inmates during interviews. Next week, once I start my own hearings, I don't think I'll feel insulted by inmate's lies and manipulations. I expect it. Wouldn't you do anything to fight for your freedom? But the result of this suspicion by this board is usually a denial of parole. While there's merit in being suspicious if you can't get at the truth, the whole notion of being lied to seems to bollix up the reviewing commissioners and places undue importance on stories that are already known to the court. True confessions don't matter here and inmates' lies tell me they want to put the best spin on their actions. I believe there are three sides to truth; yours, mine and what is probably the truest in the middle. After life on the board, I never confused the 'truth' with the facts. And here I am, launched into a system created by men to punish men. And so, armed with a day's worth of training and a lifetime of social conscience, I begin my job 'for real,' as they say.

My navigational skills become honed but there is no easy travel remedy for a state that has snow in September through April in the 'north country' or 'out west.' The risks of the road loom so large that it's common, once we land back in the office and debrief among ourselves, to tell the travel stories rather than the serial murders of the week past. My feelings of relief are often dependent on weather and I'm grateful when I get to my lodging or to a prison destination safely. But I surprise myself as my attitude 'on the job' (as the tough cops say) differs from the ones I have in personal life. On the road I think I'm invincible and wrapped in Teflon as a parole commissioner. I think that were something to happen to me, there'd be a team of troopers deployed around the state to find me...circling helicopters...and my nerves turn to steel the moment I'm 'on the job.' No one wants to lose a colleague; the board wouldn't be able to go on. I don't catch its full meaning until I'm wending my way up the treed campus that Fishkill Correctional Facility sits on (RT. 84 in Beacon). I'm following a co-worker in my car from quite a distance and have time before the interviews begin. This is still in my early years on the job when I take photos of the prisons before the mortar and brick haunt my dreams. I've pulled over to take a picture. Much to my amazement, my colleague turns around his car to see if I'm alright. "Jim", I say feeling flattered. "How nice of you." He replies, "Oh, I don't care how you are, I just can't do the Board without you." So much for collegiality.

It would be grandiose to confuse courage with authority. My shield has magic powers and I know it. Most people who see it know it also. I'm able to fend off unwanted squeegee men on my windshield, not get speeding tickets, push away muggers in the street and embarrass a circle of perhaps 50 teens at Penn Station waiting for a midnight train in the winter when a man drops from the ceiling onto the marble floor of the station. His broken body is greeted with hoots and giggles as the drunken youths, all going home to prestigious north shore neighborhoods stand around. He on the other hand, has been living in the warm duct pipes of the ceiling for the Christmas holidays. With shield in hand I stand over the man, call the police who call an ambulance, and get the preppies the hell away. I wait with the man who remarkably has suffered only a broken leg. Another rescue happens on my way to 'work' (on my way to LaGuardia to hop a flight to Syracuse). I leave home a bit early so I can grab a hot dog at my neighborhood Nathan's...a small treat before a week that promises to be tough. While I'm munching away in front of a huge window looking onto the street and thinking about yesterday and tomorrow, I notice a scene that comes alive. A couple through the window on the street, she's carrying a shopping bag trying to get away from him and he's, although silent, obviously harassing her. I put it together and think that they probably came out of the motel across the street that caters to welfare clients and I'm looking at danger. So without thinking, I get up with my shield in one hand and unwittingly take the mustard-dripping hotdog in the other and go outside interrupting the action. I ask her if she needs assistance and he steps back as I hold my shield Dracula-like, backing him up against a tree. She begs me to be good to him, her partner who's high. She's used to this, she tells me. I don't want him arrested, he needs detox. I take them into Nathan's and sit them down and call over the manager. It's tougher for me to take in the scene in the restaurant than the one I've interrupted, as all the suited up working people lunching in the place snicker at this happening. Like performance art. I am appalled! But they stop laughing as I show my badge and get to a phone to call police to have him transported to the hospital. The manager assures me he will wait with them as I have my flight to catch. Only when I get to my car do I realize the heft of the hotdog in my hand, and eat it! Anyway, courage is a reaction to fear and the shield doesn't cure that.

Life on the road may seem glamorous to some, but for me it's a constant hardship, although the work is truly a privilege. No sooner do I safely return home, (hopefully on a Thursday evening) than I tune in to the weather report to find out what the next Monday of travel will bring. And I'm beginning to look like Quasimodo with luggage wearing down my right shoulder. I have a motel policy check list: before any luggage is unpacked or a call to home made, check the heater/air conditioner, the TV, the phone, the bathroom, making sure they all work. And when finally collapsing on the bed, remove the germ-infested bedspread, which is what travel gurus tell you to do. Twelve years of wrestling with ethics; of traveling 33,000 miles per year to the state's 72 prisons; of being tossed around in the air in a 'puddle-jumper' aircraft; of checking into orange-colored, shag-carpeted motel rooms on the road; of arguing with colleagues; of eating fast food; of missing my family and friends; but most of all, of most often being alone on the other side of an issue. I've said that I'd rather be disliked for something than liked for nothing in particular. And I guess I've put that belief to the test.

One illustrious trip puts a Watertown and Utica prison on the same schedule. For me, it means that I drive my car to LaGuardia airport where I park in the long-term parking lot reserved for state workers near the Marine Air Terminal. Then stand to wait for a bus that actually takes me to the Marine Terminal where I'll wait and catch a bus to the U.S. Air terminal where my flight will get me to Syracuse. At the Syracuse airport, I rent a waiting car and drive to the prison in Watertown. After the Board finishes interviewing at Watertown Correctional Facility (up a huge hill that actually has a ski mountain aside it), where the constant drone of cars stuck in snow is background noise, we form a five-car caravan to get us down to Utica in the P.M. This means that we won't have to start out at 5 A.M. the next morning and take this trip to prison (or the grave). The five cars in a row are psychologically comforting to me but the thought that we can actually collide with each other in this whiteout doesn't help. It is the most treacherous trip I've taken as we inch along through the ice slicked road in the pitch black white-out. We drive slowly on Swan Road, down Dry Hill, onto Brookside turning right onto Route 12 south through Burrville until we find the Thruway and exit 31 to Utica. One by one we pull into one of the Econo Lodges, or Empires or Motel 6s or Landmarks or Holiday Inns that abound in the state but where the buildings are too small to even have a silhouette. No one says a word of relief as we check silently into our rooms separately and then collectively gather in the room of the Board's senior member. We fall to our knees and thank God that we have all made it safely. No one relaxes until the bottle (that often travels with a very few) is unscrewed and we all take a swig.

Some of the chummier commissioners travel together if possible, as we are all starting our trips from different parts of the state. When Kevin and I work together, we try to avoid dinners with the group by quietly going out the backdoors of the motels and finding obscure hideaways to eat. I can honestly defend myself by claiming that the cigars, pipes and cigarettes are killing me (oh, this was so long ago). One of my early and more colorful trips gets me to a little-known landing strip outside of Malone where I am assured there's a car rental. Not only is there no car rental but there's one attendant who talks the pilot down from the sky, removes the luggage and sells the tickets. While I wait for the heavy lifting to be done, he tells me there are no cars available. After all it's not really an airport, it's a landing strip! But this one man show does get me to a Ford dealer in "town" who agrees to rent me a car on a state voucher for the three days I'm there. These are the times I miss a traveling buddy, but the joys of the trust in a small town make up for it.

With all this chatter about travel, one might think the journey subsumes the main attraction. For me, as horrible as the travel is, it serves as comic relief and contrasts starkly with the sorrowful stories I can't shake. I often look down from the sky as my plane circles above the prison I'd just left, heading for home, and think about the human suffering left behind as I climb in the clouds. Most of the people in our system are the end result of poverty, lack of education, addictions, homelessness and mental illness. These factors are the greased wheels to prison. Most of the people I meet have the ability to change; only a small percentage are evil or sociopaths.

In my years in the Star Chamber, I was involved in participating in 77,000 decisions. Each one was gut-wrenching. Some were easier than others but never simple. Some of the crimes were perpetrated by people who may have been nuts. Some were committed by ordinary people. I often questioned who made me God to make these decisions and some days I argued both sides of the decision with myself. And there were days I became almost paralyzed by the toxicity of the interviews and by the often professional disrespect of my peers. In a system that is designed to separate violent people from the community, it confounds common sense that any preparation for release on parole would include taunts and vitriol to the inmates from men sitting in powerful positions. Humiliation does not heal. The fact is that but for a few exceptions, most of the other people on the board viewed power and control as their mandate, and their ways were not going to be modified by a 'nice girl' It was never apparent enough to them that they had the ultimate power of the pen.

7 | Grasping at Straws

By the time he walks in the room, there's been so much hype that it's hard to believe this guy is a notorious assassin, the shooter of Malcolm X. He looks pretty ordinary, this Muhammad Al-Aziz/ aka Norman Butler/aka #66-A-0057. Here I am at Arthurkill Correctional Facility, heading this panel for his possible parole release. To prepare myself, I've been careful to stay clear of reminding myself about the publicity around facts of the crime and my sieve-like memory serves me well. I read the file as if learning the story for the first time.

Mr. Aziz's fate had been sealed twenty years and three months earlier on February 21st, 1965, at the Audubon Ballroom in Manhattan. It was on this day that Malcolm X, who had broken from the Black Muslim sect, while delivering a speech to his followers as the icon of his new "Organization of Afro-American Unity" organization, was shot and killed. Mr. Al-Aziz was arrested for this in-concert crime at his home five days later. Today, May 6th, 1985, would be the day he'd waited for since then. It was also the third board of parole he was facing.

My route to this hearing room at Arthurkill Correctional Facility on Staten Island has seen a lot less predictability along the way than Al-Aziz' twenty-plus years of waiting in confinement brings. It's therefore a surprise, even for me, to find myself chairing this panel of the parole board. Others, with longer experience, tried to fulfill their mandate before me, but their personal opinion has interfered with justice.

Late in April, last month, all board members were summoned to a meeting that took place in the Harlem Office Building. The meeting was called to review the previous decision in the case of Muhammad Al-Aziz. He'd met his first board after serving twenty years at the beginning of December. They conducted a comprehensive hearing. In a Murder One case, the policy is to send the inmate to a panel of psychiatrists for a report, if the interviewing board is considering release. They made that decision. It also signaled to the next parole panel that the three commissioners before them believe he is a good parole risk provided the psychiatric reports come back in order. In this case, this has all happened but the second board denied release. And the second board conducted an inappropriate and appealable interview. So, subsequent to his appeal and our counsel's recommendation, the full Board of twelve votes to give him another hearing. His liberty is up for grabs now at this third hearing, this hearing that I will chair.

Although this crime is no different than others seen on a daily basis, a premeditated in-concert shooting, it is exceptional: the media is fixated on it, the racial politics beg for its attention, and the claim is made that the murder of this victim may have changed history. I always notice that the standard of punishment usually matches the importance of the victim; a person of prominence is *assassinated*, a regular citizen is *murdered*. I can't separate these observations from the case. At the meeting in Harlem, it's decided that commissioners who have already interviewed Mr. Aziz not return again, which reduces our ranks to half a dozen. 'And then there were six.' To be absolutely impartial as to who's assigned, the six of us draw straws. The short straws pulled belong now to me, Commissioner McNiff and Commissioner Leak. And lucky me, with a little more than a year of experience on the Board, has seniority over the others who also grabbed at straws. I am to be the chair of this panel.

And here I am, out the door this Monday morning, on my way to prison. It's a little over a week since the meeting. What a strange place, this Arthurkill Correctional Facility. It's a prison on Staten Island built on a junkyard next to a 'kill,' Dutch for stream. I have no idea where the 'arthur' comes from. The name alone always conjures a bloodthirsty hunt in my mind....something almost mythological with pitchforks and devils. It's also a tease in travel terms. Less than thirty miles from my door but over two hours in travel time. This gives me lots of drive time to focus on what's waiting at the other side of the Veranzano Bridge.

The bumper-to-bumper traffic allows me the vacuum I need to muse about the business I find myself in and remember the simple connection between parole and public safety. Like this Belt Parkway winding through the marshes and high-rises of Brooklyn, it's easy to get tangled up in the myriad decision-making pressures and political expectations. I stay in the backed-up traffic line even though it would be easy to wander over the interrupted yellow markings. Find out, I tell myself, what the guy did, what he did before, what he's done in these past 20 years and what his plans are in the future. But find out much, much more. What do I need to ask him without sounding like an idiot, when the minutes are reviewed either by his legal team if it's a hold, or by the press if it's a release? I will always be second-guessed, this I can predict.

Satisfied that my drill has helped, I concentrate on following the seagulls that seem to be on their way also to Muhammed Al-Aziz. A few miles over the bridge, many of them stop off at the Fresh Kills. Is it any wonder that with all these 'kills' around, one feels a shudder? This Fresh one is a science fiction-like mound built with the excesses of the populace. It's the city dump turned environmental wonderland topped with a chemist's inspired lemon-fresh perfume dolloped on the burms. The parcel still acting as a garbage cite has a huge crowd of winged customers prowling through. Is this the place or is it the New Jersey marshes that the police regularly take junkets to search for missing mob members? Among the old beautiful neighborhoods and pricey homes, this little island connecting New York with New Jersey has a very active underworld business.

Here's Bloomingdale Road, my turn off that takes me the final mile to the prison passing tank farms, scrub brush, chop shops, a convenience store and finally down to this razor-ribboned parking lot on the right. About a thousand guys live here, none call it home. Although their prison issue clothes attempt to equalize them, they are after all people as different as snowflakes. The place operated originally as a pre-fab treatment lock-up for addicts. Since our war on drugs, addicts are called felons and the place is a prison. Some of the over 400 staffers are also early employees of the Narcotic Addiction Control Commission, now turned corrections' officers. It's before eight in the morning so the trip was under two hours; could've used more time for thinking today.

As I lock up the car, I notice that my colleagues have already arrived. The reception for the parole board is almost always hospitable and this time is no different. A short walk from the parking lot to the small beige concrete bunker that serves as the first post, to certify who gets in and who doesn't, is my first stop. This little wasteland boasts activity equal to any other industrial complex: medical staff, family visitors, advisory boards, program staffers, correctional officers, inmate work gangs who work outside in nearby road crews and cemeteries; all coming and going. My little cadre of parole people are checked through with no surprises. The quick-fire rumor mill in a prison seems to leak out almost simultaneous to the facts. And so on this day we are expected here, perhaps even before I knew it, as Aziz has been transferred here from Fishkill Correctional in Orange County just days ago. Leaving the exit of this checkpoint takes us through a small pathway bordered by the cheery plantings of marigold seedlings. Once the heat and humidity settle into this neighborhood, the flowers will provide a full grown deception shading the misery inside.

Inside the administration building we take a short-cut through brown steel double doors avoiding the main corridor known as 'Broadway,' and make a right through a door that will be our interview room. Usually in this little space on regular board days, there are chairs for the many parole candidates who will sit and wait, sometimes to go nowhere. Today, only one chair for our one famous guy. No one will know how long this hearing will take so the prison has pulled in a cart with coffee, as if my nerves were not keyed up enough. I look at the faces of my colleagues as we ritually begin our morning and I see their deadpan veneer, the same that covers mine. We are all new, we are all intense and we all want justice served.

This justice thing can be elusive. And as I always remind myself, it also should never be confused with truth. People seem to want level playing fields as the translation of 'just'. These 'fields' however, have varying lengths and heights depending on who thinks one eye weighs as much as the other eye. And so as I prepare myself to 'pull' the case folder that will give me the Karnac-like answers, I focus. It's always at this time that I block everything else out realizing the ramifications of a decision. And with a spit and polish shine on my senses, I open the weighty file containing the documented facts of the life of Muhammed Al-Aziz. I'll have to guess about his less visible intentions.

We will all participate but I will be the lead interviewer. I read the well-done reports prepared by the institutional parole staff, explaining the background of this day. This is the first time I have read the full case and as I read, I flash back to the events of February in 1965. And now I read the two previous hearings in their entirety conducted by six commissioners. It's the second interview I'm most startled by, even though I'm aware of the legal finding of "bias and prejudice as evidenced by both the nature and substance of the questions and statements" concluded by our counsel as a result of the last hearing (the reason for this do-over appeal) and I wince with embarrassment as I read:

Hearing held at Fishkill Correctional Facility; February 1985
In Attendance: Commissioners Dean, Kirkland, Sherrid

By Commissioner Kirkland:
Q. You are Mr. Mohammad Al-Aziz?

A. Al-Aziz

Q. How are you?

A. Okay

Q. Used to be known as Norman Tom Butler?

A. Yes.

Q. I am Commissioner Kirkland. To my left is Commissioner Dean and to his extreme left is Commissioner Sherrid. You appeared before the board in December, is that right?

A. Yes, Sir.

Q. And they held you for what is known as a panel? In all murder cases where there is an interest maybe in releasing a person, there is an Executive Order which mandates that a panel...which means more than one psychiatrist must approve or examine the person to make sure that the person is sane, or whatever. The psychiatrist report is fine. You have done 20 years for a murder that is sort of shocking to a lot of people. You killed one Malcolm X along with two co-defendants, and one must at some point just wonder where America would be today if Malcolm had lived. He was a Statesman. He was a leader. He was psychologically uplifting to many underrated people. And was a pillar for the poor. He was a Nat Turner of the Sixties. Harriet Tubman. He was a Frederick Douglass. He was a Marcus Garvey. He was a man of time. One has to wonder what would happen if he had lived. His death certainly changed the course of history. Probably black people are more confused today than ever before. They were on the avenue or on the move of gaining their identity. Today I think they may very well be lost from lack of identity. I realize that you have a lot of letters. People recommending your release. Is that correct?

A. Yes, Sir.

Q. You have a job offer to drive a limousine?

A. Not driving.

Q. Whatever. What is it?

A. Executive position. An executive position.

Q. An executive position? And the owner of the limousine service is who? What's his name?

A. Frank.

Q. Frank what?

A. Wilbright.

Q. You have been supported by people, from some CO's, is that right?

A. Yes, Sir.

Q. Who?

A. Lots of them.

Q. What?

A. A lot of them. I don't recall their names. I don't remember all their names.

Q. You have numerous other letters. From people. Newsweek. Why?

A. Why do they support me?

Q. Sure.

A. I think they see me as a human being and not as a record.

Q. There have been several theories on Malcolm's assassination. One is that some folks felt is was the CIA. And there was a large segment of America who is appreciative of the fact that Malcolm was killed, and a large segment could include a number of people in law enforcement. Why do you think they look so favorably upon you?

A. Law enforcement?

Q. Yes.

A. I don't know. I don't think they're the only ones. Or in fact the only ones.

Q. They look favorable upon you. I am just asking you a question. Offering you a job in two places, by the way. New York City Police Department is offering you a job too. Am I correct?

A. Not just the police.

Q. I said they are.

A. He did when he was police Commissioner. When he had a different responsibility. He wasn't the Police Commissioner at the time that he said what he did. But there are some Senators and Congressmen in there.

Q. Who?

A. Datna (phonetic) for one. Al Vann.

Q. Would the Congressmen and all the rest of them be recommending your parole if you had killed a white person of a similar status?

A. Or a person.

Q. Think about it before you answer the question.

A. First of all I didn't kill him.

Q. You were convicted

A. I didn't say I wasn't convicted.

Q. You were convicted of it and we have to go according to the fact that you were convicted and my question still remains.

A. I can't answer your question that way.

Q. You can answer. You are a learned man. You have a M.A. Degree, You have done a lot of studying and you have improved your education tremendously since you have been incarcerated. I am not taking that away. You are a very intelligent person. You have written articles. A *question like that should not stump you.*

A. It is not a matter of stumping, as you said. I am a person sitting here convicted, so what could I say?

Q. My question was do you think all those folks would be recommending you for parole if you had killed a white person of similar status?

A. I don't know.

Q. In America? You really don't know?

A. I don't know.

Q. You are not as learned as I thought you would be. Your record does not reflect your true level of knowledge, and if you say you don't know—if you understand anything about America—

A. I think I understand what I am supposed to do, sit here and say...

Q. I am just asking you a question. How do you feel about Malcolm's death?

A. I think it was a tragedy.

Q. What do you think was lost?

A. More than I can talk about.

Q. Tell us. Try and talk about it.

A. I think the man was great in his time. I think he had achieved things that people don't even think about Black people achieving. And not just him. I don't even think Elijah Mohammad who was Malcolm's mentor, gave him the credit due him. But that's how America is.

Q. What do you mean, that's how it is?

A. What could I say? I mean, I am here. What could I say? You are here. What could I say? I am just trying to live according to the best way I can. Try to better myself and do the best for myself and others that I touch, that I can. And I think this is one of the things that people have seen over the years in me. I have done everything that I could do for myself and for those whom I touch.

Q. Been on work release?

A. Yes. I am.

Q. On a murder one charge?

A. On a murder one. I am not the only one.

Q. I understand that. I understand that perfectly. And I will say I have problems with it because I know that if you killed someone. A white person of similar status, you would not be getting this royal treatment. I understand that and you do too. I often wonder what kind of treatment a person got that turned in Nat Turner...caused his death. Not much is ever written about it. All we know is that another person that he trusted turned him in to the slave master. Other people that turned in John Brown. Harper's Ferry. Told them he was coming. I look around and I see the large numbers of people colored in prison today and I think Malcolm at that time was doing some things positive to keep a lot of them out of prison, and I have a very serious problem.

A. I can say that over the years I have attempted to do those same type of things, and there are some attestations to do that.

Q. I look around at the large number of Black people in prison today trying to do the best they can, and they are catching a lot of hell. You are like a hero. I am just asking questions. Ten years from now what would you like to be doing?

A. Well, it depends on how the first maybe two or three...

Q. I am sorry?

A. I think it depends on how the first two or three go.

171

I think that I have had, as you say, offers to do several things. And one of those things that I can do is in a sense what Malcolm was doing, which is to become the Iman of number Seven in New York, and several other places.

Q. You think people will trust you?

  A. Yes.

Q. Seriously?

  A. Yes.

Q. Who would you lead?

  A. Who?

Q. Yes.

  A. Whoever felt a need.

Q. What kind of people would you lead? Lead white people? Black people? Who are you going to lead?

  A. I think that whomever can accept the truth is worthy of following the truth.

Q. In addition to that, would you like to say anything else?

  A. Yes sir.

Q. Who are going to live with?

  A. Whom?

Q. Yes.

  A. My wife.

Q. And who are you a follower of now?

  A. You mean what religious community? American Muslim Mission.

Q. What is your relationship with Farrahkan?

  A. I don't have any.

Q. What do you think of him?

  A. I don't really think I can formulate an opinion about him.

Q. None whatsoever? You wrote an article on him, am

I correct?

    A. *No, I didn't.*

    Q. *Didn't I see something in here about him?*

    A. *No.*

    Q. *Okay. That was Jimmy Breslin.*

Any questions, Commissioners?

Commissioner Sherrid: *Yes. I have a few questions.*

    Q. *Mr. Al-Aziz, I would like to ask you a few questions that I would like clarified. You know, one of your co-defendants. Mr. Hagan, said in the time when he was being reviewed by the parole board that he was the killer and that you were innocent and Johnson was innocent. However, when he was asked why he didn't say that at the time of the trial, he hedged a bit. In other words, there was a question. Is he trying to get two fellas off the hook who were able to escape and he was caught? He was shot. Or if he was such a nice guy why didn't he say that during the trial, since he was caught? He went to trial saying he was innocent as well as you two. Why did he let you two take the same rap he got?*

    A. *Why did he do that?*

    Q. *Yes. Why did you do that?*

    A. *I think he was trying to protect...*

    Q. *Who?*

    A. *The Nation of Islam and its leadership. I think he was young, like I guess we all were. He being the youngest, and I think he had the spirit of the gung ho youngsters...the paratroopers...you get 17 to 19 year olds to be the paratroopers...the rangers...and so, therefore, he at that time had that type of spirit.*

    Q. *How old are you now?*

A. Now? I am 46.

Q. So you were a little older than he was?

A. Yes.

Q. Okay. But the thing is this, gung ho or no gung ho, he let according to what you are saying, two innocent men take a rap for 20 years.

A. It wasn't anything that he could do about it.

Q. Yes, he could. He could have said I am guilty and the other two aren't, right at the trial.

A. He did.

Q. At the trial?

A. Yes.

Q. Are you sure of that?

A. Yes. During the trial. Yes. It is in the transcripts.

Q. He said, I am guilty in the trial?

A. Yes.

Q. I thought he did not say that. He was convicted by a jury?

A. He still said he did it.

Q. While he was being tried?

A. Yes

Q. And that ended the trial for him when he…that means he pleaded guilty. The record does not indicate that he plead guilty.

A. He got on the stand…

Q. He was convicted. If he says in court, 'I did it', that's a guilty plea.

A. That's what happened. He got on the stand and said it.

Q. Okay. Now, the other thing I would like you to clarify Mr. Aziz, is the fellow Benjamin Brown, which was a pending case for assault at the time?

A. Yes.

Q. What was your relationship with Benjamin Brown?

A. He was a Muslim.

Q. He was a Muslim? Was he a follower of Malcolm X? The truth.

A. No, He was in the Nation of Islam.

Q. Not a follower of Malcolm X?

A. No.

Q. What was the difficulty between him and you and Johnson?

A. I had no difficulty with him at all, myself. I don't know if he had any with anybody else. I couldn't answer that question.

Q. Okay. And there is another thing I would like you to clarify. There are two statements you made. One statement you made...you were not there. You were in the hospital at the time. And there is another statement you were in the audience.

A. I didn't say anything like that. I said in the statement...

Q. I see it is in the records where you said that.

A. Oh.

Q. Forgive me for a moment. All right. Okay. There is an indication that when you spoke to the parole officer you advised him that you were recovering from a beating at the time of the killing of Malcolm X. But there is material in the folder, which Commissioner Kirkland has, that states that you admitted that you were at the time somewhat of a religious follower, but that you had denied taking part in the crime.

A. I never said any such thing.

Q. You never made such a statement?

A. No

Q. One further question since we are talking about the Reverend Farrahkan. You kept saying a few times that you are the follower of the True Faith?

A. Excuse me?

Q. The True Faith. You were talking about anybody else who follows the True Faith would be...

A. I didn't say that. I said that if a person wished to hear the truth, he could follow the truth.

Q. Okay. You said you would accept any such person in your...

A. Yes.

Q. Mr. Farrakhan is not of that kind of inclination. He has made anti-Semitic remarks. How do you feel about that?

A. I don't like the idea of saying anything about people, but I can't be responsible for what he does.

Q. Because outside of the Muslim faith there are Baptists. There are Christians. There are Jews.

A. I am aware of that.

Q. There are Blacks who are Jews. Who are Baptists. Who are Christians, just as well as Muslims.

A. Yes.

Q. How do you feel about Blacks who are members of other religious faiths or who are members of other religions? Should you feel anything different than anybody else? They have a right to have those religious beliefs.

A. Certainly they do.

Q. How about somebody who leaves the Muslim religion. A sect of it as Malcolm X did? Did he have a right to do that?

A. *A person would follow the truth. Whatever they understand to be the truth. And as long as it doesn't infringe on the rights of others, should be acceptable by other people. Their behavior or their response or reaction to it should be acceptable by other people.*

Q. *All right. One last question. There seems to be an indication that Commissioner Ward may give you a position?*

A. *Well, he offered me five or six job offers, but that's not what I intend to do.*

Q. *What did he offer you?*

A. *While he was Commissioner in Corrections, he offered me a position as a counselor when they were hiring people for that type of thing. That was when he was Commissioner of Corrections.*

Q. *How do you feel about Hagan?*

A. *I don't know. So, I don't really have a feeling about him. Using the word feeling, I don't have a feeling about him because I don't even know him.*

Q. *How do you feel about the fact that you spent 20 years for something that he admitted he did?*

A. *I don't like the idea of spending 20 years in prison for somebody. First of all, the main loss of time out of my life, not to mention a whole family that I didn't raise. I helped to raise or I helped to support...etc....so I don't feel good about it all. However, what should I feel 20 years later now? I am trying to build a life. I have no time to sit around being a coward from within because of negative feelings about somebody.*

Q. *You certainly did well while here.*

A. *Because I am not sitting around trying to worry about other people. I am trying to do the best with my life.*

Q. What are your plans if you go out at this time? What are you planning to do?

A. Well, I have a job to go to. Helping to build a corporation, where I am wanted and in fact needed. And try to develop something with my grandchildren. There is very little that I can actually do for my own children except sundry things. They are all grown up. They are having children now.

Commissioner Sherrid: *Okay I have no further questions*

Commissioner Dean: *I have no questions*

Commissioner Sherrid: *I appreciate your candor*

Inmate: *Yes Sir.*

Commissioner Kirkland:

Q. Anything that you would like to say in your own behalf?

A. No Sir. I think I have said it before.

Q. You realize a very important decision must be made, is that correct?

A. Yes, sir.

Q. You got a lot of support from a lot of big guns, you know? All those big guns will get together they probably would resolve a lot of problems out there in the community, but they don't. I wonder if all them jump on the bandwagon because of CBS's reports. I don't know. Okay. I feel America lost a great statesman in Malcolm. A great statesman in Malcolm. And I believe that it went backwards for a lot of years because of that. And we will make a decision of some sort and we will let you know, okay?

A. Yes, sir.

Q. Unless there is something else that you would like to say.

A. No.

Commissioner Sherrid:

Q. Mr. Aziz, I would like to add one thing. Commissioner Kirkland has mentioned the fact about some white people supporting you.

Commissioner Kirkland

Q. Some? A lot of them.

Commissioner Sherrid:

Q. Whatever their motives are, I don't go along with because you killed a black, whites are indifferent and want to let you out, understand?

A. Yes, sir.

Q. I don't care whether you are black or white...whether your victim was black or white. I just do it on the merits of the case, and also the fact that Malcolm X was at the time a great leader of your people, do you understand?

A. Yes.

Q. And that's a serious thing to consider. You were found guilty by a jury. You have to understand that. Whatever the motives of these white people or black people in supporting you, you have done well here. The question is before this Board is that history did change with his death, you understand?

A. Yes.

Q. And it is a serious decision that we have to make.

Now, is there anything else you want to tell us before we make that final decision?

A. *I just hope that when you are considering what you will be considering, that you also consider...you say I have done well here, and hopefully that I can be measured in a good manner. I think that I have affected thousands of people's lives, also, and I hate to say this because you are not supposed to blow your own horn, I have saved a lot of lives too.*

Q. *Your work at Attica is noted. The fact that you helped prevent some violence there. And were you in Sing Sing too?*

A. *Yes, sir.*

Q. *And were you involved in it that time?*

A. *Not involved in the sense of what happened, but involved in the sense of – I guess you could say provoking people to secure people or to—*

Commissioner Kirkland

Q. *Are you familiar with Nat Turner?*

A. *Somewhat.*

Q. *Do you know that Nat Turner was convicted of conspiracy to have a rebellion? Organizing a rebellion, is that correct?*

A. *Yes.*

Q. *And one of the other slaves ran and told the master. And he felt he could save a lot of lives by telling the master.*

A. *That's not what happened.*

Q. *You are not listening to me. I just want you to know that. Malcolm was a great statesman. He was a leader. You have done nothing to match him. Listen to me clearly.*

You have done nothing to match him. So, don't paint too many roses on your chest, okay? I am not of the mind of a lot of these folks. You are no comparison to him. The death of Malcolm has set folks back 100 years. I want you to remember that.

A. Yes, sir.

Q. And I don't care how many people support you. Anything else?

A. No, sir.

Q. Take good care of yourself.

DECISION:

Parole Denied. Hold 2 years to December 1986 Board

Reasons: Parole denied due to the gravity and seriousness of your conviction, murder first degree involving the in concert shotgun and pistol killing of a public figure on the stage of the Audubon Ballroom in New York City. You received originally a natural life sentence for this premeditated assassination which is irreversible. Your crime of conviction was aggravated by the fact that your victim was a recognized national leader and was speaking to some of his followers when he was brutally killed in their presence. Your educational and institutional accomplishments are commendable as well as your extraordinary cooperation with prison officials and the-----------------(not obtainable)

Hmmm. Not really a surprise but still, reading this for the first time, wow! Kirkland's comments have generated a huge amount of political backlash. Comments from State Senators in the *Daily News* brand him a racist and lead him to defend himself and explain his line of questioning, which he does in a searing four-page response. Sherrid, while he distances himself from the racial histrionics at interviews, does his part to get his ethnic concern on record and is a guy who believes that there is real value in interrogation even after all the evidence has been weighed at trial. And Dean, who sat silent; a decent man who I remind you is suffering from that brain tumor. No wonder there are lawsuits and problems. This parole process can be open to interpretation by its individual members. My questions have to be broad enough to answer the curiosity around the edges but narrow enough to decide if he's a public risk. Here we go.

In he comes and sits down in the 'hot seat' which by now he should be used to. He crosses his legs and folds his hands on his lap. A posture not unlike anyone would strike in a business meeting. He is appropriately quiescent while composed. I am not looking at a person who has endlessly rehearsed for this moment. He is not posing as himself. He is himself. He looks every bit of his 46 years. His comfort level is boosted no doubt by the fact that he has had a full time job outside on work release in the Newburgh community for almost a year, assisting people needing to weatherize their homes.

Trying not to be redundant but needing to be complete for the record, we repeat much of what has gone before with some obvious need for more information. I always need to hear who someone is and how they lived long before I get to the crime that puts them in the seat in front of me. People 'inside,' by definition, are defined by their crime. But if they're getting out, I need to put a whole lot more flesh on who they are. Similarly, it's important for me to check this guy's body language, his eye contact and the million unarticulated things that go with first impressions.

As a kid, he went no further than the 9th grade. Since incarceration he's received a Bachelor's in Science from Mercy College and a Master's. After dropping out of school, he was at various times unemployed but then did two stints in the Navy with an honorable discharge at the end of his service. Married in '57, father of four and not legally divorced 'til 20 years later, inside. Seems that he started following the Muslim faith after the navy and today is the facility Iman. Met a woman through ministerial services on a visit and considers her his wife today. I've got to get into this crime business... looks like no big thing but interestingly, 'bout five weeks before Malcolm's shot, he's arrested for an assault along with one of his present co-defendants. It's an actual shooting of a guy who winds up in the hospital. This guy is also beaten and says that he's home recuperating still from his beating when Malcolm's at The Audubon. Record says this shooting case is dismissed but this feels somehow connected. Better ask some more questions:

Me:

Q. Prior to your arrest on this conviction, the records indicate that you allegedly shot a Benjamin Brown. Who was he?

A. He was active in the Muslims as well. He was a member of the Nation of Islam like all of us were. At that time there were a lot of problems, ideas I could say. He along with a few other people wanted to go and, as it were, do their own thing. He opened up a place in the Bronx. All that subsequently happened because of that. In other words...

Q. Let me stop you for a minute. Understand we are trying to understand the full account here....You say a number of problems, so to speak.

A. Shifting of philosophies within the Mosque itself. When Malcolm started talking about what took him out of the Nation of Islam, namely it goes on in terms of Elijah Muhammad's fathering of illegitimate children and etcetera. So, various little factions of groups of people began to cause friction maybe and/or leave. Malcolm was not the only that left. So Brown got beat up. He tried to say that he had the correct Mosque and that he was still following Elijah Muhammed. The idea was that there was not one Mosque Temple at the time. So, when he was approached by all this, that's where this friction developed, because he was actually trying to start another Mosque in opposition to this sitting or standing Mosque.

Q. You denied being the one that inflicted the injury?

A. I had nothing to do with that.

Q. What has ever become of Brown?

A. I don't know what he's doing. I think if anybody would ask him, he would say I didn't shoot him. I didn't have anything to do with it at all.

Comm. McNiff

Q. You were well-known within the community?

A. Too well-known

Q. How were you known?

A. A Lieutenant in the Fruits of Islam. Fruits of Islam means the results of the labor or work of Islam in

184

America. People put a sinister meaning on it. Just meant the results of being taught.

Q. Were you a recruiter?

A. No, not really. I was a trainer, I suppose you would say.

Q. Did people go out and recruit like the schools?

A. No. At that time we sold papers in the street. If you call that recruiting, then I did.

Comm. Leak:

Q. What were your responsibilities as a Lieutenant?

A. Like at camp. Teach and train. Teach and train the private soldiers to live a civilized life. What happened to me, have goals and have hope and aspirations and dreams.

Comm. McNiff

Q. Did you get paid?

A. No.

Q. How would you support your family?

A. I was working and going to school.

Q. This would be like Sundays or time off?

A. Something to do after work or school.

Comm. Treen

Q. Mr. Aziz, at the time of the trial, we have certain questions surrounding that. You consistently denied involvement in this crime?

A. Yes.

Q. You stated that you were home, in fact recuperating after hospitalization from a beating that you had received.

A. Yes.

Comm. McNiff

Q. Who gave you the beating?

A. New York City police.

Q. When they arrested you?

A. Yes. I carry the scars today.

Q. This was over the Brown incident? So, they knew you?

A. Yes. That's the only reason I can account for all of this. I have no other way for accounting for it otherwise. If anybody knew or put it another way, for anyone who does know how the Nation of Islam operated at that time under the circumstances, than they knew if anything had to be done or were done, it would never be done by people in the same city, it's impossible.

Q. Hagan admits he did it.

A. He was from a different city, Mosque 25 in New Jersey. The FBI knows it and the police know it. Subsequently other investigators found out I didn't do it.

Q. Why would they say you did?

A. Who?

Q. The cops.

A. People that don't know.

Comm. Treen

Q. I try to put myself in that position. If, in fact, what you say is so and you were, understand you were found guilty of that by a jury trial, one, I would be very embittered and ask myself, "Why would people place me on the scene of the crime?"

A. They have reasons. Everybody that testified against me, the police had a line on them for one thing or another. Deportation, a crime they had just committed and didn't go forth and go to court for it. Everybody. But the people that knew me and I interacted with for years, none of them said I was there. If you know anything, you have to know how people are in the neighborhood and in communities, etcetera. The talk in the neighborhoods and the communities to this day, from then to this day is that I'm innocent. I am not guilty. I am innocent. The people who knew the intimate circumstances who will not come forth and people say do not come forth.

Q. In a sense you are saying that the police put the squeeze on others and wanted you for this?

A. They didn't have anybody else. They didn't know where to turn and who to look for. From their point of view, the streets were explosive. Anything could happen. They got pressure on them, from everybody in the world. They are trying to solve a crime. I can understand where they are coming from. The problem is justice. If I prove, or if circumstances prove me to be correct in two years from now or ten years from now or I die in here, then what will happen, because I am innocent. I didn't kill this man. So when the proof does come out, as truth and proof comes out, automatically what will it look like then? What will I look like then?

Many remarks here about the obvious conviction and moving on to questions about his involvement in 20 years inside.

Q. During the incarceration, it's come to our attention that many people working within the system have written letters on your behalf. How were you approached inside when there were problems? How were you identified as somebody who would help resolve some problems going on with inmates. Did you come forth? Were you seen as the one who could be an ally?

A. *Most of the time it was the opposite....They thought I shouldn't be considered in that manner. I did all these things myself because my people were there. I was there and my people were there. The Muslims of whom I was responsible for as their minister, their Iman. I was responsible for these people. It would be for me to do what I could to secure them and myself.*

Q. *In securing them, did that put you in a position where you breeched the trust of other inmates?*

A. *No. If that were the case, I would be dead. Can't walk up and down prisons in the halls inside prison and be against them. Absolutely not. No. For example, if I had killed Malcolm, I wouldn't be sitting here talking to you today. I have been in prison walking around for 20 years. You don't walk around in prison for 20 years...this wasn't a crime in the criminal context. Of course this is prison and this is the state and this is jail. This is not a crime in the same sense of somebody committing a crime, going out and committing an assassination or murder or robbing. This was associated with something altogether different. People understand it that way. Not like a mob hit type of thing. The results are the same. Just like in a war. Your commanding officer tells you to kill somebody. In the streets, you kill somebody. They are both killing. It's not the same, even though it's the same. People understand it as not the same. You understand it as not the same.*

Comm. Leak:

Q. *How do you characterize it then if it's not a crime in*

188

the criminal context?

A. Not just me. In the time and circumstances of what was going on in the '60s and maybe in the '50s and maybe in the early '70s. There was turmoil in the black community. Tremendous turmoil, tremendous amount of turmoil. Emotions on all levels were high. When this situation occurred between Malcolm X and Elijah Muhammed, at the time people's emotions were like that. Then you had people like Farrakan and various other ministers in the Nation of Islam making comments and statements that were incendiary. You had people at the time, younger than me, maybe more impressionable than me and moved by events and circumstances. It wasn't a sense of like, in other words, the intent wasn't criminal. It produced the same result.

In continuing lines of questions to demystify the motives for the killing and the workings of the faith, we ask if he is trying to clear his name. He says the truth is known by the FBI and that he found out through the Freedom of Information Act in 1979. Clearly it's difficult to question a guy about a crime he says he didn't do. So by the time he's finally asked why we should release him, he says:

A. I think that if we just dealt with the conviction and if somehow I were guilty, then, if there was any—maybe today rehabilitation is not the vogue. I don't know if it is or not. Most of the years I have been in prison, rehabilitation was in. It was the thing. I did everything that everybody could possibly ask me to do and more. I think that I am a decent human being. I think that the people

*who know me in this system and out, attest to that. If I
were not given an opportunity to live my life from the
point of view of a conviction and having gone through and
accomplished whatever, then what reason should anybody
have to improve themselves in prison if the person that
most can see, can't get a break. Why should anybody want
to do anything right if I can't get anything for doing right
and everybody's eye is on me?*

After making certain he had nothing else to say, he is
excused and we begin our discourse. Does he stay in to
continue his punishment for the crime he's convicted of?
Is he released or does he seem like a risk to the public? If
he's right, is he vengeful about his 20-plus years lost? Is
the crime so big that we'd be minimizing it if he goes? Will
there be new trouble from him around his belief system?
Do we add on more time for the sentence that was
originally Natural Life and later reduced to 20-Life? Is this
a murder where the guy did his minimum well, has a plan
waiting, has been out in the community working by day
for a year and is exactly the reason parole exists?

McNiff and I take the plunge and nod for a release date
in June. Interestingly, Commissioner Leak, a former
prosecutor and black woman dissents ...does she have
different sensibilities? Am I missing something? Should I
think outside of my white box?

She says for the record:
"**I most respectfully dissent in view of the serious
nature of the crime, murder in the first degree wherein on
February 21, 1965, Malcolm X was murdered in the
Audubon Ballroom in New York City. This was a planned**

execution of a major political figure. Your numerous outstanding institutional achievements and adjustment are noted and taken into consideration. However, in the interest of justice, to release this inmate at the close of his statutory minimum would serve to minimize the severity of the instant crime in the eyes of the community."

Muhammed Al-Aziz/Norman Butler was released from the custody of the New York State Department of Correctional Services three days before his forty-seventh birthday. He was in time to see the mature marigolds and geraniums lining the prison path on the day of June 24th, 1985.

Thomas Hagan was paroled at the age of 69 in 2010 after being denied 16 times and serving 45 years in prison. The third codefendant, Thomas Johnson, was paroled in 1987. Hagan has always acknowledged his guilt and testified as to the innocence of his convicted co-defendants. They all received the same sentence for the same crime committed in 1965.

8 | Unbreakable Women

Today is a really important day; on this morning in September 1986, in the gymnasium at Bedford Hills Correctional Facility, where 12 inmates gather to tell their stories of abuse to a crowd of commissioners, lawyers, senators, criminal justice officials and others who should know this stuff already. It's the culmination of years of conscious raising by the Division for Women about the impact of domestic violence in the criminal justice system. I am one among other state officials invited to hear the stories of domestic violence in the lives of women in prison. Although my co-commissioners, the 'good ole boys', aren't invited, I'm hoping that they get wind of this and realize that domestic violence is a crime. The women will be telling their own stories of extreme physical violence. For them to risk going public is heroic. I can't imagine the wounds they've suffered but I do know that even verbal abuse and manipulation gets you that feeling of fear and intimidation.

And I also am remembering Donny and why women excuse violence against themselves, confusing it with love from a very early age. At seven years of age, he was my first lesson in the myth of hurting people because you liked them. Even I knew in the second grade that something was wrong when he slammed into me with his sled, bumped into me when I was roller skating, and followed me wherever I went. I was embarrassed and felt it all had to be my fault but was powerless to change it even after I decided to 'tell on him.' It was hard for me to go to his mother. I was afraid if I told it might get worse because I'd get him in trouble. But it seemed awful to do nothing. I screwed up my courage and knocked on their first floor apartment door in this three-story town house. Mrs. Robinson seemed amused when she looked down to see me and not the least upset when I told her the problem. In fact she smiled with relief and said, "Oh, that's because he likes you". It shut me right up but it didn't make sense. Something was very wrong with this logic. How come he hits me because he likes me? I heard this same theme from others through life. Nowhere are the results more evident than in this learning lab that is women in prison.

My colleagues should know this rather than arguing with me each time they release a batterer and tell me they're not dangerous, they just have stormy marriages. They should know that being violated in this way creates more violence and that these women, some sentenced for life, were victims also. Most of the women who agree to testify are serving time for killing their abusers. This is a groundbreaking hearing; never before had hearings of any kind taken place in a state prison. But never before had The Governors Division for Women been in charge. No agency or person had ever viewed people in prison, especially 'manipulative' women, convicted murderers, as having any value or as a source of learning.

And now almost three years into being on the parole board, I see so many familiar faces in the gym. Faces that have changed little in the last ten years during which time these women have been warehoused in place while I've gone through many changes. The preparation for this hearing took months. Inmates filled out surveys, background investigations of visitors were checked for clearance, and witnesses were prepared by an attorney so that their stories could be told anonymously as not to complicate their legal cases. A great mixture of exuberance and nervousness fell over the prison as the women were forced to examine their histories of abuse: abuse of them and abuse by them, abuses that range from harassment, stabbings, murders, molestations and rapes; all occurring in their supposed safe place, home. Abuse cuts across all colors and incomes but in 1986 only the most extreme cases roil to the top of our consciousness. This hearing after all is a year before we see up close and personal the results of domestic violence on the face of Hedda Nussbaum.

Her abuser was her supposed adoring live-in partner Joel Steinberg, who over ten years managed to inflict abuse and torture in unheard of ways. His Svengali-like hold on her cost her a spleen, black eyes, broken bones, broken teeth, a fractured nose, burns, beatings, as well as taking her mind and her will. And it cost a little girl her life. The horror that existed in their Greenwich Village apartment went unnoticed despite her hospitalizations and was uncovered only when their illegally adopted 6-year-old child was struck and killed by Steinberg. He was convicted of manslaughter at trial and received a sentence of 8 1/3 – 25 years.

After serving his term of 17 years, he was released from prison in June, 2004. On January 16, 2007, the Appellate Division of state Supreme Court ruled that he must pay the girl's birth mother the sum of fifteen million dollars in damages. In his appeal papers requesting a reduction in the payment, he said that because Lisa died relatively quickly, after "at most eight hours of pain and suffering," the money was excessive! Hedda spent time in a psychiatric setting, in rehabilitation, in counseling, and in various hospitals at various times undergoing reconstructive surgery. She has worked with battered women and has written her memoir but since Steinberg's release, she's retreated and doesn't make public appearances.

What made this case a spectator sport for many people was our identification with Hedda and Joel. This couple could have been our family, our friends, our neighbors; he an attorney, she a book editor for Random House. As ugly a story as this was, people couldn't take their eyes away from the news of it; how could an educated woman find herself in this situation, why didn't she leave, what kind of woman let this happen to a child? The sentiment against her sometimes eclipsed the crimes of Joel Steinberg. If you are assaulted on a street corner by a stranger, the reaction is sympathetic. But if you are assaulted in your home, you are asked what you did to cause it. Her fractures ran deeper than bones can go.

These hearings make for an unusual melting pot. As I'm escorted into the familiar gym, I see that it's been transformed for the occasion. This is the place where so many damaged women try to work themselves back into shape and maybe today will be less athletic but no different. The chairs are tiered for the listening panelists and there's a level platform for the witnesses. There are bridge chairs around the stages for civilian observers and bleachers against a wall are down for more seating. The inmates who aren't testifying this morning are sitting on the bleachers. The officials sitting on the podium watching the women in front of them telling their stories could easily have stories of their own.

Superintendent Elaine Lord has done a good screening job, assigning the best and most personable correction officers to security in the gym. This could be any school auditorium but for the give-away clue of the state-issue uniforms the women who live here are wearing. Although remarkably, the human need to keep one's individuality shows in the many ways these state 'greens' are worn. A collar standing up here, sleeve cuffs rolled down there, pleats ironed in the front of the standard white blouse, hair plaited or piled high. And here in the first row sits Jean Harris. Her individuality is something she's maintained since long before being here; she wears her familiar girl's school headband. In so many ways, so many of us from such different places are on equal footing today. There's no entrance exam here; only an experience that makes us alike.

I know many of the inmates who are testifying and many others who are sitting on the bank of bleachers against the wall. I already know many of the stories and since I want to see the reactions of the officials and don't want to stare at the already nervous women, my best vantage point is from the bleachers. And so I choose a seat there at the bottom to hear the compelling stories experienced by these survivors.

Next to me sits Mrs. Harris. Through all the years, beginning in 1976, that I've been traipsing to this prison in toney Westchester, the question I've been asked most is, "Do you know Jean Harris?" I think I do, a little bit (as much as I can figure out the complexities behind Mona Lisa's face). I came to know her before I started on the parole board through my work-related visits to Bedford Hills. She works in the Children's Center helping mothers in prison. She is an educator after all. She's been incarcerated for six and a half years as she sits listening. The saga surrounding her incarceration is legendary as is the public's appetite for rubber-necking once the press was onto the shooting death of Herman Tarnower, the 'Scarsdale Diet Doctor.' In spite of 'Hy' being the great love of her life, she's serving 15-years-to-life for his second-degree murder. Her minimum term is about the same number of years they'd been together.

You can hear a pin drop in the gym. There are a couple of testimonies where we hear that the women never believed they were abused because their wounds weren't physical, although they certainly are noticeable. They tell us about the shouting, the betrayals, and the humiliations. There are stories I hear that could rival Charles Boyer in a "Gaslight" story line. I look over at Jean for her reaction. But there is nothing I can see that makes me think she identifies with any of it. As always, her posture is upright and her thoughts concealed.

We learn that 322 women responded to the survey in preparation for the hearings. Here are some of the findings:

Three quarters of the women indicated they were first offenders

74% were mothers

97 women were victims of sexual abuse

138 were victims of emotional abuse

41 women were married to their abusers

169 women had been abused by friends or relatives

60% of all the women responded that they had been abused

163 women said their victims had been men

13 only, had received family court intervention before the crime

21 had court orders of protection

18 had been in women's shelters

109 women had attempted suicide at a point in their lives, half of them had been emotionally, physically or sexually abused

The report noted "that 82% had not applied for or received social services suggesting that poverty was not a relevant factor in the offense." And "that social services became prominent in the women's lives, only upon the incarceration of the individual…to provide services for the children left behind."

The testimonies detailing the violence on this day are predictably hard to imagine and listen to, much less to live through.

From inmate Two we hear a classic story:

"I'm 42 years old. Prior to this arrest, I had never been convicted or committed a crime in my life. Having taken a plea to manslaughter, I'm now serving a sentence of 6-18 years for the death of my husband. We were married for 21 years."

"I was a battered woman, both physically and mentally. Physically abused to the point where I had to be taken to an emergency room on more than one occasion. Most of the time I would lie about how these injuries occurred. I lied out of shame. Believing I was the cause for these beatings. The one time I did tell the doctor my husband beat me, I was told by that doctor, "You should do something about this." What should I have done? I wasn't even aware that I needed help. There wasn't a social worker to talk to me in the emergency room.

"One night my husband started an argument with me on the roof of a five-story building. He grabbed me around the neck and flung my entire body over the side of the roof. No words could describe the terror that passed through my mind. I have no idea how long he held me there or what was said. I do know that I'll remember that feeling for the rest of my life."

"What caused these beatings? Any of the below could have caused the beating.

My 2-year-old son falling off a chair and my husband asking where I was when he fell.

Getting home 10 minutes late.

My brother driving me home from my mother's house and my husband wanting to know why my brother had to drive me home.

"But every beating stemmed from a sick jealousy that was totally uncalled for. After these beatings my husband would be very sorry and loving towards me. He would always say I'm sorry and why are you still mad at me? I would ask myself many times, "Why stay under such conditions. My feelings went from he'll change to I love him. He's sick and he needs help. Maybe I don't deserve any better. My in-laws attitude was "don't upset him." My family's attitude was 'leave him'. My friends' attitude was sympathetic. They had pretty much the same thing happening in their lives. But the general attitude was, 'so what, it's no big deal.'

"Physical abuse never left any permanent scars on me. Until it happens to someone, you could never know; the humiliation, demoralization, debasement...emotional scars that never heal. The battering of women usually goes from one generation to the next. One would almost believe it's hereditary. It's not. In most cases it's a reinforced conditioning."

"After a parent abuses a child they suffer guilt. And tell the child how sorry they are and how they love them. This is the beginning of a conditioning for that child. This conditioning goes on and it's reinforced again when the little boy at school pulls your daughter's hair or hits her. She's told, "Oh the boy likes you.""

"If our daughters grow up believing abuse is a sign of affection, they will be our battered women of tomorrow."

Inmate Three testifies:

"I would like to begin testimony by saying that I am a first time offender. I am forty-one. This was my common law husband of nine years. I am serving an 8 1/3-to-25-year term for manslaughter. I lived through nine years of physical abuse. My abuse began with verbal threats which weakened my mental abilities which caused me not to respond normally. In turn, I went through years of beatings and I mean beatings.

"The first incident began with him breaking both my jaws, and later waking up in a hospital with tubes down my throat and in my arms. I did not realize what had happened to me until I tried to talk. I was completely terrified. All I could think about was where are the children? For I had been unconscious for over twenty-four hours. My common-law husband had taken me to the hospital. What excuse had he given the emergency room staff I do not know.

"After this I received numerous beatings, such as being beaten in the head with my own shoe, receiving six stitches in my head. I remained in the hospital for a week with a severe concussion, which was one of many things that cause me to have dizziness now. I suffered from broken arms and broken fingers. Everything that could be broken was as a result of his brutality. The embarrassment of constantly going to the hospital got beyond making excuses. Finally, I had to tell the truth about all these injuries. Every time after this I reported to the hospital still nothing was done.

"Another time he beat me so severely that he was afraid that if he took me to the hospital the police would surely arrest him; semiconscious I could not talk, not walk. He locked me up in the bedroom so that my children could not see me. On the third day of being locked in that room, I looked in the mirror and my face was so distorted that it frightened me.

"I tried leaving, but that didn't work due to the fact that this was my house. I owned the house. He was my main source of support, no money, no family to turn to so I accepted his weak apology and took him back in order to survive. None of my friends would help me because they were afraid to interfere. He would say after beating me, "If you had family that cared about you, I would kill you."

The mental abuse and anguish I experienced was as horrifying as the physical. I could not talk to people, some of my friends whom I had known for years could not communicate with me either by telephone or to visit me at home."

I'm mindful as these harrowing details are relived through words, that in my role as Parole Commissioner, these women will all be treated as the perpetrators that the law says they are. There will be little room for mitigating circumstances or understanding during questioning. This parole interview business is practiced with no room around the edges to consider anything other than the final results. The continuity from my advocacy work to parole helps me better understand. Most of my colleagues are out in the cold when it comes to believing self-defense and the natural instinct is to serve as the avenger for the wronged. I shrink inside as I forecast the outcome for many of these witnesses for they will not be seen as 'wronged.' Many of these 'killers' will stay in prison long after they've served their minimum.

Unfortunately, it's less shocking to see the man in court as the abuser but not frequent, for the spouse rarely turns him in. Here's a case of a guy who received an attempted murder and assault conviction. His term was 8 ½-to-25 years. Judge Warner said at the time. "This is the most brutal, brutal, absolutely brutal; no animal could have done it any better. I just don't understand it. How a person can take another person and do that to them; I just don't understand it."

"I'm going to give you concurrent time but I'm going

to write to the parole authorities and I'm saying it now on this record that I hope that before they think of releasing you, whenever they do think of it, but that before they really think of it, releasing you from incarceration that they read the records and they try to picture in their mind what this woman looked like on the witness stand and what she sounded like on the witness stand; what the little girl looked like on the witness stand and what she sounded like on the witness stand and what the little girl said about her little brother rolling around in his mother's blood in the kitchen on the floor. I remember that too. I hope they think and remember those things from the record before they think of releasing you from incarceration".

Women rarely receive assault or attempted murder convictions in domestic violence cases because if they miss their target (the batterer) they are killed. So the women we meet today are serving long sentences, for murders.

Number Eight says:

"I am thirty two years old and I have had federal and county government jobs for 11 years. Perhaps you feel that I don't fit the description of a battered woman, but physical and psychological abuse has no color or social status. I have been the victim of both. Before the beatings began I had already acquired emotional scars. In a sense, my husband prepared my mind to accept the physical abuse I was to have.

"The mental abuse began by him isolating me from my friends my family and even my children. My husband molded my mind into a dark shadow which existed only to accept his yelling, his possessiveness, his obsession to make me his perfect wife. My family had difficulty understanding why I separated myself from them. They sensed that something was wrong, but I never confessed the truth to them. In fact, I became a very convincing liar. At this time I didn't realize that I was really lying to myself. I didn't seek help from an outside source because the idea of someone else knowing that I took this abuse could cause them to look down on me.

"The physical humiliation began shortly afterwards. Now, having totally manipulated my brain, my husband began what turned out to be daily rituals, the actual beatings. Throughout the rest of the marriage I was subjected to his fists, his throwing me against the walls, his crude beatings with furniture and other objects. He was an extremely domineering and demanding man. When his anger grew, he became erratic and lost full control of his strength….My husband would come home and start to verbally abuse me and end up hitting me with the vacuum cleaner or me being thrown around from wall to wall. In all of my eleven years of abuse I always believed that he was truly sorry as he stated after each violent attack. I actually convinced myself that he would change because he loved me or so I thought he did.

"My greatest fear was that my husband would leave me. I had lost my own self-respect. I had lost myself in his cruel and violent world where I believed I could not function again without him. After each battering, I tried to justify in my mind that maybe I deserved his ill treatment…I walked in an air of terror and fear that clogged my every breath".

All these women are serving time for taking the lives of their husbands. Remarkably, many of the women volunteer that once they were incarcerated they finally felt safe. I guess that being locked up in a prison is a place none of us would envision as being 'safe.' But if you're battered and stalked as a way of life, the absence of the abuser is a greater relief than the incarceration is a nightmare.

We're riveted to the testimonies; sympathetic but trying to be appropriately dispassionate simultaneously. As it becomes embarrassing for some to invade the privacy of these words, the panelists tell the women they are heroes to make their histories public. The mere memories conjure up visions of the undescribed murders once again. But as much as Jean and I look at each other in reaction to the lives we're hearing about, she seems not to recognize any part of herself in the stories of humiliation and disparagement as any of the motive that ultimately caused her deadly unintended consequences: the murder of the man she most loved.

One can easily translate her placid expression as peacefulness, but it is contradicted by eyes that are weary with sleeplessness set in between a furrowed brow. It is a look of worry. Her wrinkles were set long before she arrived at the front gate of the prison, or for that matter before she arrived at Dr. Tarnower's house in Purchase, N.Y., that March night in 1980. Her depression and disappointment had been building over years until her emotions took on a life of their own and a crime of passion happened in the lives of people as foreign to the concept as any of us could imagine.

The version of who she is, is best left to her own definition. Novelists, columnists and reporters have tried to tell us who she is. They know the facts of her case and they've interviewed her. Could that describe any of us fully? Could these literary sketches possibly provide enough flesh to understand the emotions that brought a studied headmistress to have a gun, travel five hours to her lover's home with hopes of at best reconciliation and at worst a final farewell ending in murder?

Mrs. Harris lived an ordinary life that some would wish for themselves, the American dream: a Smith graduate, married, adoring mother of two sons and dutiful wife. While the trappings of contentment were visible, it was a veneer that didn't last, as in time she was unhappy enough to divorce. With that stroke of the legal pen she became a modern woman, supporting and caring for her kids as a single mom. In 1965 it took some guts to be that different. She was introduced to Dr. Tarnower and a romance of well over a decade took hold. In spite of a marriage proposal, she chose instead to defer the offer and to keep her sons in their schools.

This decision carried with it the price a pioneering spirit pays for her independence; the price was allowing his independence also. For as a modern woman, she felt duty-bound to honor the arrangement with no strings attached. This meant that while she lived and traveled much of the time with Hy, she also had to accept his yen for other women. It began to unravel when after years of putting herself to the test, Jean Harris' emotions won out over her rational thinking.

In life, sometimes it's tough to reconcile what a person does with who the person seems to be. In this job though,

I seem to be aware that probably, however we look, when pushed, everyone may be capable of everything. We're more alike than we think. The difference in people is how we cope with circumstances. And Mrs. Harris' coping mechanism was at the point of no return. Her job as the Headmistress of a prestigious Virginia boarding school was in doubt and her long love affair was fading when she needed it the most. No doubt her despondence was hindered rather than helped by Tarnower's prescriptions of amphetamines and antidepressants. Her depression now had the added taint of panic and confusion. It was during this time that she bought a gun. It's pretty well chronicled that when men get angry they think to kill someone; when women get angry it's called depression and we say, "I'm going to kill myself." Jean was no different.

Of all the people I've interviewed over time, they all want to be simply 'a lunch box Joe.' They want meaningful work and love in their lives. With both of these in doubt, Jean Harris decided to end the misery. She called Hy and told him she was on her way. She packed her gun and drove the distance from her home at the school in Virginia to his home in New York.

Who knows what she was thinking along the way? Was she going to say goodbye? Did she hope he'd care enough to stop her from shooting herself? Was it a test? It is well chronicled that she'd prepared a will and that she carried phone numbers of people to notify at the time of her death.

Her trial was a well-known national drama. Her face became familiar as it replaced the fictional soap operas on day time TV. These were high stakes for an ill prepared defendant. She wore both anxiety and charm, and a mink coat. She was no less despondent and had said that she cared little about defending herself now that Hy was dead. Although assessed by mental health professionals, their findings were never revealed at trial nor was the jury given the option of a first degree manslaughter charge rather the choice of murder or acquittal. The trial lasted three months and the verdict took 8 days. Was this a suicide attempt turned tragic accident or a murder?

Her reputation preceded her into prison and it was shaped long before any verdict was cast. She was blamed for her appearance of privilege, for seeming imperious, and for her pride. Few people sympathized with her plight and once she was incarcerated, still fewer people knew her. It took little time for Jean to be assigned to work in the prison's Children's Center. Her background made her a terrific asset in the Center where parenting classes were taught, where mothers were counseled and where children, during their visits, experienced a loving environment.

One of Jean's contributions was the idea of mothers reading stories to their children on tape and sending them home. She was a gift to the children. Her great salvation was the written word. She wrote three books while incarcerated learning much about a culture that was new to her and developed a close friendship with the late author Shana Alexander. Her sons remained supportive through her years; the daily tyrannies, her health problems and the loss of three appeals of her conviction. Jean is an enigma. Since she had lost her best friend Hy, popularity was not what she was after. While she didn't have any desire to fit in, she did need to get along. In prisons, one's secrets can be used as currency by others against them and her refusal to 'confide' kept others at arm's length.

The controversy about her intentions never stopped making news. I never had any doubt. And, I've never had any curiosity to probe further. But interestingly, the parole board as a group always felt the need to launch its own criminal investigation during a parole hearing. The panel of three she sat before, conducted such an interrogation at the time of a clemency application more than a decade later. Never mind that the DA had already prosecuted the case, that the facts were heard before a judge and a jury, and that a verdict was rendered.

When she met this board to explore the possibility of a commutation before she served her full fifteen-year minimum, she wasn't believed as she explained her suicide attempt gone awry. When she described that desperate night of rage and jealousy, when her hero tried to wrestle the gun she was holding and became the target, she failed the litmus test.

This woman who had represented authority and in her time had suspended students for breaking rules was now at the mercy of another authority. With their skepticism they agreed among themselves that this sinner's additional crime was lying and unworthy of any reduced time consideration. She had a heart condition and was sixty eight years old.

Finally, as Mrs. Harris was being prepped for heart surgery on December 29th, 1992, at 70 years of age, Governor Cuomo granted her clemency. Since being released, she lived a quiet life in a New England town, with a dog named Elaine (named after Sister Elaine, always her trusted friend), close to her sons and heading the foundation she began for the children of women in prison, The Children of Bedford Foundation, which has made higher education possible for these children (There are a total of 15,000 children waiting for a parent to come home in New York). But at age 89 in December 2012, while living in an assisted living facility in New Haven, she passed away. Her incarceration allowed a peep hole in the door to prison and tells a cautionary tale to those who explode when they lock up their feelings. But sadly, this lesson comes too late for Jean.

9 | Howard Beach

The alarm clock is doing its job…pulsating in a high, piercing, totally annoying beep, beep, beep. Although, I don't think there's ever been a time I've needed it. The truth is, that I've been tossing around all night and I've been awake since 5 AM, an hour ago. It's at 5 that I usually begin to come to, with what seems to be a slow motion hoped for recollection of my just-ended dream. I know that there was a dream even though I can't seem to retrieve it. I know this because of the falling feeling that puts my throat in my stomach like gravity at work even though I'm still lying flat. The more I strain to see this dream, the more invisible it becomes. I'd like to get it out, so I can get on with the day without being haunted by this shadow, and it's creating walls in my thinking that I keep bumping into. No luck. All this thought takes a split second.

While I press the off button on the square little noisy clock, I open my eyes and let in this room that I've protected myself from. The wallpaper is the requisite pink/white/gray stripe. There's that stucco-like ceiling with water sprinklers and coming through the ceiling a chain that doesn't quite hide the insulated electrical cord for the dropped light that reflects a 40-watt bulb hanging over a miniscule round table. The table with two chairs is rammed up against the wall heating and air-conditioning unit that makes a constant humming clanking noise. In a strange way I'm grateful for the comfort of the noise that makes the heat certain. I'm more than lucky to be here in this new upstairs unit this week. There've been other rooms, in other motels, in other towns that had neither heat nor air. What rides on this recirculating air is the churned up smells of former customers...customers who chain smoke and who seem to have a habit of burning the plastic laminated bureau top. While this ersatz walnut furniture is impervious to drink rings, it can't hide the other hard-living habits that leave deep dark divots left to the imagination. Oh, if these rooms could talk!

And as I begin to sit up and kick off the snag of sheets and flimsy blanket that I'm wrapped in, the phone rings. To answer? Yep, I always answer, even though I know it's the wakeup call from the desk and there's no one on the other end. But just in case there might be a SOS from home (my son, my daughter, my mother) or a morning greeting from a friend, I always pick up. And as I retrieve the phone, with no one connected to the cord at the other end, I spy the mess of bedspread covering the industrial-strength grey carpet that I pushed to the floor last night.

I begin to focus and switch on the TV remote for the morning news. The set has had less rest than me, as it prattled on even after I went to sleep and was clicked off only during one of my waking predawn moments. The room is too warm but to my liking as it's Wednesday, December 9th, 1992, and I'm in Utica, New York... the Best Western Gateway on No. Genesee Street. I suspiciously draw open the drapes to see what disaster the weather-gods may have visited on me during the night. Good. The streets are clear even though the skies are steely. I hobble into the bathroom wishing for a tub rather than a shower. But this is not to be until the work week is over and I get into the confines of my own home. Seems like an eternity away.

When I look into the mirror as I brush my teeth, I think I kind of see what others see, but I'm never quite sure. What's a nice girl like me doing in a place like this? Before my morning makeover I look more like me, but the person inmates see is probably the typical brittle face of authority. And, I'm afraid the face that colleagues see is the friendly but always contrary person on the other side of the issue. So, as I've done every morning for eight years, I gather my emotional armor together and prepare for the day ahead. I'm on my way to hear from sixty inmates who are candidates for parole at Oneida Correctional Facility asking for their freedom. Yesterday I worked 'next door' at Mohawk with a similar group. Although I can generalize their crimes, their names, their ages and ethnicity, they are indeed individuals with stories peculiar only to them. There are so many prisons up here that are 'twinned' and sit down the road from one another. I still stumble around looking for them as they are built and open quickly in cookie-cutter-like modalities. I'm never lost for long as my colleague Gerry Burke, the sanest of us all, tells me that when I'm lost, to pull over, get out of the car, and look up. When I see a water tower headed for the sky, drive to that tower and 'bam' there's the prison. He's always been right.

I retrace my steps from the bathroom, wrapped in a towel, to the night table to collect my watch and rings. It's 6:20 and I'm still begging my dream to come out of hiding. I look at the quiet phone and decide I need a conversation to get centered before I see my public. I call my friend Linda, who I've labeled 'The Ear.' She's my listener in the absence of a 'significant other' in my life at this time (ping-pong man is out of my life…tell you later). This job does have a way of wrenching one away from average social conventions. The Ear hears my dreads and dreams at odd hours from the road and manages to sprinkle humor into the mix. During the conversation and without prompting, in walks the dream.

This dream puts me pretty much in character as I'm also on the parole board in the dream. There's a tense debating match going on in the room between myself, a strident other commissioner and a third kind of 'get along guy' decision-maker. The focus of this is the parole consideration of a twenty-something girl who clearly has mental health issues. She refuses to sit down in her chair, which is under a flower arbor, and wanders about confused and chattering in a white chiffon flowing gown. Her crime is minor, shoplifting, her punishment is major. She drifts around cloud-like, illusive, with no one able to get her to sit down and all the while we commissioners arguing without noticing who she is or what she's doing. With the dream remembered, it feels better, not such a big deal. In fact, pretty typical except that the inmates don't float around in chiffon; they wear state-issue forest green uniforms that rob them of their individuality. The bickering in the dream could be more reality than imagination.

The conversation with The Ear long ended, I'm ready to get dressed and in a cheerier mood go to the wall partition with a pole behind the door called a closet. I've always been a clothes horse and this job's amplified the attention I pay it. I've been preoccupied with my image and how it affects people after a well learned lesson when I was 15. Growing up in Boston we could drive at 16, but younger we relied on parents to get us around. My friend Annie's dad was on chauffeuring duty on a day that three of our gang were going to a movie. After we piled in the car, her dad apologized and said that before he could take us he remembered he had some work to finish up at his office. His office was at Brandeis University in a close-by suburb where he, Dr. Abraham Maslow, a world renowned sociologist on staff, was doing research. Once we were in his office waiting room he asked us separately to help him with a project. We had to identify professions of people from pictures he showed us, essentially mug shots. After each of us had a turn he came out with a long face admitting that he'd jumbled up the results and asked us for a do-over. Although we quietly grumbled, we complied. Our original look at the headshots took place in a room with a hanging exposed light bulb over a chair and table that sat next to a bare cot with ticking mattress and no windows. The repeat performance, we were asked to do (showing the same faces) occurred in a sun filled room with blue curtains, a table with a ruffled tablecloth and yellow daffodils. It's no surprise that while the first group were all ID'ed as scurrilous horrible people capable of who knows what, the second group were all upstanding professionals. Those results are still quoted today as I discovered while I was doing research for my master's degree, identified by name. Never forgetting that connection between environment and mood, I sometimes ask for flowers to be placed on a board room table.

So I pick my clothes carefully trying to define myself plus relaxing the parole interview. I used to make a concerted effort to mimic the stark surroundings until I ultimately discovered this was a mistake in prison. In lock-ups you could be sized up in a minute. People institutionalized love to see outsiders come in dressed in the latest fashions. In fact, they have better taste than most considering that many have 'boosted and jostled' and could tell designer 'knock-offs' from a mile away. From their window on the world they see mostly clergy, staff and uniforms and their sense of 'time' is frozen by sameness. So civilians are a treat. What I learn goes beyond style; I learn authenticity. I put on my navy belted suit over a ruffled blouse on this day.

Well, it's already 7, and I'm salivating for my first cup of coffee. Of course there'll be about six more throughout the day, but the first is always the best. So as I look around the room, I have to decide whether to pack and check-out in the hopes that maybe this is the last day of the board, in which case, do I want to drive the Thruway from Utica to Long Island and get home at about 11 tonight in order to wake up in my own bed? Or, should I stay here? Maybe we won't be finished and then I'll have to check in again. Maybe it will snow and I won't want to drive through the night after a day of sitting and reading files and interviewing people. Ah well, I can always check out tonight if I want to; best to stay here for now. And so I grab my keys, check the room, take my day-runner and board-count (the number of interviews awaiting) and face the day.

In the lobby at the front of this rabbit-warren-like motel there's a lunch room. It's not bad at all and one can select from the modest breakfast selections set out daily on the counter. There's the familiar TV blaring news touting

Utica. "Alive with Activity" it says. I think, "must be a different Utica than the one I know." Since the advent of the prison industry in this Mohawk Valley, there's been an influx of drug dealing following the Thruway up the prison corridor, according to locals. I select some low-calorie food and wait for my two colleagues to show up. After coffee and out of my isolation, the day is beginning to look much cheerier. I count my blessings; I'm staying in a place that's devoid of orange shag carpet, I'm working with good guys, I'm not caught in a blizzard (yet) and we had a great dinner at Johnny Appleseed's next door last night.

Before my two colleagues enter the lunch room, I look around to check out the public. Business people mostly. I'm so used to trying to figure people out that I cast around the room and begin to invent their characters; who are they and what are their stories? Here come Tom and Israel, my co-commissioners. We have to do the job as a trio so we're inseparable this week. I'm chairing the panel as I'm senior by many years to both of them. Tom Biddle, always wearing a smile and a grey knit vest, is a retired village justice from upstate Newark. He acknowledges that his appointment was a way in which he could retire within three years with his most recent salary determining his retirement entitlement. He is enthusiastic with a small town charm and banter with inmates that reflects an absence of cynicism and life lived as though drawn by Norman Rockwell. He even has a daughter named Buffy. But his politics are polar opposite to mine.

Israel Gonzalez is also relatively new to the board and junior to Tom. He's from the Rochester area having worked with youth. He is serious and well-intentioned in his work. Both these men are great additions to the board. They conduct dignified interviews with parole candidates and are willing to discuss decisions. No bullying or power plays this week. This differs from most of my other experiences on the board. As Israel and Tom and I discuss our plans for the day over coffee, we decide we should each take our own car considering we may finish the board and make a break for home. And so five of us stride out into the courtyard of the motel and get into four cars. The other two people are court reporters who alternate throughout the day, recording every grunt. The board cannot go on without them and they also add a human ingredient when one makes eye contact with them when ridiculous things are said. We could all play poker.

Like yesterday when I was again reminded of the many things I learn from my interviews with inmates; some of them are hilarious responses to stupid questions that we are perfectly capable of dishing out. At Mohawk yesterday I was into my preachy maternal-like line of banter to a guy when I said, " If you had stayed home that night, if you'd kept away from those guys, if you'd listened to your girlfriend, none of this would have happened." To which he responded, "If, if, if. If I had pots and pans, I'd be a kitchen!" His obvious reference was the 4 wheels and car thing, but more importantly, I realized how ridiculous I sounded. He had gone out that night. He had been involved in a crime. He was sitting in prison. It seemed that I could dole out better than that for a litmus test of his readiness for the world. And the very skinny mobster who I asked why he wasn't a target of the flying bullets (suspecting he was in on the hit), answering "I was standing sideways." And the philosophical guy who said "life is a mystery and a miracle ...putting aside the clock and the calendar." I always write these things down; there's way too much to trust to memory.

And so, our small caravan of cars is wending its way west onto Route 365 to Oneida Correctional Facility and other people's misery. There is a lot of sorrow warehoused in central New York with at least four prisons housed within shouting distance. The U.S. Geographical Society says that the exact center of New York is near Building #2 of this forty-five building campus. I've told you about Gerry's advice that if lost on a highway looking for a prison, look up for a water tower and follow it. That's usually the bull's eye. Oneida borrows their stone water tower, built in 1898, from adjacent land at Mohawk. We don't need to look up, we know where we are.

We turn left onto Lamphear Road, then right onto School Road and find the prison on the right. As we turn into the parking spaces, the feeling is that of being in a black and white documentary. Despite the chaos that takes place in all institutions, the perimeters always seem dead. Being December, the ground is frozen and has patches of mud with a murky steam that rises. There are stone gargoyles carved to scare off evil spirits. Although Oneida is a classified medium-secure facility, it is still surrounded with razor-ribbon fencing. There is no sparkle dancing off the wire today. There is no sunshine to bounce back and the only reflection is the barren grey skies. This befits an institution that has been known by various names over time since the beginning of its construction as the county Alms House in 1825. The most agonizing of titles was in 1894 when it served as the Rome State Custodial Asylum for Unteachable Idiots. Despite different incarnations, it has always served as a place for the poor, the criminal, the insane, the handicapped and the disabled. Although it is thought to be a place since 1988 where we separate criminals from society, the residents still are the poor, the incompetent and more and more, the mentally ill. The state bought this institution from the county in 1893 for $104 thousand dollars. The Department of Corrections got the place in 1986 for $45 million and has spent $62 million on renovations and $8 million on new construction.

One by one, in our parking spaces and out of our cars, five of us assemble at the locked metal gate that opens to take us through an outside mesh enclosed alley to the locked door of the lobby. After we sign in and show identification to the officer on duty, we wait for an escort. On this morning we are greeted by the senior parole officer who's been working with offenders for years and against all odds has retained his humanity. He takes us through the building to a back door that exits onto the campus and we weave our way around buildings and up sally ports to the final stop where the parole hearings are held on the third floor of yet another antiquated building. It's 8 in the morning and we have reached our final destination; a marble-floored hall pointing us to the conference room used for parole hearings.

We walk past already waiting inmates who have been called out of their cells earlier this morning and escorted here. They sit on bridge chairs lined up in the hallway. They're waiting for their chance to get out of jail; some have been waiting twenty years. They check us out as we walk by and I nod and say 'good morning'. Mostly they are treated as if invisible. Wow! It's always hard for me to realize that I have the power to make this kind of difference in people's lives. Having worked with prisoners before this position, I'm keenly aware of the parole-carrot that inmates see almost as soon as they're sentenced. And, I know the fears and hopes they feel in the months and weeks leading up to what may be a five-minute presentation.

As we enter this old, large, well-windowed room, I smell the coffee and donuts that accompany the hearings throughout the day and I see the centerpiece: the long table where I sit in the middle, Tom, number 2 man, to my right and Israel, number 3 man, to my left. The court reporters set their machines up on the other side of the table where they can see and hear us and the inmates. On chairs behind each of us sit boxes of folders, maybe 20 each, trying to tell the entire story of the life of the person who will be judged by us. On the table before us we have a calendar that gives us the marching order of the day. Taking it from the top, we always begin alphabetically with initial appearances (first parole hearing), followed by reappearances (repeat interviews after denials) and all other types of categories (special requests, witness protection, legal appeals) requiring consideration for parole. Our huge calendar sheet has the name of the applicant/inmate, the crime, the dates and other guides for our translation. The cases are dealt among us; 1 – 2 – 3, beginning at the beginning. We will also be referring to a stack of 'book copies' that are condensed copies of each case the other two commissioners will review from in-depth original files. We are expected to read and prepare our (every third) case and participate in the other interviews as well.

We will sit at this table until 5 or 6 this evening; studying, interviewing, eavesdropping, caucusing, writing, judging, and arguing. I ask a few familiar questions of the parole staff who also sit in the room as I grab my first case. I want to know if there are any unusual circumstances in any of the upcoming cases, if we should expect people out of order as it happens with prisoners who may be coming from keep-lock or protection or absences because of out to court or transfer status. Mostly every case is treated similarly with no discussion until their turn comes closer. Today there's also a sociable exchange between us and the staff about parole rumors and the usual suspects. And with this the tone of the day's mood is set. The staff is always eager to get going and I think they view the hearings as part show business and part professional participation. After all, we're dependent upon their reportage for some of our information. Simultaneously I say my own private version of a serenity prayer hoping for the courage to make appropriate decisions. Decisions that are based on paroling practices, not guided by peer pressure or politics.

And we begin! The stories will come spilling out through the day like a string of pearls. Alfonso Alvarez is walking in the door toward the table and takes the seat in front of us – the hot seat. A stark wooden chair; no arms, no excess. No mistaking this for comfort. He's nervous and that's a good sign. But I know he wonders if being an 'A' is a disadvantage. Are we cranky, are we fresh slates? I recognize him from the corridor a half hour ago. He looked different among the others, somehow bigger. He makes eye contact with us all waiting to be lead to the person he'll be talking to. It will be me, but we all say good morning. He's lucky today as the usual style of the majority of commissioners is to sneer, snort or just ignore a civilized greeting. I always feel that I have the power of the pen and confrontation as an interviewing technique doesn't fly. I'm mostly alone in this belief but not today.

And so I go through the paces with Mr. Alvarez to decide whether he'll be risky to release and if he is, why. Of course I have to begin with what brings him here: his crime. I go over it very mindful that all this will be on the record and I better be absolutely sure of what I'm talking about and I invite him into the interview; after all, it's his life. He's denying everything. I'm thinking, 'Hey, the court sentenced him, finding him guilty. I'm not getting more mileage out of beating him up.' But I'm curious here about truth. I factor in the truth quotient but I rely on fact. I'll let his mother worry about truth. In the next five minutes though, I want to get some sense of who Alvarez is. We talk about his prior record, what he's done in prison over the past three years, who his support system is, what his plans are. Like most other drug dealers, when asked what his dream looks like, he can't answer me. I think he thinks I'm tricking him. After some coaxing, he describes the life of 'lunch-box Joe'… a family and a job. And I go into my 'dirty sox' routine; that life has some highs and lows but mostly if it's done right, it's a lot of dirty sox. Can he deal with that concept? Who knows, but in the world of molesters and serial murderers, he's looking pretty good to me. I tell him we'll let him know and he leaves the room, backing out. I say to staff 'open date' and neither of my colleagues disagrees. So Alphonso is going to go back to Brooklyn in two months at his minimum allowable date of his three-to-six-year sentence. He'll be supervised and he's got to look for work, keep a curfew and stay clean. It sounds easy; it proves to be impossible this time.

Now comes Norbert Aswalder, a burglar since 1972. He's talking to Tom explaining an ongoing crack habit. In this crime he took 2 bathroom sinks and a toilet and traded them for four years of his life. This is the third time he's been in state prison and it's a hell of a toll at the tune of forty thousand a year for tax payers. I've glanced at the book copy and interject my voice a couple times for the record. But in general, Tom is doing this interview, asking all the obvious questions while Israel and I are reading our next cases. Norbert's not the worst guy. Kinda harmless but does he stay in with taxpayers paying the freight collectively? Or does he go out where we know he'll continue to use drugs and then individuals will pay through robberies, assaults or burglaries? He's inside the guidelines, does okay inside, is responsible for four kids, and expresses all the right stuff. There ought to be a better way to change this guy's habit but I'm stuck with what we've got.

When he leaves the room we have a difference of opinion as to whether he stays or goes come February. We chat and ultimately agree that he stays, until he reaches his conditional release date. That's a year from now. So on a two-to-four-year sentence, he's doing three years. He's not getting any discretionary time off through parole. He's doing every second that the law demands but in prison. What a price to pay for some sinks! Even I know there's something wrong with an equation that when x-amount of time doesn't work, we do more of it! What?

It's about 8:55 and I'm checking to see how much time we're taking for interviews. Two interviews in twenty-five minutes. Seems we'll have to be a little quicker. There are no 'B's' today so up steps Mr. Corado. He is a tall man, 25 years old with no priors. This is a tricky case where the victim gets shot but Corado says it was self-defense. He takes the case to trial, gets acquitted as it's found that he was protecting himself and pleads to weapons possession. So this guy is lectured about weapons ad nauseum and gets to go home.

Now with the first three cases done, we pretty much have our rhythm down and the morning seems to catapult along with people's lives hung out, hoping they come clean, one by one as if on a clothesline. We take a break when the 'kitchen' delivers the food on a rolling cart even though it's far from noon. Oneida happens to be the "cook/chill" capitol of the state and including the eight of us in the room, there are 58,065 inmates in 61 other facilities who get the food that this facility prepares. I can never understand how many inmates are thin considering this diet consisting of some kind of mystery meat, heavily doused with gravy and mashed potatoes. There are those who are wary of the ingredients. They hear about mouse droppings, urine and other delectables and they keep a clear barrier between 'them and us' in their eating habits. I happen to love the food but I'm the only one who admits it. In combination with the couple of greasy donuts I've downed, I go easy on the calories. Even though I sit most of the day, I still seem to nervously burn up the carbs.

After some stretching, back-bending and chit chat, Act

II begins. We stopped at 'H' on the 'initial' calendar before lunch and we're ready to continue. It's pretty clear that we'll have to come back tomorrow morning. But then again, you never are sure. Once this decision is made, our pace slows a tad. I'll make some calls to friends to reorganize my evening plans for tomorrow night. Good thing I didn't check out and better yet that I left my heating unit running. Better to be overcome by heat when I go back to the room, than by a dank, cold, cigarette-smelling room. We keep talking in rotation and pulling our cases. There are the usual addicts, burglars, scam artists. I scan the calendar and notice that a Jason Ladone falls to me. A Manslaughter 2 and consecutive Assault in the first degree. Familiar?

As I read the folder it begins to come back to me. This is a notorious case that really made the neighborhood of Howard Beach code for racism. Even before he enters, I know every ounce of my notions of justice will be tested in this one. Well, 'mother told me there'd be days like this' or as they say, 'That's why we get paid the big bucks.' My shoulders slouch but I draw a deep breath to fill my form and tell staff to bring him in the room.

In comes an ordinary, scared-looking kid; average height and build, fair complexioned, pale, tense, not knowing what to expect, his mouth dry with nervousness, about 22. Some mother's baby. I always am amazed at the havoc one being can cause. He sits down in the chair, absolutely harmless.

Me: You're Jason Ladone?

Ladone: Yes.

Q. Mr. Ladone, my name is Commissioner Treen. With me are Commissioners Biddle and Gonzales. And you're serving an aggregate sentence of five years minimum and fifteen years max, two and a half to seven and a half years for assault in the first degree and you were involved with two codefendants and several others in a racial attack during which a victim was killed when he was struck by an automobile. That occurred while he was being chased. And, another was beaten about the head and body by a baseball bat, fists and sticks.

A. Yes.

Q. So, we'll talk about this, Mr. Ladone, your background, what you've been doing since you've been incarcerated and what your future plans are. What you've handed me is a certificate of earned eligibility. We know that the Department of Correctional Services issued this to you. So, we'll return this to you. This is your copy. You can keep this. We have one in the file.

A. Thank you.

Q. I'm going to put the crime, in longer detail, on the record and you can speak. You were 17 at the time this occurred?

A. I just turned 16.

Q. When I look at the probation material, I guess that was done a year later in preparation for the sentencing. Alright, you just turned 16. I read that you were at a party that night. That one of your codefendants had left to take a girl who was at the party home. Had seen some African Americans at a parking area of a pizza store.

A. Yes.

Q. And a fight erupts and these guys are your victims. As I said, one brutal assault, and the other, in trying to flee, running across the parkway, was struck and killed by an automobile.

A. Yes.

Q. The deceased was Michael Griffith and the man who was assaulted was Cedric Sanderford and there was a relationship in that the deceased was the assaulted victim's stepson. He had been living with the deceased's mother. They were people out, their car broke down, they pulled into the area for help. That's their story. So, what would you like to say with respect to this crime, Mr. Ladone?

A. I was young. It was peer pressure. I guess at the party, I just, what happened was to impress girls and stuff like that. Be a part of a group. I didn't mean to hurt nobody. Very unfortunate and I'm very sorry.

Q. Of course this was a notorious case. The racism, it's all about racism, pure and simple. There are all kinds of letters in your folder from family, from professionals who have been enlisted by your family to prepare documents and so forth. Was it bail or were you released in your own recognizance?

A. Yes, I was bailed.

Q. And for a period of time, that was the time your mother sent you to Long Island to live with your aunt so that you were out of the neighborhood.

A. Yes.

Q. Where you worked in a supermarket during that period of time. You took this to trial. Your codefendants, one received ten year minimum and 20 year max. And the other received a six year minimum and an 18 year max. I guess as I understand you signed up to get a GED at a school while you were out on bail. But, because of the trial, did not do that.

A. Right.

Q. And you were remanded, I guess when a verdict came February 11ᵗʰ of 1988.

A. That's right.

Q. You have no prior criminal history?

A. No ma'am.

Q. At one point you said maybe you were doing drugs.

A. Yes, ma'am. At the first year of high school. Again, I got involved with the wrong crowd and at that time, my mother and father were going through a divorce and I didn't know how to deal with the hurt and I guess I used that excuse to get high and stuff.

Q. And the grades started going down and you dropped out of school and got a job?

A. Well, yes. I wanted to get a car and stuff, you know.

Q. What about you do you think, made you identify and choose these people as your friends? You said you wanted to impress. Why? Why weren't you good enough?"

A. I was home alone that night. Actually, I was home, I was with my mother. But, I wasn't with my girlfriend. I don't know, she was going shopping or whatever she was doing. I wanted to see if a friend wanted to go to a movie, something like that. He said he was going with his girlfriend. So, I went up the block, crossed the boulevard to the Bow Wow Restaurant and played video games and stuff like that. I went there. Got hamburgers and fries and I was playing a couple of games and a friend of mine came up to me and said that this Steve Shaw is having a birthday party and it was a surprise. So, he asked me if I wanted to go. So, I was not doing nothing, I might as well go and check it out. I was there and had a few beers and hanging out, talking with the girls and stuff. And that is when the incident started. It was just acquaintances, I guess people in the neighborhood.

Q. As the crime evolves, you get involved in this gang for sport, hunting people for sport and that is how the community saw it.

Commissioner Gonzalez:

Q. If, in your judgment, the individuals were walking down this particular street, were not African Americans, would you have attacked them?

A. No sir, probably not.

Q. So you specifically attacked them because of their heritage, color?

A. I was young and drinking and I didn't know no better. Now that I'm here, incarcerated with different people of races and color, I see things a little differently now. I feel I've grown to understand people and nationalities. I didn't know no better. I didn't mean to hurt nobody.

Q. "You said you were around 16 at the time? You just turned 16?

A. Yes.

Q. You were trying to impress others, specifically girls?

A. Yes.

Q. Impressing others to a degree where you would be a part of someone's death, is that the way you wanted to impress them?

A. No, sir. I didn't want to hurt nobody.

Q. Alright.

Me: Why don't you bring us up to date on what you've been involved in doing, Mr. Ladone, through these almost five years?

A. I took some general business courses, computers.

I received my GED diploma. I took some electrical, some plumbing. I was in a more or less self-help program and ASAT (alcohol and substance abuse treatment). Mr. Bickenstaff, he was the ASAT teacher who came up to P.C. (protective custody). He recently pulled his back out; because I had a month or so to go to complete that course. I liked it much more because it was training, therapy. It was nice. I did that. I was out on crew, porter work. I was working my 12 steps with an outside sponsor.

Q. Twelve steps in terms of?

A. A.A.

Q. Okay.

Commissioner Biddle:

Q. Are you in protective custody most of the time?

A. Yes, sir.

Q. That was not true throughout? That was a result of an incident?

Me: "You want to tell us about that?"

A. I was in J-Dorm and that morning I was having a visit and I was proceeding to get ready for the visit and out of nowhere the officer told me to pack up, I was moving to G-Dorm which was the mess hall dorm. It had twice as many inmates in the dorm, all the way back. I was a little leery; it seemed funny to me because I was getting along pretty well in J-Dorm. And, it seems I had not too much to say, I tried to speak to the Sergeant, a Lieutenant through the daytime in the dorm in the visiting room. I came back that evening and I knew a couple of guys, we had a talk. It didn't seem like it was nothing. And a black man confronted me, what I was involved in, where I was from, which was nothing new. And it was throughout my whole

233

time and I tried to talk to him, like you know, to make him understand that I'm not really a bad guy and stuff and shook hands, whatever. I didn't think anything of it. People told me something will happen and I really didn't think nothing of it. It was something I always hear and I will try to talk my way out of it.

Q. So, go ahead.

A. I went to sleep and I don't know what happened. I just felt heat, hot something burning. I guess it was a mixture of oil and water because it was slippery, my hair was wet.

Q. You had hot oil and water thrown on you, that was in June of '91 and since then you've been in protective custody.

A. Yes.

Q. Is there anything else that you want to let us know about throughout your period of incarceration that you feel we should know about?

A. I don't know if it would make a difference to you, but in V-Dorm, it was July 8, me and an officer, we were walking down to go to chow and an inmate, we saw that he was hanging and he was unconscious at the time. He happened to be a black male and I didn't feel, I felt I should help. I wanted to help. I felt bad. Since me taking a life and stuff. I felt glad I was able to help and save that man, something positive I did.

Q. How old are you now?

A. Twenty-two.

Q. What do you see for your future, Mr. Ladone?

A. I see for my future, as soon as I get out, if and when I get out, I will probably go back to plumbing. I had a good rapport with my boss. I liked it a lot, that type of hard trade.

Q. Plumbing and Mechanical Corporation?

A.   Yes, Steal-Marr Plumbing and Mechanical Corporation.

Q. Home would be back in Howard Beach?

A. Yes, ma'am. Also, I'd go to my A.A. meetings and N.A. meetings.

Q. Howard Beach has irrevocably been changed as a result of this and the reputation. Do you anticipate any problems returning to Howard Beach, if and when that time comes?

A. No, ma'am. Not at all. I learned my lesson. I feel terrible."

Q. Your mother of course, is still there?

A. Yes, ma'am.

Q. Okay. Are there any other questions?

Commissioner Biddle

Q. What type of work do you hope to do eventually?

A. Plumbing. In growing up when I was a teenager, I worked in a supermarket, bakery gas station. I also worked with a friend of my father's in home improvement, which he did a little bit of everything. Sheetrock, tiles, plumbing, electrical, framing. All of that was a little too much, confusing. I came across plumbing and really liked it.

Me: Okay. Are you satisfied that you said everything you wanted to say to us this morning?

A. Yes, ma'am.

Q. We covered it all, okay. Mr. Ladone. We'll discuss this, we'll make a decision in a few days. Thank you sir.

A. Thank you.

And he's gone from the room. Although we have the power, it doesn't mean it's easy to use it. We all sense this one is a debate. This guy is a model inmate, not likely to harm a fly in the future. But, his participation in a crime that incensed the black community seems to scream for more punishment, but only if one were thinking about political fallout. I think retribution is a luxury we can't afford. Tom, my colleague who's in the trenches of the 'right' side of the political spectrum, translates his parole mandate in a narrow way; look at all the facts and decide if the community is at risk if Ladone goes home. This is amazing, I think, because I agree with this Conservative. I can't tell all that's going through his mind but he says he thinks he should be released. Israel is unconvinced. He seems to think that release looks like a reward and is against that message. The sentence is 5-15 with parole having discretion until the conditional release of ten years is reached. This is a bias crime after all.

I am pretty certain about my decision here, but I talk it through as much to hear myself as to tell the others. I think, parole is not forgiveness, it's serving your sentence but in the community on supervision. My job is not to mete out compromise between the victim's suffering and the inmate's punishment. I'm not hired as an avenger for the community. The court heard the facts of the case and sentenced the kid. I enumerate; he has no priors, he cut an inmate down inside saving his life, he had hot oil thrown on him, he's in P.C. so he's not likely to be learning anything more, he's got strong support in the community, he was out on bail with no trouble for a while and judging from the interview, not likely to j-walk in the future. And not incidentally, he's got an earned eligibility certificate from DOCS (this is awarded to people who have less than a six-year minimum as a presumption of release).

I go into my philosophical mode to myself. I want to do justice. I don't want to continue the toxicity of this case, which was to treat people who are different, differently. I want my deliberation to focus on the merits of this particular inmate without resentencing. I believe people go to prison as punishment, not for punishment.

We sit and talk about more of our opinions for a while longer. I know this is an important case and will probably make the headlines somewhere. Well, Tom and I agree so we cue for an 'open date' and the remainder of the decision is recorded.

"Open Date
2/3/93
Curfew to be imposed and enforced by parole officer
Drug needs evaluation. No alcohol. Some (seek, obtain, maintain employment)
Inside the guidelines
Defer his certificate of relief pending street evaluation by PO
Commissioner Biddle concurs.
Commissioner Gonzalez descents.

Commissioner Gonzalez:
"I dissent, based on the fact of the nature of the instant offense, which resulted in the death of the victim; and number 2, the admission of the inmate if in fact the victims had not been Afro-American, this incident would not have occurred."

Sensing a strain in the room, I move on with artificial buoyancy. And move we do, onto the 'reappearances' and 'special considerations' until all the men are seen, all the decision rendered, and the week's board is over. Israel, Tom and the reporters decide to head north to their homes. My drive is at least five hours and at this hour I opt to stay the night.

Driving back to the motel solo, I review the day and the week of work. I feel satisfied that I made proper decisions and continue to believe that the job is misunderstood by many of colleagues as well as the public. I've long stopped recording my beliefs as I did as if it were a professional diary, when I began this position. But I still remind myself on a daily basis what I'm supposed to do.

And speaking of doing; to eat out alone as I often do, or grab something to take back to my hotbox and watch a night of TV? I'll do the latter and stop at a submarine joint. My room is as warm as I expected and I spread my feast on the round table under the 40-watt. I'm in time for the 7 o'clock world news. And, what a world it is. In spite of it all I sleep like a baby.

I'm up early in the morning ready to get on the road. My suit case is one of these double zip things on a hanger that's more than paid for its life. I hate it, but it does the job. I load it up dashing from the bathroom to the only other room to collect all my stuff. Once in the early days, I left a gift teddy bear in a motel room in Dannemora and never want to repeat that embarrassment again. I'm packed, I'm checked out and I am on my way. I've listened to the forecast but the weather bands are so varied between here and the city that I never know what I'm in for.

It's always great to get home. Drag my luggage up stairs, look at the mail, hear my phone messages and resume life. Once home, I always feel like I've imagined the other me, sitting in prisons, judging people. But tonight I know that the private me and the professional me are the same person when the phone rings and it's the Chair of the Parole Board. He wants to know how I could have made the decision I made on the Ladone case. In spite of all my feminist training, my life growing up as a girl betrays me and I'm immediately flummoxed thinking maybe I did do something wrong. He says that there've been inquiries from the 'top,' shock from the special prosecutor who had plans to go up the political ladder, and that the word is if this guy were to get out there'd be riots in the streets. He asks if I noticed recommendations from the DA, the judge, the victim, etc. I respond limply, because after reviewing one hundred-plus cases this week with equal concentration for each, who remembers? Evidently the Special Prosecutor called outraged about the decision (and evidently he has ambition to become governor). The upshot of this call is that there'll probably be a recession ordered (a legal hearing after a release date is decided that brings new information to the case not known at the time of the parole hearing) and if so, a new decision rendered and release blocked.

After the call, I get a grip and count the ways in which I know this was a good hearing and release decision. I almost don't want to know about the aftermath of the rescission and the denial of parole. What I do know, is that there is certain to be one! Ugh, politics. I fall into bed and turn on the news to see what the weather Gods have in store for next week. And so it goes.

AFTERMATH

As I study files and books to tell an accurate story of what happened twenty-two years ago, I finally find out about the rescission hearing.

The original parole interview I held was on December 9th, 1992, at the five-year minimum of a sentence that began in February of 1988. At that hearing he was granted a date to go home on February 3rd, 1993. On December 16th (about six days following the phone call) an e-mail arrived at the prison from the Counsel for the Department of Correctional Services to the Inmate Records Coordinator. The e-mail alleges that the time calculation is inaccurate and the legal minimum parole eligibility date for Jason Ladone is really April of 1995. On January 14th, 1993, the sentencing judge held a hearing on the sentence and affirms that the sentence begin from March 11th, 1988.

Still, as a result of the Department's time calculations, the Division of Parole schedules a rescission to hear the facts. That hearing is held at the prison on March 17, 1993. Ladone was represented by two attorneys. The Division was bound to abide by Correction's calculation and find that he is not eligible for parole and take his date from him. The missing information that comes to light is that although Mr. Ladone was sentenced on February 11th, 1988, he remained free on bail pending appeal until he entered prison on April 23, 1990. Ladone's date was adjusted to a first parole eligibility of April 14th, 1995. At the time of the rescission hearing, his date of release was taken away and the hearing commissioners denied him parole for two more years. He returned as a 'reappearance' on February 6th, 1997, when he was again denied discretionary release for two more years. On February 1st, 1999, he again met the board and was denied, intending him to be released at the legal end of his term. He left state incarceration on April 14th, 2000, seven years longer than I intended.

The crime occurred on December 20th, 1986. The trial took 353 days to lay out the case, with a special prosecutor called in. The jury took 12 days to deliberate. The verdict was reached on January 23rd, 1988. Jason Ladone was sentenced on February 11th, 1988. He received two sentences for the two convictions of Manslaughter and Assault. The incident at Howard Beach happened in December of 1986. Nineteen years later, in April of 2005, his sentence of five-to-fifteen years was completed. This was a hot case.

10 | Geranium Justice

It's the kind of Friday afternoon in August that clichés are made of with promise and humidity filling the air. The streets of Manhattan are sizzling with the unspoken excitement that only a summer end of the week getaway day can bring. Osmondo Gonzales has this dream as he looks at the clock where he works at the West Side Tool and Die Factory. Despite wearing his yellow and black paisley bandana knotted around the curls on his head, the perspiration runs from his dark hair to his neck and beyond. His damp denim shirt and industrial strength green pants hang on his stooped frame as he glances at the clock. It says 4:30 - time to go!

There's a buzzer in all our heads that tells us we can relax come a certain time on Fridays; school's out, work's over, it's playtime. We can do whatever we want. So many choices; we can spend time with family, we can sleep late, make a date, have a fling, maybe suspend the usual routine for two and a half days! Osmondo is no stranger to these expectations for he's living a middle class, lunch-box Joe life now with all the ordinary hopes this brings. But there are a few gaps in his kind of middle class life: no big family, little money, no friends (just 'acquaintances') and more than anything, just a few months now on work release to prove he can do it. He's practiced this regular life before but it didn't work; it's never easy for him to face the Friday test. The 'after-work rule-free day' when good behavior sometimes takes a holiday itself.

Osmondo's days of suspended animation on the count

at Greenhaven Correctional Facility are behind him. He's certain they're over! He knows this because after five months of commuting back and forth to Lincoln Correctional Facility at the head of Central Park on 110th Street a couple days a week for drug testing as a 'day reporter,' followed by two months on the job has given him the confidence he needs to allow himself to be frisky this steamy afternoon. So far, so good, no trouble, seven months! He put in a good week at the factory; kept up with the other guys, didn't piss off his boss with any smart remarks. This has been going on for almost nine weeks and for him, this is an eternity! Things were rocky, as they always are when he first gets out. He couldn't find work, he was terrified he'd get caught up with the old crowd; he got grief from his PO who seemed to stalk him at all hours of the day and night and threatened him about a violation if he didn't get a job. Ozzie wants the same thing for himself but "it ain't no easy thing." Half the time he feels people look at him like they would an insect and the other times he isn't even noticed. He goes through the same motions each new beginning. He reports to his parole officer within the first 24 hours and within the first week goes to the required job training interviews and programs. He's so sick of this... he knows it so well, he could teach it. In the past he's always ended up flipping burgers in spite of everything he knows. And the last time, when he did go to the job, he flipped with a mix of arrogance and humiliation until the day came when someone realized he wasn't there and when he finally showed up, he's fired. He flopped the life test and he absconded. Nope, he didn't leave town, he didn't commit a crime, he just gave up; stopped reporting, stopped working, stopped getting out of bed, got picked up at his mother's house after a month and got sent back to the big house until his conditional release date on the 2-6 year burglary.

And about a year after he's paroled, there's this new felony that he's doing time for and on parole today. His record goes back twenty years. He's a burglar...and a heroin addict. This time he's serving 5-10 years for a burglary he committed where he got property valued at $250! The court didn't see any merit in separating him from the public for any fewer than five years so at the price tag of two hundred thousand (!) dollars to the taxpayer for pocketing $250 bucks, he's sent away. He goes around the circuit: Cayuga, Mid-Orange, Great Meadow, Green Correctional Facility, Hudson, Fishkill, Clinton, Adirondack and then Lincoln work release again about four years into the sentence - close to a year before his parole date. 'This time's gonna be different.'

He thinks he knows who he is but when he looks in the mirror cleaning up before leaving the factory, a stranger peers out at him. It's all begun to take its toll. He sees a guy who could be 60-something looking at him but he knows he's 47. His sloped back and gnarled hands are testimony of his many brawls. He never thought much about his face before, only if it could be identified in a lineup. But as he washes up getting the grit off his hands and arms, he gives more thought than usual to himself. He's been a bundle of reflexes for as long as he can remember but lately he seems to be making room for new thoughts to surface. Finally, at his age he's been practicing making plans, having intentions and hopes, believing he can be in charge of his own life. He used to think he was a thief because he took things but lately he thinks maybe

245

he's been kidding himself and that he takes things because he's a thief. Since his girlfriend Mena's kid was hustled at school, he's begun to think about the outrage of that. He never understood it when people corrected him when he said that "he caught a case" (like the flu). In fact, if his new line of thinking is right, he gets what they mean. That maybe he has some control over what he does. Nobody is more surprised than Ozzie that without invitation, a conscience seems to be creeping in to his spaces.

"Hey, I'm not a bad looking guy," he thinks, as he wonders how he'll fill the night. His once rugged looks qualified him as a heartbreaker although the only hearts truly broken were his and his mama's. He says this while he grins broadly at himself to catch all sides. Back in the day, that smile that started as a small crevice slightly upturned on the left side and slow to spread, was choreographed with the unashamed bold gaze of his gorgeous, seemingly dilated, amber rimmed brown eyes that belied the life he was living under his features. He had a way of listening to you that made you believe you were all that mattered. Those eyes. That smile. When he went for the interview set up for him by his PO at the tool and die factory, there was no smile because he was listening for the moment he would be told there was no job for him but to check back in a few months. Those words were never uttered. Instead he was asked when he could begin. And right then he started to make a new plan for himself.

As he leaves the side door of the factory on his way to his next bid, the toughness has seemed to leak out of him. To the west the sun is beginning to think about going down and in preparation it's sending out rays to prepare for the next couple hours of salmon skies. Ozzie's heading east: his mother's house where he'll come in, change and go out. He's in no rush, mom is used to his comings and goings and this time he's kept his curfew of 9 PM on weeknights and a bit later on weekends. But he has nothing really to do and no place to do it. He needs special permission for anything out of town or out of order. He walks east on 23rd to Tenth Ave with no particular map that'll get him home to east Harlem other than his steps following whatever his eyes like to look at. He's feeling pretty proud of himself. The sun going to bed, the heat, the good feelings and possibilities make Ozzie's mouth water.

The odds are against his success. The reach of Ozzie's record defines the long arm of the law. It started with arrests for auto thefts in the '70s. Until the '80s his crimes were mostly done outside; fights in the street, joyrides, possession of drugs – a record that reflected the neighborhood he was in. But then he started going inside, like into other people's homes to commit his crimes and this advanced him to the burglar status he is today. With consistency he'd become a magnet for hot property. He's kept the NYPD in job security with his felony convictions, so far. Sorry to say that could mean there were other break-ins no one but Ozzie may know about. He's spent so much time in the system being questioned, arrested, booked, arraigned, detained, bailed, returned, plea bargained, sent away and locked up, that I can't figure out if this is his real life with interruptions at home or if it's the other way 'round. None of the consequences has changed his behavior because he's never had anything to lose by going away. If nothing changes, nothing changes!

Enough musing about his sins of the past, he's not doing it anyway: I am as I'm reading his record for his latest try at freedom.

And so with his curly mouth whistling a tune he begins to trek cross town. Although he's put in an honest day's work, he never feels like the rest of the folks on the street. He wouldn't stop at any of the watering holes in this neighborhood or at the Chelsea Diner. He's wearing his blue collar workman clothes but it's more what's on the inside of him that keeps him from believing he could ever fit in here (or many other places). He's always afraid of making mistakes; what to say, how to eat, what to wear. He suffers from institutionalization. Granted, this is no one's fault but his own but he does long to be recognized for who he is. Believe it or not, I've met Ozzie–he's a sweet guy.

So, with a wicked thirst and no structure to obey but his own, he happens to see a liquor store and as if by remote control, he quickly buys a pint of gin. Opened, but in the paper bag, he slugs it down little by little while crossing town. "This is the life," he tells himself, satisfied for the first time in a long time – even if it's momentary. He reaches the east side more quickly than he thinks possible. While strolling he's become the center of his universe; he hasn't noticed the others on the street and barely the traffic mayhem during the Friday shuffle. I think this is because by the time he gets to East 57th Street, he's drunk!

Enter Mrs. Wallace who is returning home from a day of shopping with expectations of her own for a wonderful evening of fun and frolic with her husband and friends in this magical town. While buzzing herself into her brownstone down the street, she glimpses Ozzie (who's an unusual sight on this street) weaving in her direction. Uh oh, what's this? Remarkably, Ozzie says the same thing to himself as he notices the most beautiful potted geranium he's ever seen! Mena would love it! A slight hindrance as it's behind a built-out glass hothouse resting on the balcony of this lavish private brownstone. Ozzie feels that it would be no problem to mount the front steps, climb the fret-worked, steel black railing, and gently remove one of the hinged windows to take the flower. Without a second of thought, he reflexively begins to dismantle the terrace glass but cuts his arm. Dam! Mrs. Wallace thinks the same thing and calls the police. When the guys arrive from the precinct they find Ozzie in the bathroom with a towel and a sweatshirt wrapped around his arm to stop the bleeding. So much for his plans for the weekend!

While I'm tracing Ozzie's days through his transcripts while he waits in the hall for his hearing, let me tell you about what my days have been like. They've also had their ups and downs during the six years Ozzie's been in stir since the aftermath of the big geranium heist. While he was back there on the terrace taking up gardening years ago, I've also been making changes along the way in my personal life. Today I'm going to meet Osmondo for the first time (I don't know anything about him yet). I have this plum assignment within an easy commute to my office and my home on Long Island this week at Queensboro Correctional Facility; another of the state's work release sites on Van Dam Street in Long Island City on the other side of the 59th Street Bridge. There's a reason this is happening. I'm waiting to be called off the road for a meeting in the city with someone (don't know who) in the administration about a sexual harassment suit that

I've informally initiated. The insult of this ongoing harassment at work has spilled into my decade-long relationship at home making me less patient and understanding. Since I can't control work, I decide to make some changes in my personal life.

Tired of the failed promises of living happily ever after with Roy, I've decided to stop waiting for a permanent life with him, and still seeking the American dream with the picket fence, I've sold my original small safe sanctuary and moved up to my dream house on the other side of town. I remembered the 'nobody's gonna rescue me mantra' of long ago and am getting on with it. It's easy to stagnate when you're in love and hopes feel like realities. But the scales have tipped here and it's up to me to change the imbalance. So, for as long as this on again/off again affair worked, I remained charmed and connected although I've spent half the time disappointed and abandoned. I have my friend 'The Ear' hearing my laments from the road, but Roy's been my best friend; he's been my weekend spouse who knew nothing but what I've taught him about 'justice' making him appropriately biased and always on my side. It's not only how I felt about him but how he's made me feel about myself and I haven't been feeling so hot for a while. I've stayed too long. He was as much my secret as I was his. His infernal struggle with guilt, which paralyzed him, represented the very values he had that made me love him and are the very reasons that I'm now leaving him.

On this day that I'll meet Ozzie, and in spite of waiting to be summoned to the meeting, I'm looking forward to going home after work to my new place and tending its beautiful gardens and pond. I'll be able to see my kids and friends this week. By the way, we've all obviously survived my parenting over this time from my long distance life on the road, stretching from their young adulthood to their full independence. While I'm able to tell you about my thoughts and happenings, I'm not comfortable telling you their stories; they belong to them. But that said, their joys and sadness are also mine regardless of their age. Good parenting is supposed to develop roots deep enough so that wings can sprout; 'roots and wings'. In my family's case, I've always worried that the view of the kids is that I was the one who took wing. Single parenting has a way of amplifying mistakes. In spite of having a title before my name, I have no special powers to protect my children from all the dreads I know and read about each day in case files.

While Jim has gone the distance of college, trying on various jobs landing solidly on his feet with a fabulous marriage and career and morphing into a mother's definition of a Renaissance man, Heidi has been hijacked by Svengali. She is living out the adage that 'the shoemaker's children go barefoot.' I was now a sage when it came to domestic violence issues but had no influence in my grown daughter's own situation except to confirm for me all the signs and symptoms of her abuse that I knew so well. I lived each day in fear for her. It was made worse by the stories attested to by the inmates before me! In spite of my begging her father to step in (which he never did) and approaching the 'boy's' parents, nothing changed his disposition or threats. The dynamic was a text book case where because of fear, she staunchly defended her boyfriend and avowed love. Domestic violence doesn't only happen between two people; it affects the entire family. I wasn't going to tangle with a guy who carried a 'piece' to my nephew's wedding, when the others wore boutonnières. I considered connections that could break a couple of his limbs but the thought of ending up literally on the other side of the table myself didn't sit well. In the end I could only stand by in spite of my best efforts. Stripped of my work life, I have the same muscle as any other citizen: zilch! Until I kidnapped her. The day came rather spontaneously while I was on a staycation (the kind I liked best as a respite from travel and talking). A friend who knew the situation was with me when we hatched the scheme to go to Heidi's house and forcibly remove her. In spite of the years of her inability to leave, this 'assistance' worked. We are beholden to my friend Don for our lives. I spent that vacation shadowing my daughter while I tucked her away in a place I'd hoped was secret and safe, notified police and got her to support groups. Domestic violence is a toxic health issue that erodes every part of oneself...but it is curable. My daughter is living proof.

And back to my present reverie, thinking of my plans at being able to go home after work. I'm also relaxed to be reviewing this all-male board at Queensboro because it will spare me from arguments that arise when my male co-workers interview women. Coming on to this board as the first white woman and youngest member in a mix of 'good ole boys' (and one woman who's toughness made them look like babies) may have seemed like a leg up for an added dimension of employing justice, but it hasn't played out that way. The blend of paternalism and entrenched macho law enforcement values is a 24/7 effort for me to overcome. Most of my decisions need to be defended regardless if I decide to release or deny; it's often challenged by an exclusive few of the ten men who have toxic influence. Nowhere has this been more profound than in judging women. Most of my colleagues have a real bias assessing female offenders. Although I feel expert in working with women, I've come to dread what's become for me the machinations I practice in my interviews hoping to cover points that will lead my co-commissioners into agreement. My colleagues find women's stories are rarely believable, they are mocked, and their physical images are scrutinized in ways that men are not (a mirror of the free world) and they are always labeled 'manipulative.' The forgotten piece seems to be that 'they' are 'us' and I'm none of those things. If they dress their best for their presentation they're suspect, flirtatious. ("Who does she think she is?"). And conversely, a shy sad woman will reflect the possibility of someone about to make poor judgments and hook up with the first bad boy. The overwhelming majority of the women in prison are there as a result of a life trail that's been laid out by some guy. Fear, intimidation and bullying from the board doesn't bring out the best in people sitting in the hot seat hoping for freedom. And on my side of the table, any style of interview that seems the least kindly causes raised eyebrows, harsh words, and contrary opinions from my peers. Straying from the majority opinion and peer pressure immediately puts my decision making in doubt and I became one of those suspect women myself with my rulings frequently overruled.

When I was narrating a Court TV parole hearing of Leslie Van Houten, one of the Manson Family, I recall after the broadcast a male co-worker calling my attention to her using her feminine wiles based on her matching lipstick and nail polish. This was his message that she was dangerous! I do admit to the importance of being tuned in to the nuances of a person's 'style' and body language; there's no second chance for a first impression. Clothing regulations make individual statements pretty tough but personal attitude does come through; the jailhouse tattoo, the association with drug culture evidenced by that lengthy cocaine fingernail that leaves me questioning. I did indeed weigh in for Van Houten's parole denial citing my reasons for continuing to doubt her safety based on the bizarre multiple murders she committed that forever questions her judgment to me. She does remain in prison but not for the color of her nails and lips. I've also sat through the repeated indelicacy of Dragonlady asking a candidate if she was proud of working on her back!

Forget for a moment the suspense I've put you in waiting to meet Ozzie. He's been waiting for almost six years now for this parole interview so I'm going to keep him in the hall a few minutes longer because it seems a brilliant time to tell you about that sexual harassment suit! As the 'odd man out,' except for a most appreciated couple of allies politically in the bunch, I was flabbergasted when the most disgruntled member of the board professed an 'interest' in me! Surprisingly, this is the very guy who's been my biggest critic and who asked from day one if with my social work background I intended to take inmates home with me! His advances occurred during a board way up in the nether regions of the Adirondacks when over dinner he shared way too much personal information. Believe me I understood the strange loneliness of the job and filling in the gaps by hearing about other people's lives, but his interests put me on guard. This guy endeared himself to inmates by telling them they were like the 'flotsam and jetsam' of the ocean (that will modify behavior, right?). In comparison to a black woman who had been appointed to the board and always treated appropriately, I became a traveling daughter/wife in this guy's mindset. I could think of no way to use his advances to my professional advantage. The opposite happened.

I have had vast practice, as do most of my friends, in experiencing the backlash of the feminist movement. And I did know that there were benefits of this inequity, but if my assets got me in the door, I felt that my talent had to keep me in the room. I got my job at the newspaper (and probably others) because of bias. But the flip side of being treated as an asterisk and not viewed seriously left my generation fighting a war. I'd been denied a byline at the newspaper, I'd been compelled to date customers when I was in PR and I always seemed to be the one who washed the coffee pots, but this current struggle in my position was vastly different; it often cost people their liberty. This because I rebuffed someone's advances and became the enemy thus paying for it with my parole decisions often being overruled! I sat around thinking I imagined all this, that I was weak, that this was politics, that I should be flattered by his attention. When I finally called it by its rightful name, sexual harassment, I knew I hit the nail on the head. This is the '80s; it's an unfamiliar state of affairs legally, although not behaviorally. There are no policies in place for any agency and the parole officers don't know if even telling jokes is considered harassment. Nobody's clear, but when you're the target you know! And I knew!

I became overwhelmed with embarrassment, shame

and fear and wrestled with how to get it to stop while keeping it a secret. My first stop was to the Division of Women. Their counsel was a new hire who miraculously enough was the attorney I had used for my second divorce. This was less coincidence and more providential I think. She had nurtured me during those dark days with Joe and here again I found myself in another horrible situation needing support, confidence and legal advice. I'd come to the right place for validation but they couldn't do anything but pass this information up through the administrative ranks and advise me to get a lawyer. I contemplated stopping my complaint and just toughing it out but as the story leaked out; people came to me and said that if in my position I didn't follow through, it would be terrible for all bottom and mid-level employees experiencing similar humiliation. I was called to the Criminal Justice Coordinator's office – the very same man who had originally interviewed me for the job in Albany. He was well-versed with the circumstances and seemed to have done his homework with respect to handling such a problem (a man ahead of his time). He told me that the problem needed 'some gray hairs' to intervene and asked me to hold up on my lawyer's notice to the state. I've gladly given him time for the next step. One of the things that's happened is that as other commissioners learn of this, they've become part of a fraternity that steers clear of me and empathizes with the villain who they see as the victim. My friend Kevin advises me to drop it because my harasser has clout. He tells me his brother is some kind of insurance mogul. That doesn't seem like any big deal to me. It turns out that his brother is indeed the CEO of the most infamous company of the day; a billionaire, an international businessman, member of numerous boards and foundations and the obvious reason that my nemesis was awarded his political patronage. And with that success, what a window I have into their probable sibling rivalry. I have every reason to believe that I was going to beat this David and Goliath story despite the money and political intrigue.

So I'm in a holding pattern this week waiting for an answer from some gray hairs (I hope they're not going to be mine quite yet). But okay, now I'm about to start the board. There are three of us working together. We're going along at a pretty regular pace and with good humor. It's about 10:30 in the morning; we've been at it a couple of hours and we're up to 'G'. And I pull my next case and in comes Osmondo Gonzales, like a skeet shoot.

He's an affable guy, polite, open body language, a smile, looks about 60-something but after my introductions I look down at his file. Wow, what a record...four felonies going back forever. And I ask him what he did to get here this time. He tells me he took a geranium and got 6-Life! I wince knowing that he must be adjusting his truth; this cannot be. But in the context of his body of work as a burglar, what else could the prosecutor recommend? This is where the system does more of what we know doesn't work! I learn everything I've told you about him from his record and our conversation. I get that he seems to separate his intentions from his deeds and as much as he and his lawyer tried to explain away the geranium, he had broken into someone else's apartment. Mrs. Wallace and the whole neighborhood think that he got a break taking a plea. I cannot deny his parole, nor do I want to. His guideline range for the crime is from 20-36 months and his sentence has him already serving 72! He's been on work release again and doing well. The reports say that his record reflects "utter disregard for the criminal justice system." This is true. This flower didn't come cheap. I've sat on some mystifying cases and legal conundrums but a lifetime sentence for a potted plant leaves me asking questions about what could have been different. It's very easy to criticize the system but until there's a better solution, pot shots are worthless.

At home on Wednesday night I get a call from the chair of the parole board's secretary telling me to come to a meeting that's being held at the cafeteria in the Marine Air Terminal at 1:00 pm the next day! The head of the agency is a youthful wunderkind on his way up politically and the very same guy who gave differing advice during the case of Teddy Martucci, when he labeled me an 'emotional woman.' If he's the designated mediator, there's no gray hair but I'm glad to be getting on with this anyway. When I get to the café I find my harasser (Commissioner X) who has, of course, also been summoned. My heart stops and my breath comes in spurts; what did I think was going to happen? How silly of me, how petty, how weak.

Mr. X. and I don't approach one another until the Chair comes in to the building and signals us to sit down with him. Ah ha…this is why we're meeting in such a strange place; he's flown a little commuter plane down from Albany and has only enough chat time until it turns around and flies back. And he begins by admonishing and swearing at *me*! "What the fuck (!) is wrong with me? Why didn't I just go into his office and tell him to knock it off, where was my head, what was I thinking, how juvenile could I be?" I am all the '-fieds'; stupefied, mortified, horrified. But I just sit there and take it thinking that this is a deftly rehearsed politically challenged performance because it's too stupid and too wrong for it not to be deliberately planned. It's got to be a tactic he's using in order to spare and appease the real wrongdoer who has the power. With all these admonitions I sit there feeling a modicum of relief as long as this guy is called on it. Even in negotiating a truce here, I'm the one humiliated.

In the aftermath of the airport rehab I succeeded in putting people on notice and sounding the all-clear bell. My demands were met and they were simple: that I never again work in the hostile environment that was created and that the agency have sexual harassment training for its staff and parolees. For the Chair's part: upon leaving me speechless in the airport he called the Division for Women to give them a complete retelling and report on how well he did. He is clever! We've come pretty far from that logic today; it's never been one of the ways to handle what's now viewed as a civil rights case.

This was quite a week capped off for Osmondo Gonzales and me. But the lingering questions of justice on so many different levels remain for me long after.

11 | Looking For Justice

"Forgiveness is not an occasional act. It is a permanent attitude." These words were said by Martin Luther King.

Sitting at Wende Correctional Facility outside of Buffalo, in the town of Alden, the original site of the Buffalo County Jail, is a dreary proposition. Sorry Buffalo but it is as dreary as the Buffalo weather. In large measure this is due to the special classification of inmates needing attention; the deaf, the disabled, the mentally retarded. Although, the room that we hold our hearings in is cheerier than most because due to the acute disabilities of some of the parole candidates, there are often interpreters or correctional officers who know the inmates well and can sit in with them. That advocacy lessens the tensions. At least this is my experience.

As I read the stories of their lives and crimes, I wonder sympathetically how much their disabilities have shaped their behavior. And subsequently, how I evaluate their parole risk. Arson seems to be a common crime scene here. But when 90B2220 walks in the room, I know him. Everyone knows of him. Shavod Jones.

It would be impossible to have ignored his crime reported by the media five years ago. In Central Park on July 12th, 1986, Detective Steven McDonald approached Shavod Jones and two other 'kids' about bicycle thefts in the park. These three young boys, between the age of 13 and 15, looked suspicious and started running away when the two police officers went towards them. The boys split up and scattered. When Det. McDonald found them hiding in some bushes and started questioning them he noticed a bulging sock on Jones. When he probed this he was shot. Three bullets hit him; one in the head above his eye, one hit his throat which caused him to have a speaking disability and the third shattered his spine, paralyzing him from the neck down leaving him a quadriplegic.

The take-away of this tragic event and the following media blitz is not the shooting of a cop but that Steven forgave Shavod! Steven was a newlywed with a child on the way. He spent eighteen months hospitalized when his wife Patti Ann, gave birth to their baby, Connor. Steven has written during that time:

"I wanted to free myself of all the negative, destructive emotions that this act of violence awoke in me – the anger, the bitterness, the hatred. I needed to free myself of those so I could be free to love my wife and our child and those around us. I often tell people that the only thing worse than a bullet in my spine would have been to nurture revenge in my heart. Such an attitude would have extended my tragic injury into my soul, hurting my wife, son and others even more. It is bad enough that the physical effects are permanent, but at least I can choose to prevent spiritual injury."

And here's the shooter five years later sitting in front of me asking to go home. As I read the records about his history and the years he's spent in prison, I'm astounded to see that there's been correspondence between Detective McDonald and Shavod and more. The kid had been living with his grandmother and it seems that Steven has been of help to her financially so that she could take the long bus trip to see her grandson. In fact Steven planned to visit but the complications of his travel arrangements prevented it. A couple of years into his 'bid' Shavod had telephoned Steven and his family to apologize. In Steven's words, "...the young man who shot me called my home from prison and apologized to my wife, my son and me. I told him that I hoped he and I could work together sometimes in the future. I hoped that we would travel around the country together to share our different understandings of that act of violence that changed both our lives, and the understanding it gave us about what is most important in life."

My interview with Shavod Jones is not unusual for a hearing at Wende. He makes little eye contact, seems disconcerted, and above all says very little and makes practically no reference to the crime. To me, it feels that he has little capacity for understanding or regret. He seems totally unprepared to live competently in the community. Steven has written as part of an explanation as to who he was to Shavod:

I was a badge to that kid, a uniform representing the government. I was the system that let landlords charge rent for squalid apartments in broken-down tenements; I was the city agency that fixed up poor neighborhoods and drove the residents out through gentrification, regardless of whether they were law-abiding solid citizens, or pushers or criminals; I was the Irish cop who showed up at a domestic dispute and left without doing anything, because no law had been broken. To Shavod Jones, I was the enemy.

And here I am, across the table from him, another enemy.

This is an easy decision for me. I deny parole to him. His behavior fueling the crime and media hype have nothing to do with my decision. It's his behavior during the hearing that speaks loudly enough for me to conclude that he still seems alienated.

Shavod was to spend a little over eight years in prison. He did meet another board two years after he met me and was again denied. He got out on his conditional release date of September 6th, 1995. He went to an approved residence in East Harlem and kept a curfew of 10 PM. It was short-lived. He kept the curfew for two nights, but on the third, his first Saturday home, he died. As a passenger on the back of a motorcycle doing wheelies, he was thrown when it crashed into a couple of parked cars and died a few hours later in the hospital. Ironically he was being observed by one of his supervising parole officers at the time. She was sitting in one of the cars that was hit. Some might say this was "karma." I say it was continuing risky behavior by a kid who had little to lose.

Most days over these years on the job there are people with stories that burn themselves into my memory and they never shake loose. Since I live in the New York environs, I'm often called upon to do those hearings that have to be held in city hospitals; the hearings of the sick and dying who are barely able to speak and for whom I have to make a record so I answer for them. One of these cases was that of a man who had only hours left of life and was waiting in his bed at St. Claire's Hospital with the priest at his bedside. He was but one of many victims of the early wave of death by AIDS. The officers hustled my co-commissioner and me off the elevator into the prison ward as time was of the essence. Against all odds, this man felt he died with some dignity – not as a prisoner, but as a parolee. Another visit to St. Claire's hospital to a man on his deathbed coming into the heavily policed hospital room as the priest was giving last rights; at the end of a long parole board hearing day at Sing Sing being ushered in the dark through the underground tunnel system and up flights of stairs to the hospital to 'interview' a stroke victim sitting under a hanging 60-watt light bulb; the woman who'd served 22 years whose mother was in the last stages of cancer and whose daughter was paralyzed. These were not only medical cases but those for whom the system had failed. Our prisons are peppered with the aged, the infirm, the feeble as well as those who have the potential to aid our communities. People we over-incarcerate.

There is a piece of the decision-making puzzle that no one admits to: instinct. How can you articulate that? You can't. You definitely can't when a decision you make goes bad and hits the front page; you can't when you try to persuade your colleagues about your reasoning; you can't when you're called on the carpet. It's hard to tell yourself what that nagging internal, but certain, feeling is. But don't we all size people up? For me I allow my gut instinct to play a role – it's the percentage I allow it that makes the difference. We are humans in a people business after all. If machines could do it, machines would do it.

The extraordinary sadness and gore takes its toll; but not for everyone. Not all of my colleagues react similarly; in fact only a couple do. One of them, my friend Kevin, a former priest himself, uses his compassion/understanding (rightly) as a factor to throw into the mix for decision making. My only other ally is 'Big Joe' who is (wrongly) as biased toward the disadvantages of the inmate as the other sixteen are against, acting as avengers. I'd like to believe that their callousness is because they think showing any sympathy amounts to a betrayal to the victim.

And not all the commissioners act unlike our customers: one convicted of six counts of perjury stemming from the questioning of rigging the release of a political donor; the other arrested in a sting operation at a motel where he awaited two children with whom he arranged to have sex. My mother used to say, "Every dog has his day and sometimes you're around to see it." Although I wasn't around for either of these events, I did work with one of them; he was my biggest detractor who had pitched tirades in hearing rooms over my decisions and tried to get my reappointment blocked. The other, the pedophile, had an impressive history as a state assemblyman and former TV reporter, and was known for his stand for tougher penalties for sex abusers with a reputation for firmness on the parole board. The papers reported that upon his sentencing in the summer of 2010 he read a prepared statement in court, his voice taking over the courtroom not unlike the way state lawmakers hold forth on the floor of the state Assembly. But on this day, Ortloff claimed to have a "normal, healthy sex life," admitted he had committed adultery for 20 years and even quoted Shakespeare. He repeatedly blamed the Internet as the vehicle to his downfall into infamy. I cannot imagine what his reaction to this defense would have been to one of his former customers across the table from him. Both these men experienced firsthand what they'd been dishing out. Sadly, they are both also guilty of corrupting the integrity of the Parole Board. Two well-respected Commissioners also lost their reappointments. Their crime was their courageous decision to ethically release a worthy person in a high profile case in spite of political and media pressure against it. The law says that we "sit at the pleasure of the Governor."

I continue to remind myself that I am not an advocate for parolee or victim; that parole doesn't mean forgiveness; that I am not voting for guilt or no guilt, that happened at sentencing (I am not the jury). And I always know that retribution is a luxury we can't afford. I am fast burning out. But this is a job that allows for no 'down time,' no debriefings. This is like that of a race horse who continues to run with no time out until put out to pasture. I need a vacation.

I have long suspected the dispassionate attitude that pervades the board now is a culture that existed long before I got here and will continue long after I leave. And aha, I'm right. Here's a case demonstrating a total lack of empathy …not to mention failure to follow the statute. It was reported in the *New York Law Journal* in October, 2006 (a decade after I'm gone) by John Caher. This is the case of a 76-year-old, half-blind, diabetic cancer victim and stroke survivor having undergone two surgeries for prostate cancer and removal of an eye for a malignancy. The crime of murders occurred in 1968 with the conviction of 25-L imposed. He was denied parole at his first hearing, he was denied parole at his second hearing two years later whereupon he appealed based upon the imbalance of deliberative factors putting more weight upon the commission of the crime than upon all the rehabilitative efforts; academic achievements, humane initiatives, program development, future plans, administration's respect, etc. As such, he won his appeal and parole was ordered to hold what we call a 'de novo' hearing, which is a fresh hearing that would date back to the time of the last erroneously ruled hearing. However, when that third hearing occurs, once again a panel of three, in spite of a court's corrective insight, denies this aged addled guy release, although it's a sure bet he's not a threat to the community. So he appeals again and with astonishing results the court orders his direct release from prison with only a stop along the way to speak to a parole board to make sure nothing's happened new since the last hearing which would change the picture. When the decision was issued by the court, his lawyers said:

I am not aware of any case in which this was done, but I am glad that Justice Friedman issued this order. It's clear that the Division of Parole will just continue to deny him parole. Someone needs to tell the Division of Parole that enough is enough and it is time to release him.

About my need for a break, I have for a while had my eye on the possibility of getting a fellowship from a foundation called *Windcall.* If I understand this correctly, the award is time on a ranch in Montana doing nothing! Could this be? Yep, it be. They say they are "a supportive environment to explore the unknown with the space and time to build new visions or to find again what feeds your soul." The Institute's mission goes on to explain, "All over the country, organizers and activists are leading heroic efforts to resolve long-standing social, economic and environmental problems…..." In short, rather than the typical grants awarded to agencies, they are giving the individuals within the agencies some nurturing to continue their work. I didn't quite imagine that I could be in the queue as a finalist after I wrote my application essay; I didn't rebuild the Gulf Coast, I didn't defend immigrant rights, I didn't fight for affordable housing or improve the environment and I didn't do many other heroic things but I did know that the job was robbing my soul and my energy. Each weekend that I was home I was sick and when I went to consult the doctor he said sarcastically that the easy fix was to get a weekend job to keep me on my toes. I still feel the work is an enormous privilege and that the toll is neither the hardships of the road or the scars of the stories but the courage it takes for me to combat the attitudes of my co-workers. This is politics in both a small and large 'P'! And I do believe that the sifting through of human lives, one by one, on their way to the possibility of transformation is important work.

I did get the fellowship and arrived in the Gallatin Valley in Montana in the early spring with the snow still on the mountaintops framing the ranch and the grass still crisp in the morning. I had been warned about the cool temperatures and packed accordingly but found soon enough the down quilts and the electric towel racks, the chef that comes in to cook the meals, the art studios and the computer rooms, the barn for movie viewing, the pond to fish, the horses to ride; and I was expected to do nothing! It was extraordinary. There were two other recipients there with me who had never been further than a few miles out of a city centre where their work was, toiling through different kinds of homeless and hunger issues. In this respect I felt a bit of an interloper portraying myself as worthy of the award. Unlike them, I had seen magnificent countryside before, I collected a healthy salary and my soul was suffering from other people's misfortunes, not mine, after all. In spite of my guilt I was definitely on an equal footing with them and our friendships blossomed; a black female housing advocate finding safety for people found in dumpsters and huddled over street grates, a radical Latino playwright who brought theatre and inspiration to the streets of the poorest slums and a white female parole commissioner. Some trio we were. We discovered we had everything in common. We rented a car and saw Yellowstone, swam in hot springs and visited Native American lives during the stay. I was not prepared for what I found when I entered a church/community building on an Indian reservation where we went to witness a Pow Wow; there on the wall of the entrance was a full-page newspaper article tacked up about their hero, Steven McDonald! He was their God. Here comes this 'synchronicity' again. I must meet him.

When it was time to come home we promised to keep in touch. We knew we wouldn't but we also knew that we would always take a part of each other with us through our lives extracted from the exchange of our stories and our feelings. I missed my work and wondered who was 'minding the store' in my absence. I felt I had abandoned people. My time out didn't renew me; it just delayed my determination to make the difference I wanted to make in the system, more fair justice. And I wanted to meet Steven McDonald for the conversation about courage I needed for this to happen.

And in May of 1991, when I get home I'm just in time for a new policy that will confuse everyone further, victim impact statements – in person. This ratchets up the politicization of parole to a new pitch with the insinuation of victims meeting parole commissioners. Their written statements have always been encouraged and factored into our decisions. Their input has been helpful to them and more fully describes the story and the effects of their victimization. But does this help me make a decision... that story was known during the trials when the sentencing time was assessed. But here we are so many years later again equating inmate time with victim pain. Are we now resentencing? Could you read this letter and then release the man she's talking about? Let alone meet her and hear what she has to say. Read it and weep:

Dear Parole Board,

I don't think I have to give you explicit details for the horrible reasons my father is incarcerated. I'm sure you have that information available in your file. I don't have to tell you about the bruises, black eyes, fat lips, cuts, cigarette burns, whip marks, or broken teeth that were given to me by my father's hands. You see most of the scars go away after a while. The scars that will never fade are the deep scars he left in my heart, in my soul and in my mind forever.

This addition of a personal interview with the victim is prompted by a new movement that's stirred by the belief that there's nothing level about the playing field of our justice system; that after the offender serves the time s/he's free while the victim is forever captured by the crime. It's become a powerful political force that's been a long time in the happening. The majority of the offenders are paroled while the victims' impairments last a life time. While the advocacy and support groups give much needed strength to the victim, they also place emphasis on tracking the offender who's incarcerated. I have many questions about the value of this but it's inappropriate to ask any of the victims I meet about this. I wonder if this focus prolongs the suffering, if it keep the experience alive and vivid over the years? But I can't measure the satisfaction of revenge. Is anger necessary for healing? We need some experts here and the parole board is not that. I suggest we use a mediation process that's useful and is used elsewhere; a meeting between victim and offender. Could explanations, apologies, intentions aid the victim?

While this has worked in other jurisdictions, this one isn't going to be one of them. In fact, parole usually directs the parolee not to be in touch with the victim. And the Department of Correction certainly doesn't condone it. Reconciliation is a highly sensitive area of work and requires special skills. But for a few examples, this rarely occurs; the human heart isn't socialized for this. No one is turning the other cheek; we are looking to trade eyes. But Steven McDonald has done this and has said,"….had I sought revenge, I would have been a dead man already."

And I worry that the agency's new policy will give the victims false expectations. But this is a developing policy and I shouldn't be too critical even though I feel this is a ruse that the Division is using to quell the victims frustrations and is not thought through. There is no guarantee that their interview with a commissioner will prevent a parole. They believe that they will be meeting the actual commissioner who will be interviewing the inmate. That could be the case but it would be strictly a coincidence. The plan is to select victims of certain crimes (rarely a criminal that anyone would release regardless) and set up an interview with rotating commissioners. I make the suggestion that a social worker be hired to interview the victim and submit a report for the file. This is another one of my ideas that goes nowhere. Maybe I'm being selfish but hearing the suffering of the victim so many years later and then judging the offenders risk puts me between a rock and a hard place. The stories of the victims are agonizing and we have no training for this other than our sympathy. It seems so wrong to me to dabble with their emotions. Of the ten or so I've conducted I'm careful to stay clear of agreeing with the inevitable characterization of the inmate, although I certainly agree about the crime. The victims are haunted and are reliving the worst incident of their lives, having rehearsed for this day. The challenge for me is to gather facts empathetically and not get stuck in the sadness. I remind them that I want to know what's occurred in their life since that day. The crimes leave them stuck in time. The damages are life long and carry with them chronic hospitalizations, nightmares, permanent fears and life altering pain. When I write the report for the file I record the events in a fairly sterile, objective style for the reader, no editorializing…this is hard to do. It reads like Jack Webb wrote it ("The facts, Ma'am, just the facts."). It's not enough that the parole board makes the tough liberty decisions in spite of political heat, public opinion and latent personal bias, but now we carry the face of the victim with us. We need to do something more for their pain but our job shouldn't be trying to balance pain and punishment. This is an impossible job. Have I mentioned before, that when I was being considered for the parole board years back I asked what the actual job was and was told that a 'parole commissioner stands between the Governor and the gun." Boy, was that ever an apt description!

And after many inquiries and conversations I'm finally looking forward to meeting Steven McDonald. We've arranged to meet in a school building on a weekend morning to have the talk I've so long hoped for. By necessity he arrives with an entourage that includes his health worker, his driver and an additional person. He is considered at all these meetings to be on duty. He's still employed as a detective by the police department and does his work 24/7, every minute of the day, talking and living *peace.* To say that from the instant he appears I know him to be 'divine' is not hyperbole. For the agnostic that I mostly am, I recognize him to be godly. As I again explain my admiration and motives he simply talks about his belief that he sees his tragedy as a blessing that has allowed him to become a tool for nonviolence. We meet for no longer than he is able, which is under an hour and I see the extraordinary strength and courage required to forgive; to take back your own power, to have love conquer anger, to rein in revenge. For most of us the view of forgiveness is interpreted as passiveness and an inability to confront. But I learn from Steven the work it takes to reclaim the 'stuff' that's taken from you as a victim and fully live.

I was able to meet Steven once more a couple of years later in his home. For the first time I met his wife who of course is every bit his equal. He has a shrine of sorts where he spends his quiet time praying but I suspect those times are limited, for he is a busy and sought after lecturer and writer; all in the hopes that his aura will attach itself to us mere mortals. His wife encouraged him early on to begin speaking about gun violence. In 1995 he met with Pope John Paul II. And in the ensuing years he's spoken at two Republican conventions. In 2004 he was promoted to detective first grade. He has become a noted public speaker, mainly on behalf of the NYPD, peace initiatives in Northern Island, the U.S. Navy, and with students about violence and forgiveness. His wife, Patricia Ann McDonald, was elected Mayor of Malverne on Long Island on March 2007 and his son has joined the police force. Steven writes:

Forgiveness is a topic that people need to hear about today more than ever. As human beings we need forgiveness, whether we are giving it or asking for it. And people make up countries. So that means countries need forgiveness, can offer forgiveness. Forgiveness is really about our own healing. We may experience slight offenses, or they may be profound. But in the end it is our choice, and it is the survival of our own souls that is at stake.

The parole Victim Impact Unit officially grew up in 1993, a couple of years after it started. It formalized its policies and protocols, developed staffing and training. And as victims are included at the outset of the cases, it seems 'just' perhaps that this consideration continues. Maybe, I think, just maybe this is fair. We talk to the inmate long after the crime to get a more recent update; does this help the process of justice to employ the same rule with the victim? However, the residual affect to both victim and offender last lifetimes regardless of parole outcomes. And unfairly, the public pressure that is placed on the parole board does propel decision making. And there are so very many human beings serving 20-30 years, being denied release over and over because they're politically hot crimes or the victim is high profile.

There've been in the annals of parole and continues to be, decisions that become legend. And the Board's decisions in some cases have been characterized as fatally flawed, illogical and irrational. Some member's decisions are more flawed than others depending on how they interpret their job. Is it retribution, deterrence, rehabilitation, incapacitation, reparation or denunciation? These decisions make history in the courts and resultantly set the standard for cases to come. While these cases are always an embarrassment showing the ineptitude of the Board, they provide direction for future deliberations. And the arrogance of discretion requires reminders about the limits of power every so often.

These were the notable words that were said by a colleague in an interview with an offender:

"Society itself has no answer for how much is enough (time). We don't have any answer. God doesn't tell us. He certainly didn't give the knowledge to know with certainty how much is enough for killing somebody…And yet in a few minutes, sometime today, this afternoon, this panel is going to decide how much is enough with you.. We are going to make a decision because we are in a position. That's our job to do. And we are going to do it. But I want to tell you humbly, it's not written in stone. We don't know how much is enough. We don't have the answer. You're not the same guy that you were when you were in the fast food restaurant…you're not the same guy now. And the victim (name change), he wouldn't be the same guy either; he'd be 22 years older….you pose a dilemma to us."

This case was denied parole in spite of exemplary rehabilitative efforts during his years incarcerated. And the parole denial was appealed with a successful outcome and parole granted. The court concluded that the board misunderstood its duty saying:

The establishment of penal policy is not the role of the Parole Board or any other administrative agency and these remarks reveal a fundamental misunderstanding of the limitations of administrative power. The torturous and difficult decisions involved in determining the appropriate penalty to be imposed for the commission of a particular crime is fundamentally a function which belongs in the hands of the elected officials to be performed in open and considered debate. It is the province of the legislative process, except insofar as the legislature has entrusted, within certain parameters, the imposition of individual sentences to the judiciary. The due operation of those processes has seen fit to punish petitioner with a sentence of 20 years to life. The role of the Parole Board is not to resentence petitioner according to the personal opinions of its members as to the appropriate penalty for murder, but to determine whether, as of this moment, given all the relevant statutory factors, he should be released.

One of the more common sticking points is the line of questioning that insists on confessions and remorse. This becomes a catch-22 when the parole candidate denies involvement which then results in a parole denial. The Judge's decision on appeal of such a case included this language: "Clearly, it was not the role or the power of the Board to exact a confession from petitioner, or to make him grovel as he uttered phrases of remorse for conduct he believed he was not guilty of."

Some of the other considerations that act as either mitigating or aggravating factors, that really shouldn't be in the paroling deliberation, is whether the sentence was the result of a jury trial or a plea (the plea carries a lesser sentence usually), and if there are multiple convictions, do they run together, concurrent, or consecutively, has he cooperated with authorities? While it's not the business of the board to tack on time, it's done in this thought process to conclude if the punishment's/time's been enough. I know, I look at these things too. Such was the case ruled on by Judge Emily Jane Goodman who ordered a new hearing in the case of a man who had three sentences running together; the overriding one for attempted robbery being 8-Life. It was noted that the New York Code Rules and Regulations for such crimes carried a sentence of 2 ½ to 4 ½ years. This inmate, who was 58 and had accomplished a bachelor's degree, a master's degree and a doctorate in theology to attest to his rehabilitative efforts, was denied six times for a total of nineteen years spent behind bars; quadruple the recommended maximum term under state sentencing guidelines. He wasn't given parole until two years after the judge stepped in. And again in another case carrying a term of 18-L where the candidate had been denied release a total of ten times (!) 20 years more than the minimum set by the court. This man was released only in late 2011, while the grudging lead commissioner chided the judge's decision to follow the law, confusing legal definition with the morality police. It's hard to keep justice on track.

I've been involved in a few suits and I'm sure have kept the legal department, awash in appeals, busy myself. It would be uncommon not to have denial decisions appealed by our customers. I learned in a hostage training course I took that the healthiest thing a prisoner can do is plot an escape. The second-healthiest seems to be to appeal legal decisions not in your favor. Appeals are appropriate in a place where time stands still. The first step in an inmate's rebuttal to a parole denial is an administrative appeal. Our desks were overflowing with requests for review of these appeals. We were made aware of case appeals more as an educational tool rather than any active involvement as we had 'absolute immunity' and the state represented us in court. One of the cases of mine that I watched and was mindful of was that of a music rapper. I knew even during the hearing that this one would end up in court. There was confidential information that I couldn't reference either verbally or in writing in my reason for his denial. But he did say in the interview that he had written lyrics to his rap 'songs'(?). This in the early days of rap. His crime, which totally eludes my memory, was one of violence but had nothing to do with his music profession. I read the confidential info which were his alleged' lyrics' found in a cell search. They read like menacing threats to all "white bitches" when he was released. Even if they were put to a tune and I could hum along, I wasn't so sure that I was looking at a song and not a threatening letter and I wasn't about to take a chance on him. Tricky stuff. Evidently I fashioned an inadequate denial which made it to court.

I usually kept my lid on during interviews…not too hot, not too cold, just right. People ask if I'm frightened working in a prison. The answer is no! Every single person wants to get out and as such is not going to make an enemy of a parole board member. In twelve years I've experienced only one threatening incident and that was from a man who had psychiatric problems. During a non-confrontational hearing at Sullivan, he spat in my face. I must say the great parole staff took it much more seriously than I did. After all it was coming from a deranged person. Ten months after I denied his parole, he was conditionally released from state prison and civilly committed to Kingsboro Psychiatric Hospital. I got notification of this at home and was happy to hear that he was being supervised carefully by staff but that he could abscond at any time from the hospital…he was no longer anybody's prisoner. Freddie never did follow through on any of his threats. And then there was the start of a riot at Green Correctional where I sat as Chair bookended by my two colleagues who thought I was deaf when the guns in the tower over us started to fire and I continued to interview an inmate. I figured that if we interrupted the hearings, all hell would break loose with the bunch of inmates outside our room waiting for us. And so I continued and took a break only when the noise settled down. It never developed into anything.

And on my road looking for justice I experienced the bonus residuals that a title and a shield could bring, some were really good and always unexpected:

On a weekend train trip to visit family in D.C., I struck up a conversation with my seatmate; a new minister at St. James Episcopal Church. Upon hearing what I did he offered a million dollars from a fund for social justice to put into programs for offenders. Using a cell phone and jumping out of my seat with excitement, I put him immediately in touch with a friend who tailored a program preparing parole candidates for 'the' fateful interview for parole and incorporated the program in an existing not for profit criminal justice agency.

Reading about the rapes and atrocities in Bosnia written by Newsday reporter Roy Gutman, I called Newsday to inquire if I could speak with him as I wanted some information. I wanted to know how my network of women's rights groups might cable the victims in sympathy. I was told that they would patch me through to him in Bosnia! Of course I used 'Commissioner' when I introduced myself. He shared with me all the answers I wanted. What evolved was a speaking tour among many friends before human rights audiences that raised enough money to build a school there. We did reach the women through connections with reporters and clergy and told them that, "We heard your screams and we're going to help".

On Sundays it wasn't unusual that I went the mile from my house to Old Westbury Gardens to wander among the walled gardens on the 200-acre estate. This place is on the National Historic Register and upon entering you were immediately restored. Still living on the grounds at this time was the 93-year-old granddaughter, Peggy Phipps Boegner, of the original builder and owner. Her home, also on the grounds, was a mansion in its own right built for her as a wedding present by her father so many years ago. The grandeur of the place smacked of royalty but when you explored you knew you were in a family home where children were reared and orphans fostered during the war. Mrs. Boegner began a foundation expressing that her "main objective has been to preserve the charm and beauty of the Gardens in the tradition of my parents during their long and happy time and sometimes to give a sense of delight and beauty to the gentle, welcome visitors." So moved was I that she would invite all these strangers into her still private place, I wrote her a thank you note. I told her what I did for a living and how being on her grounds mended my soul. Within two days her secretary called me and invited me to her home for tea! It was a memorable experience (obviously) with the conversation turning to her curiosity about skinheads, the current culture and politics. I had hopes that she would accept my invitation for dinner in return but that never happened.

And my highlights wouldn't be complete unless I told you about the other notable 'vacation' I took when I joined the Israeli Army through Volunteers for Israel for a little getaway. This was the veritable busman's holiday. I was single, not the type for a cruise and not the body for a bikini clad Island destination so I thought it time to better understand my heritage. With a bit of persuasion after rigorous screening, I convinced the agency that I was really interested in going, was Jewish and had good intentions. It was designed for people to take the place of reservists who could then go to the front. They were very particular about who they allowed on these nefarious trips. They accepted me. My shield however, got me designated as the group leader on the army base and I was responsible for the volunteers' grievances and activities apart from the work we were assigned. Too much to say about this time in history but it was perhaps one of the best things I ever did.

And the glint of the badge never escaped the attention of the more notorious inmates currying favor with new appointees. In my case a three page single typed beautifully written letter arrived on my desk when I was a couple of years on the job. The letter was penned after he served twenty two years and that was twenty eight years back (!). He remains there today still for the most brutal murders of three women but his notoriety came from the fame of one of his victims: Kitty Genovese. While she was being killed, the story that's now being disputed is that the neighborhood heard but did nothing. He professed to have my biography and wanted assistance with the name of a publisher for a book he was writing about the system. I could be of no help but answered his letter as respectfully as he asked. His crimes didn't make his complaints or requests any less valid. And I remembered a Chinese proverb that said, "Whoever opts for revenge should dig two graves."

12 | Redemption

The call came to me at home on a Friday morning telling me that the power of my signature was finished at the end of the day. And that I should get into the office and look over a few more cases before the end came. I thanked the caller who was deeply embarrassed while I breathed an almost audible sigh of relief. I'd been waiting for the inevitability of this for the last six months as my two appointment terms of twelve years ran out six months ago. And with a Republican governor, I knew that I was merely a seat holder until he needed someone for his own reasons. You don't go into politically appointed jobs thinking that merit gets you there or will keep you there. Even with all the difficulty of the work, I was prepared to continue if that's the way it went as I've always believed it was a bigger calling for me than just being employed.

The seat was needed in order to pass a health bill that was being blocked by an upstate Democratic legislator. She was offered my seat on the parole board after having it made clear to her that the 'machine' would make certain she would not win her incumbent election. She was left little choice but to step aside. It was smooth sailing for the health bill. I instructed the secretary to send a 'thank you, good luck and farewell' memo to all the parole staff in prisons and around the state that I had worked with. Remarkably, this had never been done by anyone before. The consequences of that phone call relinquished the power of my John Hancock which may have granted or denied an inmate release. It may have been a new start for one of the 55,000 persons doing time. I like to think that my signature had been currency for fairness. I didn't go into my office that day or again.

I got to central office in Albany within a few days and did all the usual handshaking and small talk. It was all very amicable. I turned in that magic badge and a deeply flawed vehicle from the state's fleet. As I started my experience on Amtrak, so it ended while I did an about face home on the descending track of power. And, as I settled myself in the normally comfortable train seat heading south to NYC on January 13, 1996, I wasn't happy. On this trip home I remembered the northern route, the familiar faces of day-trippers from the city to the capital who are dependent on government money; either lobbyists for agencies, executive directors scraping and bowing for 'member item' awards, private sector contractors going to bidders' conferences and a variety of the usual political sycophants. Today I recognized no one. I was going in the 'other' direction. I had many thoughts knowing that I was officially unemployed.

I was a private citizen and in so many ways I was relieved of the heartache and responsibility and the uphill battles sitting on the other side of the table. As the train traveled on its route through the lower elevation passing Sing Sing Correctional, I thought of all the injustices that had occurred during these years. My friend, "The Ear", is on the train with me. I tell her all about it. There had been the death of my college roommate's son due to the perception that a recommendation from me, a woman, was too emotional and rather than release, he died shackled to a jail hospital bed. There had been the hotly and often contested hearing of one of Malcolm X's assassins. There had been a protracted sexual harassment mess aimed my way. There'd been the political outrage of one of the Howard Beach defendant's decision. But for all the controversial cases, there were thousands of more ordinary stories recounted in shame and received by those listening in disbelief. There were the confrontational styles, the insults, the put-downs, the pontificating but mostly the disconnect between authority and those hoping for redemption.

Throughout my comings and goings in jails and prisons over three decades under the auspices of several different employers, I came to know the faces and stories of many people. The blur that's created by the sameness of uniforms and the cacophony of thousands of people's noises tends to make one ignore what's in plain sight – that this horde is individuals stacked one upon another. The cases of the less notorious criminals are eclipsed by the sensational few that are made famous by their very actions. The vast majority of these prison-cities are filled with hapless individuals who became their own worst enemies as they took victims with them. There's the familiar show and tell of the neighborhoods sport of machismo that ricochets throughout generations and the obedience of the girls turned out. Remarkably for many, prison became the first place that they've stood still long enough to grow. This is not an endorsement for lengthier sentences that would let the roots sink deeper but a sad indictment of their lives in the streets.

I've met and held on to many of the friendships I made on the inside….some are out and some still in. I recall sitting in a circle on a Saturday morning with inmates at

Bedford Hills Correctional Facility and students of mine from a class in criminology I taught at Queens College. As we went around the room we all introduced ourselves; who we were, what we did and why we there. One woman who had already served fifteen years sitting in her prison greens said that she worked for the Department of Corrections and was a counselor in the children's program. And she was! This was a woman who knew that she was so much more than one action in her life would define her as being. That day as we left, there were hugs and kisses and promises to correspond. It changed not only the opinions but the careers of many of the students. It was like leaving a prayer meeting.

And so too have these friends changed me by showing me what accountability, gratitude and remorse look like. All these people are responsible for the taking of human life…all inadvertently. If anyone believes that criminals do their time with never a look back, they are mistaken. In spite of some of these crimes being committed thirty years ago, there is not a day that goes by that each of these people doesn't remember with shame and grief the impact of their actions. And each one has dedicated his and her life to the betterment of others. These people could have been the poster children for parole: people who were all long-termers, who matured while incarcerated, who maintained loving families and loyal friends in the community, who were incapable of malice, who never incurred a 'ticket' over the years, who showed true expressions of remorse and took leadership roles in whatever programs were offered. These are people who now live compassionate lives and would be your friends. For those who are in the community; they've all landed impressive positions in places where their education and experience make a difference for others in that ripple effect that Robert Kennedy talked about. They all live their lives on purpose. Yet these same people were denied parole by different boards over time, again and again (which interestingly enough is how I met each of them through advocacy after I left the Board). They each filed appeals; some with the help of pro bono attorney clinics and some paying huge amounts to lawyers who had worked in the past denying parole before making a living rebutting all those reasons! These are the missed opportunities to reward redemption. The following was written in a prison newsletter by one of these remarkable friends who needs no attribution as he knows who he is:

"Tell Me People Can Change"

"After my last Parole Board hearing I was telling a dear friend about my preparation for the Parole Board, and about my experiences during the hearing and after my denial. It was my second appearance and the second time I had gone through the hope and denial process. My friend told me that many of our peers had commented on how strong I was being. No one could understand how someone who had worked so hard to make amends by serving others for so long could have been denied for a second time. Everyone thought the decision was unfair, and many were losing hope of their own chances. But I knew I had changed, and I knew others had changed too. My friend suggested I write about my feelings as a way to help others, both those on the inside and those on the outside, understand how today's blanket 'get tough' parole policy has been affecting those of us in prison.

My first reaction was that I knew many in our society did not believe prisoners suffer enough. I thought why would anyone want to read about the pain of an incarcerated man? Then, after much thought, I decided that if nothing else I could help others prepare for the challenge they too would eventually be facing when they appear before the Parole Board.

After almost two decades of feeling remorse and performing outstanding accomplishments many in the community and behind these walls felt I should have been released at my first parole board. On the contrary, that was not the case for my first hearing or my second. They are experiences I will remember for the rest of my life.

When I was incarcerated for taking a life, at the age of nineteen, I understood I would be doing a minimum of sixteen years before being considered for release. I also understood that if I turned my life around for the better I would be released to return to my family. During this time deserving individuals were being released after serving their time in exemplary fashion. In view of that, for the next eleven years I did everything possible to make myself a better person who would contribute to the healing process of the neighborhoods like the one I left behind. I also believed it was one way I could make amends for my crime. Then in 1995, the parole policy was made tougher.

At one point I refused to believe a person who had worked so hard to demonstrate his remorse, who had matured so much and who could be of such benefit to the community would be denied parole. That was like telling me people cannot change. Therefore, for the next five years I continued from behind these walls to give back to the free community and also to those around me. I assisted dozens of men to return home and become true examples of loving fathers, caring husbands, responsible sons and community providers.

When my time came to appear at the Parole Board I made sure the person I was, would be seen through a well compiled portfolio and my sincere words. The night before the hearing I told myself it was all up to God now and I should give myself a good night's rest. Nonetheless, my anxiety and the fear that that I would not be understood prevented sleep. I tossed and turned the whole night. The morning of the hearing my stomach was in a knot. As I walked to the hearing room all I could do was ask God to keep me strong. Then came the wait on the bench outside the room. I thought my nerves would crush me until finally I heard my name called. I thought the hearing went well. But I would have to wait several days before I knew the decision. As the days passed my uneasiness continued to build. To add to the suffering, the decision was not delivered on the third day as expected. I knew my family was also in suspense. But the final decision was heartbreaking. I was denied parole for two more years.

I did not want to call my mother to give her the news since it was her birthday. Instead, I called her to wish her well and to tell I still did not know my fate. I believe my pain was greater because I was making my family suffer. I had already caused so much pain to the family of my victim. Now I was again making things difficult for my own family. To have my hopes and dreams deferred, to continue with the uncertainty of not knowing when I would go home was one thing, but causing my loving family further pain was devastating.

The pain of knowing I would not be returning home and that my family would have to endure two more years of struggles was destroying my heart. I had prepared dozens of men who were doing great things in the community, so how could I not be worthy of release? The statement I kept hearing in my head was the Board does not believe I have changed. Yet, I will continue to pray, wait and hope for the day the Board will believe that we do have the ability to change."

My transition into other work still had me profiled as a magnet for trouble and troubled people. After my title and shield were turned in and had no benefit to me, I took possession of a new job in a new office but the stories kept coming my way such as the meeting with the tall dark stranger who I'd dared to hope about on first impression and tell you about now:

As I leave my office for lunch miraculously the elevator is waiting for me at the end of the hall. This is a trip you can count on taking half an hour longer than it should what with the time it takes the elevator to creep up and down the twelve floors. I'm lucky. I'm on the 7th floor. Another miracle; only one other person on the down elevator. Not that I noticed (much), but he is a snappy looking 50-something guy in the New York uniform of all black, chiseled features, holding a Starbucks coffee that he doesn't seem to need to get his motor going , and an incredible line of banter. As the elevator descends slowly, I know his taste in shoes (Manolo Blaniks), that his name mimics a toney store, that he is a born and bred west-sider who'd spent the last years in California but was back for his mother's funeral, that he's wrecked his BMW on the West Side Drive the day before, that he'd just come from his therapist on the 7th floor, but mostly that he's grateful I'm speaking to him. Well, it's all very heady and as I'm taken through his paces I think, "They should pay me for just walking around in public diagnosing people," or "Is this guy for real and I've just seen too much?" I break through his words like a gust of wind and shout, "I've got one word for you: Paxil!" He swivels around, pauses, really looks at me and then rambles on about the effects of Prozac on his manhood. I decide I'm right to be suspicious and that he's definitely Mr. Wrong. This is a pick-up, this is a nut job, as usual. But still, as we reach the lobby and I race away to catch the subway, I hold out a little hope that this is just a harmless, eccentric, New York Woody Allen moment, and that if I lived in the Midwest, I'd imagine this goes on all the time in this city.

The next day a dozen long stemmed roses are delivered to me at the office with a note gushing gratitude from Him. My staff at work is titillated by the possibility that this could actually become a spectator sport. In truth, I know down to my toes that this is a bizarre thing and that there's a story here. The most romantic thing that could happen, I think to myself, is that I never hear from him again and that indeed it is one of life's quirky moments reserved for retelling when I write that book. Two days later a collect phone call from the Westchester County Jail comes through. I accept the call because I'm in the rehabilitation business, only it's not a client. It's Him. 'Til the last skeptical but hopeful second when I ask him what he's doing at the jail, I'm praying that he's some kind of cracked wizard on staff there. Not so.

"What are you there for?" I ask.

"A misdemeanor"

"Oh?"

"Some woman says I was stalking her"

"Hmm (some surprise). I want to thank you for the roses and wish you good luck."

"Ya know, it's not the twenty days. I can do that. It's the time left on federal parole violation if they bring me back. I did 11 years and it would kill me to do any more."

With a mixture of personal disappointment but professional smugness, I pat myself on the back for being right.

"Well, best to you," I say "and thanks again".

Just to confirm my diagnosis of elevator-man, I go online to 'inmate locater' at the Department of Correction website and voila, there he is: a slick talking white-collar con man on parole for a federal offense. I don't talk to people on elevators anymore. And my building mate, his therapist, clearly has his hands full.

But I continue to work after all these years in the trenches of justice feeling less than satisfied knowing that not one thing has changed since I started my work...that my theories inspired no one and that my interpretation of my mandate was fairly unique among my colleagues. The Star Chamber still sits.

EPILOGUE
Where Are They Now?

1 | In The Beginning

<u>Mark David Chapman</u>: Chapman had his seventh parole hearing on August 23rd, 2012, and was again denied release...to be reviewed again in two years. He is at Wende Correctional Facility having served 33 years on his 20 – Life conviction. The reason for denial reads as follows: "The panel notes your prison record of good conduct, program achievements, educational accomplishments, positive presentation, remorse, risk and needs assessment, letters of support, significant opposition to your release and all other statutory factors were considered. However, parole shall not be granted for good conduct and program completions alone. Therefore, despite your positive efforts while incarcerated, your release at this time would greatly undermine respect for the law and tend to trivialize the tragic loss of life which you caused as a result of this heinous, unprovoked, violent, cold and calculated crime."

<u>Town X, Maine</u>: The town of my coming of age now boasts 1,100 year 'round residents but swells to 60,000 in the summer. Anti-Semitism is non-existent.

<u>Bellevue Hospital</u>: The jail psychiatric outpost of Rikers Island was consolidated with Metropolitan Hospital at the beginning of 2011 to treat and evaluate acutely psychotic or severely retarded inmates with a 104 bed capacity.

<u>Gloria Hiroko Chapman</u>: Remains married to Mark Chapman and has family visits with him as she has done throughout his incarceration.

Attica Correctional Facility: Vincent Mancusi, the Warden at Attica responsible for the conditions leading to the 1971 riot, died at his home in VA. July 5th, 2012, at the age of 98.

2 | Teddy Boy...'She's Just a Woman'

Mt Ida Junior College: Transformed from all girls junior college/finishing school to a coed undergraduate and graduate liberal arts college grown from 5 to 23 buildings.

Dean Hanson: Alive and well at 79 living with his second wife of over forty years.

Annette Martucci: Passed away at too young an age literally sick to death by the tragedy of her son's death.

Ted Martucci: Passed away in June, 2011, hastened by the years of mourning the deaths his son and wife.

Cooley's Anemia: Remains a rare life-threatening blood disorder requiring regular transfusions and leading to heart trouble.

Joe Mullholland: Died February, 2002.

3 | Attica and Other Riots

Heidi Hanson: My daughter lives happily ever after in a remote mountain village in Vermont with her dog, Violet, and friend Peter, and is a brilliant floral designer.

Jim Hanson: My son lives in NY with wife Jeanmarie, daughter Molly and two dogs, Hunter and Dublin, where he has love and purpose in his life.

NEWSDAY: Moved to Suffolk County, owned by Cablevision, circulation outlets spread widely throughout

Long Island and Queens. Gone are the shenanigans. The history of the birth and growth of the paper is recounted in Bob Keeler's book; "Newsday: a candid history of the respectable tabloid."

<u>Joe Treen</u>: Died suddenly at the age of 66 in June of 2009, leaving a wife and adopted daughter.

4 | Rikers Island, The Wonder Years

<u>Rikers Island</u>: Grown to ten separate jails housing 15,000 inmates on its 400 acres and boasting a new progressive corrections commissioner from Maine made famous by his reduction of solitary confinement use.

<u>Sister Elaine Roulet</u>: Her house is a victim of Hurricane Sandy but as a survivor, she is rebuilding to continue retreats through her latest program, 'Our Journey.'

<u>Warden Pat Perry</u>: When last heard he was appointed the first inspector general of Putnam County, NY.

<u>Dan Pachoda</u>: Legal Director of the Arizona ACLU.

5 | The Men Who Got Away

<u>Bill Arico</u>: Deceased, fell to death in prison escape attempt.

<u>Georgio Ambrosoli</u>: Deceased, target of mob hit

<u>Michele Sindona</u>: Deceased, cyanide poisoning.

<u>Henry Hill</u>: Deceased, natural causes helped by risky lifestyle.

<u>Maria von Somebody</u>: Once returned to Spain, wrote that she was marrying a bartender.

<u>Barbara Allan</u>: Continues her tireless leadership of Prison Families Anonymous.

The Boss: Remains in investment banking and philanthropic works.

Oscar de le Renta: Maintains his iconic fashion house.

6 | The Star Chamber

Parole Commissioners: The original twelve members of the Board with whom I served have all died, save two.

7 | Grasping at Straws

Arthurkill Correctional Facility: Sits empty and for sale by the state, being considered for retail development

Norman 3X Butler/Muhammad Abdul Aziz: Worked for seven years at a drug rehabilitation program and was briefly appointed as the chief of security to the Nation of Islam's Mosque No. 7. Along with codefendant Thomas Johnson/Khalil Islam, released from prison in 1986, they attempted to get the government to reopen the Malcolm X murder case, for which they had always maintained their innocence. The third codefendant, Thomas Hagan, attested to their claims stating that he was responsible entirely. After serving 40 years, Hagan was released in March, 2010. Johnson died at the age of 74 in 2009. The Justice Department decided not to reopen their case in July of 2011.

8 | Unbreakable Women

Ronnie Eldridge: Hosts a weekly public affairs television show, 'Eldridge & Co.' and is a former Member of the New York City Council.

Hedda Nussbaum: Advocate, lecturer, author; new book, "Surviving Intimate Terrorism", married within the past few years and left the New York environs.

Elaine Lord: Remarkably transformed from Superintendent to counselor/mentor for homeless women at "My Mother's House" run by Sisters of St. Joseph.

Jean Harris: Died quietly on 12/23/12 in an assisted living residence in Conn.

Twelve Witnesses: Responsible for policy and legal changes regarding violence against women after the epiphany that was their testimonies.

9 | Howard Beach

Jason Ladone: A family man in his 40's doing honest work for NYC.

Howard Beach: A neighborhood that has less than 2% black population.

Cedric Sandeford: One of the 3 victims; passed away in 1991.

Timothy Grimes: The second surviving victim, himself serving time in VA for a violent shooting crime.

10 | Geranium Justice

Osmondo Gonzalez: (not true name) Served another bid for burglary.

Leslie van Houten: Denied parole for the 20th time June 5, 2013, and will reappear in 2018.

Roy Burke: The last love of my life reappeared in 2008 to an unwelcome reunion; soon after he became terribly ill – his fate is unknown.

My Harasser: Deceased.

11 | Looking For Justice

<u>Steven McDonald: As</u> a NYPD detective he continues to inspire a nation speaking on reconciliation and against violence; Patty, his wife, is Mayor of her village of Malverne, NY; son Conor is a police officer.

<u>Victims Impact Unit</u>: Today a staffed unit with seven employees who facilitate victim input and track inmates for victim notification.

<u>Roy Gutman</u>: Foreign Editor of McClatchy Newspapers, Pulitzer Prize winner for Bosnia reports and other honors.

<u>Peggie Phipps Boegner</u>: Died in 2006 at 100 years of age.

12 | Redemption

The culture of the Parole Board has never changed. There are different faces, different names, and the same ethos. I continue to advocate for policies and people who suffer most from a system that replaces legalities with political, pressuring influences. But perhaps some change agents are beginning to notice along with the tide of winning appeals, judges' scrutiny and more public comments and condemnations of the broken parole system. The New York Times said in an editorial on February 17, 2014, that in order for change to occur there has to be a "fundamental reworking of both the board's process and its culture". That sounds like a lot of work when all they need to do is consider risk, not guilt.

After I left the Board, I ran two criminal justice

agencies before deciding, once my mother passed away and my doctor retired, that it was time to take my dogs and go do my work back where I first became socially conscious. There is a lot to do. I am an activist and work with political campaigns. From afar I'm in close touch with the people and issues that I still feel so privileged to be a part. Clarence Darrow said, **"You can only protect your liberties in this world by protecting the other man's freedom. You can only be free if I am free."** I agree.

Barbara Hanson Treen

39356006R00190

Made in the USA
Charleston, SC
05 March 2015